Educational Leadership and Pierre Bourdieu

Pierre Bourdieu was one of the most important thinkers of the twentieth century. He argued for, and practised, rigorous and reflexive scholarship, interrogating the inequities and injustices of modern societies. Through a lifetime's explication of the ways in which schooling both produces and reproduces the status quo, Bourdieu offered a powerful critique and method of analysis of the history of schooling and of contemporary educational polices and trends.

Though frequently used in educational research, Bourdieu's work has had much less take up in Educational Leadership, Management and Administration (ELMA). *Educational Leadership and Pierre Bourdieu* argues that ELMA scholars have much to gain by engaging more thoroughly with his work. The book explains each of the key terms in Bourdieu's thinking toolkit, showing how the tripartite concepts of field, habitus and capitals offer a way through which to understand the interaction of structure and agency, and the limits on the freedom of an individual – in this case, an educational leader – to act.

Educational Leadership and Pierre Bourdieu offers an analysis of dominant trends in ELMA research, examining the kinds of questions asked, projects undertaken and methods used. It provides alternative questions and methods based on a Bourdieusian approach, further readings and a range of exemplars of the application of these tools. The book will be of interest to those whose primary focus is the utility of Bourdieu's social theory.

Pat Thomson PSM, PhD, FAcSS is Professor of Education at the University of Nottingham, UK. She is a visiting professor at the University of the Free State, South Africa, Deakin University, Australia, and The University of Iceland.

Critical Studies in Educational Leadership, Management and Administration

Series Editors: Pat Thomson, Helen M. Gunter and Jill Blackmore

This series draws on social and political theories from selected key thinkers and activists to develop critical thinking leadership tools. Each text uses the work of a particular theorist or theoretical approach, explains the theory, suggests what it might bring to the ELMA field, and then offers analysis and case studies to show how the tools might be used. Every book also offers a set of questions that might be used by individual leaders in their own practices, and in areas of further research by ELMA scholars.

In elaborating the particular approaches, each of the books also suggests a professional and political agenda which addresses aspects of the tensions and problems created by neoliberal and neoconservative policy agendas, and the on-going need for educational systems to do better for many more of their students than they do at present.

Titles in the series

Deconstructing Educational Leadership: Derrida and Lyotard
Richard Niesche

Educational Leadership and Hannah Arendt
Helen M. Gunter

Educational Leadership and Michel Foucault
Donald Gillies

Educational Leadership and Nancy Fraser
Jill Blackmore

Educational Leadership and Pierre Bourdieu
Pat Thomson

Educational Leadership and Pierre Bourdieu

Pat Thomson

LONDON AND NEW YORK

First published 2017 by Routledge

2 Park Square, Milton Park, Abingdon, Oxfordshire OX14 4RN
711 Third Avenue, New York, NY 10017

Routledge is an imprint of the Taylor & Francis Group, an informa business

First issued in paperback 2018

Copyright © 2017 Pat Thomson

The right of Pat Thomson to be identified as author of this work has been asserted by her in accordance with sections 77 and 78 of the Copyright, Designs and Patents Act 1988.

All rights reserved. No part of this book may be reprinted or reproduced or utilised in any form or by any electronic, mechanical, or other means, now known or hereafter invented, including photocopying and recording, or in any information storage or retrieval system, without permission in writing from the publishers.

Notice:
Product or corporate names may be trademarks or registered trademarks, and are used only for identification and explanation without intent to infringe.

British Library Cataloguing in Publication Data
A catalogue record for this book is available from the British Library

Library of Congress Cataloging in Publication Data
Names: Thomson, Pat, 1948– author.
Title: Educational leadership and Pierre Bourdieu / Pat Thomson.
Description: Abingdon, Oxon ; New York, NY : Routledge, 2017. |
  Series: Critical studies in educational leadership, management and administration series
Identifiers: LCCN 2016025059 | ISBN 9780415603553 (hardback) |
  ISBN 9780203818213 (ebook)
Subjects: LCSH: Bourdieu, Pierre, 1930–2002. | Educational leadership—Philosophy. | School management and organization—Philosophy.
Classification: LCC LB880.B6542 T56 2017 | DDC 371.2—dc23
LC record available at https://lccn.loc.gov/2016025059

ISBN: 978-0-415-60355-3 (hbk)
ISBN: 978-1-138-60970-9 (pbk)

Typeset in Galliard
by Apex CoVantage, LLC

Contents

Acknowledgements   vii
Series foreword   viii

1 Introducing Pierre Bourdieu   1

Bourdieu's approach to education 3
Bourdieu and a system of unequal education 6
Bourdieu's conceptual frames 8
Is it all just reproduction? 21
Where next? 22

2 Introducing ELMA – educational leadership, management and administration   23

Education – a global/local affair 23
Educational leadership and governing 26
Bringing Bourdieu to the changes in the education field 29
The ELMA field 31
Governing and ELMA scholarship 32
ELMA concerns and questions 32
ELMA and its methodological bases 37
*The take-up of EEIR and leadership studies as part of
   governing 42*
Where next? 43

3 Bringing Bourdieu to ELMA   44

Using and misusing Bourdieu 44
Bourdieu and educational research 50
ELMA and Bourdieu 52
*Designing a Bourdieusian ELMA study: a hypothetical
   proposal 55*
Where next? 59

vi *Contents*

4 **Why do headteachers want autonomy?** 60

Part A: the phenomenon of headteacher desire for autonomy 60
Part B: a Bourdieusian sketch 69

5 **What do leaders need to know? The doxa of the thoroughly modern manager** 76

The context of the case study 77
The NC leadership training framework 80
Bringing Bourdieu to the qualification modules 88
Outside the doxic black box: misrecognition 94
In conclusion: what does this example show us about what
  Bourdieusian thinking might offer to ELMA? 96

6 **New practices and old hierarchies: Academy conversion in a successful secondary school in England** 98
RUTH MCGINITY AND HELEN M. GUNTER

Introduction 98
Policy games 98
Capital exchanges 103
Summary 110

7 **Thinking with and against Bourdieu** 112

The limits of social theory 112
The limitations of Bourdieu's toolkit 115
Implications for ELMA scholarship 124
A future ELMA agenda? 126

8 **Finding out more about Bourdieu** 129

Introductions to Bourdieu 129
Bourdieu on schooling 129
Bourdieu and education 130
Bourdieu and language, literacy and education 130
Bourdieu and ELMA 131
Bourdieu on academic practice 131
Extended reading about Bourdieu 131

References 133
Index 163

Acknowledgements

This book has been a very long time in the writing. I have always found writing with Bourdieu to be very difficult and it just 'takes as long as it takes'. In this instance, taking as long as it takes has been a matter of years, not months. I have therefore to thank my co-series editors, Helen Gunter and Jill Blackmore, as well as co-authors Ruth McGinity and Helen (again) for their patience. I am grateful that they continued to trust that this book would see the light of day. A grovelling apology must go to Anna Clarkson and the team at Routledge, with thanks for being prepared to hold onto the book despite serial missed deadlines. A very special thanks go to Helen and Shaun Rawolle for reading the very nearly final version of the book and providing helpful feedback. All errors and interpretation issues that remain are clearly mine. Finally, thanks to my partner Randy who has put up with the never-ending moaning about the never-ending writing project and, as always, has administered appropriate quantities of tea, sympathy and hugs.

Helen and Ruth would like to acknowledge the ESRC for funding the theorising and fieldwork reported in Chapter 6, specifically the Knowledge Production and Educational Leadership project (RES-000–23–1192) and the ESRC CASE Project title: *Modernisation through personalized public services: an investigation into localized school policymaking* (ES/GO39860/1). They would like to thank the staff and students of Kingswood High School/Academy for their participation in this research.

The book reuses a paper which first appeared in 2010 as "Headteacher autonomy: a sketch of a Bourdieuian field analysis of position and practice", in *Critical Studies in Education* 51(1). The paper is updated and has new, additional commentary to highlight its methodological approach.

Series foreword

Imagine yourself walking into the foyer of the Department of Education Victoria, Australia. In front of you is a wall on which a series of names are displayed ceiling to floor. You glance quickly and note the following: Edward de Bono, Richard Elmore, Michael Fullan, Andy Hargreaves, Maria Montessori, Linda Darling-Hammond, Daniel Goleman, Kenneth Leithwood. Now imagine yourself in England. You decide to go to the website of the state owned leadership research and training National College and you find a section called Key Thinkers. When the screen changes you find yourself looking at a list which contains many of the same names.

Today, both of these things have disappeared. The names on the wall in Victoria have been removed and the National College website has been revamped. But they were both in place for some years. Seeing them made us wonder how it was that the very same people were being lauded on both sides of the world. We noted that both lists were dominated by North American men. In the Australian case no Australians were listed, and in the case of England, the English names were in a minority. Would this happen if we were exploring a leadership space or place in Los Angeles? In Edinburgh? In Cape Town? In Beijing? In Buenos Aires? In Toronto? It is interesting to think about where and where not we might see similar listings.

We are sure that we would not have found this thirty years ago. While there was an international circulation of educational ideas and texts, the development of a celebrity leadership culture promoted by international gurus with modernizing know-how is a new phenomenon. It is worth considering why this might be the case. We think of four possible reasons:

1 Leadership now encompasses all aspects of 'continuous educational improvement'. All professionals (and increasingly children and young people as well), are identified as leaders, doing leading and exercising leadership. Head teachers, or principals, are deemed repositories of leadership that they do or do not 'distribute' to others to enable 'delivery' to be 'maximized'. All educational professionals are spoken to or about as school leaders, often without reference to role titles, and so just about everyone is potentially included as a consumer of leadership ideas and models.

Series foreword   ix

2   There is now a much greater focus on leadership development. All education policymakers understand that if policies are to be implemented then they need leaders at the local level to make that happen. Many have also decided that they only need to provide directions for change, and frameworks for what is to be done, and then devolve to the local leader the means to secure the necessary resources.

3   Systems now assume that they need to be seen to be using 'world's best practice'. National governments are highly conscious of their place in international league tables and their national credibility rests on being able to show some kind of 'continued improvement'. They are extremely vulnerable to media portrayals of 'failing' schools and/or systems. They believe that there are international 'solutions' to local problems that may appear to be not dissimilar to problems in other jurisdictions.

4   There now seems to be a leadership industry made up of knowledge producers and popularizers located in private companies, universities, and schools. This leadership industry has made significant interventions in all spheres of activity, including in education and in educational leadership. What is on offer from a select range of academics and consultants, the travelling policy entrepreneurs, are tailor-made as well as off the peg 'solutions' to individuals, organizations and governments. These solutions are sold as transnational, evidence-based and transferable.

The readiness of the leadership industry to provide policy solutions creates a situation in which it seems, if one examines the kinds of training on offer to potential school leaders, that there is a one-best way to do leading and leadership, and to be a leader. The promotion of leadership, policy anxiety and entrepreneurial activity is not necessarily, we suggest, a virtuous circle. We call this conjunction the Transnational Leadership Package (TLP).

The TLP is not a homogenous body of work or people. It is derived from different national and cultural settings. It draws on a range of intellectual histories and practice traditions in different national contexts within the field of educational leadership, management and administration (ELMA). There are distinct but interrelated intellectual lineages within the field of ELMA, which can be backtracked from contemporary concerns to particular historical contexts and theoretical origins. We call these lineages paradigms. ELMA paradigms cannot be easily disconnected from each other, either theoretically or chronologically, as different approaches were developed differently in different places and at different times, in response to the failure, or lack of explanatory power, of earlier paradigms. The ELMA paradigms, each with their own internal logics, can be roughly depicted as:

1   The US adoption of the Ford manufacturing, Taylorist principles of **scientific management** (standardization, specialisation, synchronisation, concentration, maximization, and centralization), as the 'factory model' to emulate in schooling during the 1920s. Its later renditions are the school effectiveness

x *Series foreword*

and school improvement movements (SESI). SESI is now interlocked with education policy through the imposition, across the entire public sector, of private sector market principles in the form of New Public Management. The core principles underpinning the resulting managerialization and marketization of schooling are competition and compliance, efficiency and effectiveness. School rankings and comparisons are central to this push.

2   The post war **human relations movement**, again largely US driven. This movement recognised how supportive social relations and participative decision-making informed productivity. This human relations paradigm is re-emerging in the 21stC in the therapeutic turn in education. Emotional intelligence and managing interpersonal relations and intercultural communication are now seen as core leadership skills rather than a display of weakness. This paradigm informs the move away from the provision of public service through institutions towards brokerage, contracts and partnerships. Notably it is visible in the organizational and pedagogic discourse of personalized provision.

3   The US **theory movement** of the 1960s sought to establish ELMA as a value-free science. This paradigm has been ever present in ELMA, but has gained new clout through the contemporary focus on large-scale quantitative studies, evidence-based/informed practice and data-driven decision-making. Prime examples of this contemporary trend are the involvement of TLP in the *No Child Left Behind* policy in USA and *Every Child Matters* in England.

4   The **experiential** or **pragmatic perspective** of the UK tradition, which derived from a strong practitioner orientation and apprenticeship model of leadership. This has recently re-emerged in the 'what works' discourse in England, as leadership accreditation and training provisions were taken up by governments, and as teacher education was pushed back into schools.

5   The **socially critical, neo-Marxist** and **feminist perspectives**, emerging predominantly from the geographical margins of Australia, New Zealand and Canada during the 1980s and 1990s. These are now being reinvigorated with the revival of social justice as a leadership issue in the 2010s, given the marked growth of educational inequality in both developed and developing nation states. This book series is located within this tradition.

There is now a convergence of the ELMA paradigms. This has occurred at the same time as neoliberal policies have spread from the Anglophone nation states to Asia, the Middle East, Mexico, South Africa and South America. Key aspects of the neoliberalist agenda are virtually enforced by international bodies such as the IMF, World Bank and OECD, and results of international standardized testing such as PISA are now a crucial reference point for policymakers in most countries in the world. This policy spread has been made possible in part through the advocacy work of knowledge and 'know-how' entrepreneurs whose activities inform and are sometimes commissioned by these international agencies. The result is that there is now a coming together of the ELMA paradigms through preferred

Series foreword xi

models such as transformational leadership, which is simultaneously about delivery, an emotional commitment to the delivery, and a predictive evidence-based process to that delivery. Tactical and pragmatic mediations may occur in some countries such as England, but in the main ELMA paradigms inform and communicate vision and mission for localized implementation.

ELMA can now be understood as a transnational field of educational research, with a recognizable lexicon, key players and logics of practice. This is the case regardless of whether we are looking at the TLP, other ELMA scholarship somewhat separate from it, or socially critical scholarship. Across ELMA generally there is a trend towards both standardization and normalization in relation to what constitutes good leadership through the development of leadership training programs and professional standards nationally. This represents a shift away from post-occupancy professional development to leadership preparation, in some instances requiring certification. Scholars from the fifth paradigm are also positioned by these developments and engage in the kinds of critical, deconstructive and reconstructive work that is the purpose of this book series. Indeed, we have briefed our authors to engage in this process so that the problematization of the field of ELMA and its relationship with the TLP are essential to engagement with theory and theorizing.

The convergence of ELMA paradigms has also been actively produced by particular scholars and professionals through a process of selective eclecticism and appropriation of a set of concepts in response to the multiple and complex challenges of school leadership and to opportunities offered by anxious governments. This process of production, its agents, and its outcomes, collectively form what we refer to as the TLP.

The TLP is not the same as ELMA. It brings together concepts and practices that were formerly confined to particular localities and institutions into a particular 'saleable' form. The result is an assemblage of ideas and activities, which focuses primarily on the needs of educational systems and national governments. These do not necessarily meet the needs of individual schools, their students, or their communities. The product is in fact constantly repackaged and contains a few genuinely new ideas but plenty of normative rhetoric on the urgency to buy and use.

The TLP consists of three mutually supporting strands:

1   A set of policy prescriptions based on the experiences of consultants working in contractual (and often informal) partnerships with governments and agencies in particular jurisdictions, mostly North America and England, but also now including PISA success story, Finland. There are ready-made sound bites in this strand combined with the authority of 'best practice'.
2   A series of meta-analyses and effectiveness studies, whose impressive statistical manipulations mostly boil down to saying that if you want to improve students' learning, then you have to focus on how teachers and classroom practice can 'deliver' higher outcome standards, and not on networks, teams or devolution of funding since these alone won't produce the desired test result improvements.

xii *Series foreword*

3 A cultural professional deficit where the identification of problems, agenda setting and strategizing is perceived as rightly located outside the school, and where notions of professional agency are reduced to tactical localized delivery. Some TLP manifestations have taken up the Finland exemplar to argue that a well-qualified and intellectually active teaching force is vital, and that too much emphasis on testing and league tabling is counterproductive. However, the role of leaders remains the same in both versions, as does the primary goal of system needs.

The TLP provides a (largely) Anglocentric policy flat-pack of policy 'levers' that will produce the actions and effects that count in national elections and international testing. While modern but cheap, it is worth 'buying into', largely because to be seen as different is risky. However, there is considerable debate about whether these objectives meet the needs of schools, communities, teachers and students in countries as diverse as Denmark, New Zealand, South Africa, Canada, Wales and Singapore. At a time when populations in many countries are also becoming more diverse and less egalitarian, it is also not clear that the TLP is up to the challenge.

We are not arguing here that the international circulation of ideas and people is to be discouraged. Obviously, finding out what others are doing can be very helpful as means of generating new perspectives. The debate and discussion that occur when people with different positions come together are a Good Thing. However, we think it is ironic that at the same time as national governments and transnational agencies are concerned to maintain diversity of plants, animals and habitats, precisely the opposite is occurring with education policy ideas and practices. 'Good' leadership features prominently among one-best global prescriptions and representations. Many ELMA scholars not in the TLP, as well as those from critical paradigms, suggest that there is no one-best way of leading or changing a school and that the models of transnational 'success' need to promote diverse approaches that are tailored to local needs histories and circumstances.

We take the view that what is needed in education in these times is more than PISA envy and 'what works'. Prescribing a set of steps that governments and leaders can take, regardless of wherever and whoever they are, eliminates one of the most significant educational resources we have – our capacity to understand, analyse and imagine within our local contexts. It is a fine irony that these intellectual practices are precisely the ones that education systems are designed to inculcate in the next generation.

In these times, those who are engaged in *educational* leadership need, more than ever, to think about their work – its purposes and processes and well as its effects and outcomes. Our emphasis is on the *educational*, where the knowledge, skills and processes that constitute professional practice are located in teaching and learning; these provide the basis for leading and managing. This series of books aims to support this kind of reflective *educational* work. Each volume will focus on the work of a particular social science theory and theorists. We draw on scholarship from sociology, anthropology, philosophy, politics and cultural studies in order to interrogate, interrupt and offer alternative ideas to the contemporary versions of TLP and the broader field of ELMA. The series provides theoretical and methodological options for those who are engaged in the formal study of educational leadership, management and administration. It provides alternative resources for naming, framing and acting for those who are engaged in the practice of educational leadership, management or administration, or who are providing training and policy for practising educational leaders.

The books and critical thinking tools

This series of books might at first glance seem to be very removed from the kinds of pressures that we have described. However, our motivation for generating the series is highly practical. As series editors, we come to, and hopefully have informed, the field of ELMA from different intellectual and occupational histories.

Together, we take the view that now, more than ever, leading any educational institution requires intellectual work. Educational professionals must, in our view, be able not simply to follow policy prescriptions. In order to do the work of leading and leadership educational professionals need to be able to critically analyse policy directions; assess and evaluate their own institution and its local national and international contexts; understand how and why particular educational issues come to be centre stage while others are sidelined and to communicate this to others; and call on a rich set of ideas in order to develop directions for the institution in particular and for education generally. This requires, among other things, a set of critical thinking tools. These are not all that are required, but they are an essential component of professional practice.

This series draws on social and political theories from selected key thinkers and activists to develop some critical thinking leadership tools. Each text uses the work of a particular theorist or theoretical approach, explains the theory, suggests what it might bring to the ELMA field and then offers analysis and case studies to show how it the tools might be used. Each book also offers a set of questions that might be used by individual leaders in their own practice and some possible areas for further research by ELMA scholars.

In elaborating the particular approaches each of the books also suggests a professional and political agenda, which addresses aspects of the tensions and problems created by neoliberal and neoconservative policy agendas and by the ongoing need for educational systems to do better for many more of their students than they do at present.

Pat Thomson, Helen Gunter and Jill Blackmore
Series Editors

1 Introducing Pierre Bourdieu

Pierre Bourdieu (1930–2002) grew up in rural France. He came from modest circumstances. His father, the son of a peasant sharecropper, was a poorly paid civil servant who ran a rural post office in a remote village in Bearn in the Pyrenees. Bourdieu's village primary school classmates were the children of peasants, shopkeepers and craftsmen. His early academic success was largely due, he suggested, to the encouragement of his father, rather than his teachers (Bourdieu, 2007). Bourdieu left home as a youngster to become a boarder at the regional lycée in Pau, where he was, by his own account, far from a model student. He was only able to take his baccalaureate exams because the school headmaster intervened in a dispute between a feisty young Bourdieu and a senior member of staff (2007, p. 90). As a child, Bourdieu benefitted from both family and institutional support, a point that was not lost on him in his later career.

Despite his rebellious habits, Bourdieu went on to win a scholarship to an elite school in Paris, where he was prepared for entry into the prestigious Ecole Normale Superieure. From there he went to teach in a lycée, and then, via military service and university teaching in Algiers, he gained university posts in Lille and Paris. As a university academic, he undertook a substantial body of empirical work into social systems, cultures and structures. He died an internationally renowned social scientist whose writings inspired and grounded the work of numerous other scholars around the world.

A stellar career. From humble beginnings to international academic superstar. Bourdieu can be seen as the very epitome of the success of a meritocratic school system through which bright children from any background can rise to the highest levels of achievement and social acclaim. Yet this is an interpretation that Bourdieu strenuously rejected. He argued that, unlike him, most children from working-class and rural families did not succeed and ended up in much the same social and economic position as their parents. This was not because of any lack of merit on their part but because the school system was designed to work in this way. Furthermore, he suggested, even those who, like him, had 'made it' against the educational odds, were still scarred by the experience.

In a reflection on his own life, written not long before he died (*Sketch for a self-analysis*, 2007), Bourdieu described how, as a child, he developed a strong sense of his own otherness and class position. His mother's family were landowners

2   Introducing Pierre Bourdieu

with a drive for 'respectability'. But his mother married 'beneath her station'; her family was critical of her husband's anarchistic politics and his lowly position, and their antipathy produced ongoing tensions in the Bourdieu home. At school, the young Bourdieu was very conscious of the ways in which regional city children looked down on those from isolated, rural areas and on his own ambiguous position, sandwiched between the children of the more affluent middle class and those from poor and peasant homes. He was also acutely aware of the difference between the regimentation, the competition among and the hard punishments meted out to boarders and the apparent calm encouragement of the classroom. He described himself as exhibiting 'a mixture of aggressive shyness and a growling, even furious, bluntness' (2007, p. 89) which often landed him in trouble. His parents could not understand why he had so many difficulties at school since it seemed to them that he had opportunities that they themselves could never have hoped for.

Bourdieu's feelings of 'out-of-place-ness', and his troublesome ways of dealing with them, did not go away when he found himself a provincial young man in the French capital, his dress and speech giving away his social and class origins. He wrote that he regularly felt compelled to attack those he saw as the comfortable and arrogant 'bourgeoisie' and to defend his own self and position against what he perceived to be their contempt. He described his life as marked by a 'strong discrepancy between high academic consecration and lowly social origin' (2007, p. 100).

It is suggested that much of Bourdieu's work can be explained through the lens of his unease with his own social mobility (Reed-Danahay, 2005), and there are certainly resonances between the feelings of classed otherness he describes in his autobiographical sketch and his notion of *habitus*, which is explained in more detail later in the chapter. Yet Bourdieu dismissed the notion of autobiography, arguing strongly that, even if his work was concerned with issues which arose from his own life trajectory, he was not interested in his own singularity and exceptionalism but in social and historical (re)production at scale.

Bourdieu was also critical of higher education. It might be assumed that as a successful student, teacher and researcher he would unequivocally promote the values of a university education. This was not so. Bourdieu acknowledged that he loved the solitude of scholarly work, of immersing oneself completely in a book, but he was also painfully aware of how privileged he was to be able to spend time in this way. He resented what he described as any 'submission' to the education system – obeisance and deference to a world of examinations, prizes, inaugural lectures, thesis committees, commendations and recommendations. Bourdieu consistently argued the value and necessity of intellectual work, but dedicated considerable energy and time to critically interrogating the conditions under which it was usually conducted.

Although Bourdieu was trained in part as a philosopher, he became interested in social science when in Algeria, and his first significant publications were focused on that country. His analysis of the deep hierarchies and injustices of colonised Algerian society led to him to advocate for, among other reforms, a broadly based and equitable education system. Bourdieu saw the emancipatory potential of education, as well as its reproductive logics (Grenfell, 2007).

As a social scientist, Bourdieu deliberately chose to study 'everyday' social, political and cultural life – education, politics, real estate, publishing, art, literature, journalism – rather than the lofty philosophical topics in which he was trained and which were commonplace among his peers. He seemed to revel in this scholastic contrariness, suggesting in his autobiographical sketch that his choice of research agenda was indicative of the ways in which he had spent his life rejecting educational 'conformism' (2007, pp. 100–107). He, of course, also acknowledged the fine irony that it was this very academic orneriness that brought him widespread recognition and acclaim.

Education can be seen as the backbone of Bourdieu's life, and it was a key theme in his writings. In this chapter I signpost the tenets of Bourdieu's work on education and then use this to point to the major elements of his approach – his key ideas and terms.

Bourdieu's approach to education

Bourdieu began to write about education in the 1960s (Grenfell, 2008) although much of this published work appeared later in their English translation (see Figure 1.1). He wanted to examine whether the French school system was 'democratic' in the ways it proclaimed itself to be. He sought to not only document but also make sense of the kinds of knowledge and learning that was variously made available to French children and young people. Bourdieu wanted to show how the French school system worked, not simply to produce elite distinguished scholars such as himself but also, and at the same time and through the same practices, to perpetuate the very uneven successes he witnessed in his own environs and in French society more generally.

It is important to recognise that Bourdieu's question about the democratic nature of the educational system emerged from a particular historical context. Since the French Revolution, the national imaginary of France was enshrined in a narrative about the importance of equality and democracy. The French school system, established at the end of the 19th century, was underpinned by rhetoric about universal, secular and free schooling; it was also tightly sutured to political and social expectations that education should provide equal opportunities for all children. This was understood to mean the provision of a core and common curriculum, with advancement through the system based on demonstrable attainment. If children were offered different learning opportunities, so the narrative went, then inequality would be inbuilt at the outset. The modern French school system retains this universalist approach, with a common curriculum taught in all schools and some additional choices available in some locations and levels. There has never been a divided secondary system in France and a subsequent struggle for comprehensiveness. The French education system, and the rhetoric surrounding it, is thus very different from the history of grammar and secondary schools in England, the German post-primary four-track system, or the technical and high schools of Australia.

4   *Introducing Pierre Bourdieu*

Key books about schooling
Bourdieu P., and Passeron, J C. (1964) *Les héritiers* Paris: Les Editions des Minuits
Bourdieu P., Passeron, J C., and de Saint Martin, M. (1965) *Rapport pédagogique et communication* The Hague: Mouton
Bourdieu, P., and Passeron J C. (1970) *La réproduction: Élements pour en théorie du système d'enseignement.* Paris: Les editions de Minuits
Key books about higher education
Bourdieu, P. (1982) *Leçon sur la leçon* Paris: Les Editions des Minuits
Bourdieu, P. (1984) *Homo academicus* Paris: Les Editions Des Minuits
Bourdieu, P. (1987) *Questions de sociologie* Paris: Les Editions des Minuits
Bourdieu, P. (1989) *La noblesse d' état. Grandes écoles et esprit de corps.* Paris: Les Editions des Minuits
Bourdieu, P., and Wacquant, L. (1992) *Réponses: Pour an anthropologie réflexive* Paris: Seuil
Bourdieu, P. (2001) *Science de la science au réflexivite* Paris: Raisons d'Agir
English translation: schooling
Bourdieu, P., and Passeron J.C. (1977) *Reproduction in education, society and culture* (R. Nice trans) London: SAGE
Bourdieu, P., and Passeron J C (1979) *The inheritors: French students and their relations to culture* (R. Nice, trans) Chicago, IL: University of Chicago press
Bourdieu, P., Passeron J C., and de Saint Martin, M. (1994) *Academic discourse* (R. Teese trans) Oxford: Polity Press
English translation: Higher education
Bourdieu, P. (1988) *Homo academicus* (P. Collier trans) Cambridge: Polity
Bourdieu P., and Wacquant, L. (1992) *An invitation to reflexive sociology* (L. Wacquant trans) Cambridge: Polity
Bourdieu, P. (1993) *Sociology in question* (R. Nice trans) London: SAGE
Bourdieu, P. (1996) *The state nobility: Elite schools in the field of power* (L. C. Clough trans) Cambridge: Polity
Bourdieu, P. (2004) *Science of science and reflexivity* (R. Nice trans) Cambridge: Polity

Figure 1.1 Key texts by Bourdieu on education

But Bourdieu saw the French educational system, with its rhetorical commitment to universalism and meritocracy, as very far from the ideals it espoused. He was struck by the contradictions between frequently expressed democratic goals and the material outcomes of schooling. In reality, the majority of children and young people who succeeded at school were the sons and daughters of those who were themselves well educated, who were comfortably off or wealthy and who had social status and were well connected. Bourdieu argued that, as a social institution, the entire educational system worked to produce – and, thus, to reproduce – the social, economic and cultural status quo. It did not live up to its promises – to treat each child as if they are a unique individual, to promote children solely on the basis of their achievement, to fulfil each child's potential, to allow each child equal opportunity to succeed and to inculcate common and democratic values and learning.

This insight is, of course, not Bourdieu's alone. Nor is this educational inequality confined to France. At the time that Bourdieu was writing his seminal studies of French education, scholars in other locations were also focusing on the very same phenomena. From the perspective of the 21st century, it is perhaps difficult to appreciate the combined effort and impact of the work of 20th-century postwar educational sociologists (e.g. Bowles & Gintis, 1976; Freire, 1972; Jackson, 1960; Jackson & Marsden, 1966; Karabel & Halsey, 1977; Sharp & Green, 1975; Young, 1971). We are now accustomed to seeing contemporary national and international test results and analyses which attest to the resilience of the inequitable social, economic and educational nexus (e.g. Berliner, 2009; Gorard & Smith, 2004; Hirsch, 2007; Raffo et al., 2008). But at the time, these new sociologically oriented empirical and theoretical studies were shocking, disruptive and coincident with populist political movements geared to holistic social change.

Bourdieu's goal was to provide a generalised explanation of social inequality – he wanted to do more than simply produce evidence. He wanted to build theory through empirical work on and in an education system in which teachers and administrators believed that they were acting equitably, but the results were almost the opposite. There are two important things to note about Bourdieu's approach to studying educational inequality:

1 Bourdieu did not see that 'the problem' lay with education staff per se. He did not see teachers as duplicitous hypocrites; he sought an explanation that did not attribute blame to individuals or groups of people. He sought a *social* explanation. In doing so, he was addressing a larger theoretical debate within the social sciences, namely how it is that social structures limit and frame an individual's capacities to act and make decisions. Given that people are not brainwashed or conditioned like Pavlovian dogs and that they do demonstrably make choices, how can human action be explained? Too much emphasis on structure denies agency to individuals. Too much emphasis on the individual leaves out the ways in which social structures frame and shape what individuals can do. This conundrum is known in the social sciences as the structure–agency quandary. It was a quandary that Bourdieu could not ignore.

2 Bourdieu's approach differs substantially from scholars who were, at around same time, establishing the basis for what we now know as the school effectiveness (SE) movement. These scholars sought to understand how much of the difference in educational outcomes could be seen as 'caused' by the individual school (Coleman, 1966; Levin, 1970; Rutter, Mortimore, & Maugham, 1979). The SE quest was to ascertain the characteristics (factors) of schools which were able to go against the odds and thus to inform educational policy and action within schools. By contrast, Bourdieu's agenda, and that of other critical social scientists (e.g. Apple, 1979, 1982; Corrigan, 1977; Holt, 1964; Kozol, 1968), was to understand what schools did to produce and reproduce the broader social, political and economic system, and to use this to consider change both in and beyond schooling. This critical quest often meant taking a closer look at curriculum making, classrooms and schools in action – and this is what I briefly do now.

6 *Introducing Pierre Bourdieu*

Bourdieu and a system of unequal education

It is neither simple nor quick to sum up how Bourdieu theorised the ways in which the French school system worked to produce and reproduce the status quo. Because the final section of this chapter introduces Bourdieu's specific terminology and concepts, it is helpful to have a picture of his general line of argument first. A long time ago I found one way to do this, through story (Thomson, 2002, pp. 1–2, 4). This little narrative is still the best way I have to present the gist of the Bourdieusian thesis.

Imagine two children about to start school. They are both five years old and are eagerly anticipating their first day. Imagine that each brings with them to school a virtual school bag full of things that they already learned at home, with their friends and from the world in which they live.

Thanh and Vicki

Out first child is a boy called Thanh. He lives in an extended family where he has been chatted and read to in Vietnamese and Chinese since he was very small. He has watched Australian television, visited shopping centres, and worked with his family in their restaurant – doing small tasks like collecting dishes, giving out menus and change and washing vegetables. His parents spent much of their lives in separate refugee camps and were not reunited until they got to Australia. Thanh's father carried a nguyet (a guitar-like instrument) with him on the long walk from the town where he was born to the camp in Thailand, and had kept it safe until he reached his new home in Australia. When he is not too tired, he plays it, and Thanh loves to listen to the traditional songs handed down through the generations. He also loves to hear his older brother and sister talk about school. His parents' formal education was disrupted by the civil war, but both of them are literate in two languages and treasure books. They have worked long hours and several jobs to finally open, with the help of the hui, *the community financial system, the restaurant, where they now work most days and nights. Thanh comes to school with three spoken languages in his virtual school bag; a love of music; an understanding of the restaurant trade; a capacity to get on with a wide range of people; information about Vietnam, China, Thailand and Australia; and an understanding that school is important.*

The second child is Vicki. Her parents are both university educated, and Vicki's mother runs a small catering business at home, supplying gourmet cakes to cafes. Her father is a teacher in the local high school and is currently researching his Irish family heritage. She is the oldest child and has one younger brother. Vicki has been to both preschool and child care and has already begun to read, much to her parents' delight. Vicki loves to help her mother and regularly plays with the family computer and the database of recipes, customers and accounts. Vicki also has a small dog, and her current ambition is to be a vet. She watches a lot of television and can sing along with all of the advertisements, much to her father's disquiet. She loves being read to at night and knows that her parents will expect her to join in and comment on the connections between the illustrations and the story. She knows that when she is read to, she is expected to sit still and listen. Vicki's school bag consists of spoken and written English, well-schooled reading behaviours, knowledge about the white colonial history of Australia and understanding about popular culture, animals, business and the computer. Both children's school bags contain roughly equal but different knowledges, narratives and interests.

Thanh is going to a state primary school in a neighbourhood known to demographers as one of the poorest in the country. Vicki is going to a state primary school in a leafy green part of town. Vicki's parents think that they will send her to an independent girls' school before she starts high school. Thanh's parents hear lots of stories about the local state high schools but think that Thanh will probably go to one not too far away, where there is a uniform and where some friends' children have already graduated to go on to university, a profession and a life of something other than the long days in the restaurant trade. They are determined that Thanh will do his homework and work hard.

Vicki and Thanh have different life worlds, but their life trajectories are connected and differentiated through the school system.

Educational differences between Vicki and Thanh become apparent in their first year at school. Vicki is advantaged in her classroom. She feels comfortable with its rules and modes of operation. She already knows about book behaviours and is not shy about asking for help, whereas Thanh feels awkward, and he is also embarrassed about his occasionally clumsy English. What he knows about restaurants and music is not necessary for success in his classroom. Even within the first few weeks Vicki starts to 'outperform' Thanh in almost everything. Thanh has a knack with numbers his teacher says, which is what she has been told by friends she can expect of 'Asian' students. There is nobody she can ask about this, and because she is anxious to help Thanh succeed, she allows him to spend more time with numbers than with those classroom activities with which he is struggling.

Vicki's virtual school bag contains lots of things she is able to use in school every day, whereas Thanh is only required to open his virtual school bag for arithmetic. Thanh's teacher is not unaware of this, but cannot find the time and space in her busy and crowded classroom to organise alternative learning activities for him – and all of the other individual students with their particular school bags of difference, their unique interests and their knowledge. The probabilities that Vicki will do well at school and go on to university like her mother and father and that Thanh will end up in the family business are already being brought into reality through the mediating practices of schooling.

The key things to take from the story of Vicki and Thanh are:

1   children do not arrive at school as 'empty vessels'. They already have a complex set of 'stuff' – knowledge and skills, ways of being and doing things, expectations and hopes, as well as different pressures and supports – that comes with them through the school gate. This is variously recognised and used by the school. Some already advantaged children's 'stuff' just seems to 'fit' more easily with the ways in which the school works.

8 *Introducing Pierre Bourdieu*

2   there is nothing apparently untoward or unusual in what the school or the teacher is doing. Yet it is clear that there is a high probability that these two children – and others like them – will end up with very different kinds of education and life chances. It is as if the school system itself is designed to recognise and build on only some children's sets of 'stuff'. It is as if the schooling game is rigged against some children right from the outset; this has little to do with individual children and everything to do with broader social relationships of class, culture and gender.

This story of Vicki and Thanh and the processes of reproduction of privilege set the scene for the introduction of Bourdieu's key ideas.

Bourdieu's conceptual frames

Through his ongoing empirical studies, Bourdieu developed a suite of inter-dependent concepts to make sense of the ways in which schools produce and reproduce inequity. It is important at the outset to understand that Bourdieu's 'thinking tools' work together. They are not stand alone ideas, but are interwoven in any Bourdieusian study. For explanatory purposes, I will however deal with each major concept separately. I begin with the notion of field and then work through other key 'tools' – capitals, habitus, logic of practice, doxa, illusio, misrecognition and reflexivity. I refer back to the story of Vicki and Thanh as I go along.

But first, a caveat – Bourdieu's concepts were developed through empirical studies – for example photography (Bourdieu, Boltanski, Castel, Chamboredon, & Schnapper, 1990), art (Bourdieu, 1991), science (Bourdieu, 2004) and politics (Bourdieu, 1998c). While it is possible to discuss his concepts and to indicate how they are used, they make sense as they are developed in, with and through specific data sets and projects, over time. Bourdieu's conceptual framework is intended to be applied to a specific problem, supported by the generation of particular kinds of data. I point towards this in this chapter. However, Chapter 3 focuses specifically on the Bourdieusian toolkit as a methodological approach. It is very important to read the remainder of this chapter knowing that a further elaboration of the conceptual frame as a methodological approach is still to come.

Field

Bourdieu conceived of society as consisting of multiple interlocking and overlapping spaces that are at once social, cultural *and* material. He called these spaces 'fields' – for example there is a field of government, a field of politics, a field of art and a field of education. Fields can be thought of as little 'social worlds'. Taken together the various fields constitute an overall societal field of power. Each individual field operates according to its own set of rules, but each is also shaped by, and itself shapes, the overall field of power. There are similarities and differences

Introducing Pierre Bourdieu   9

between fields. Bourdieu talked of each field being *relatively autonomous*, but there are also important *homologies* (commonalities) across them.

Bourdieu suggested that the overall field of power is geared to support the (re) production of national/global economic and social regimes. Every other field has a particular part to play in making the field of power. For example the job of the field of politics is to legislate and regulate in ways that will support the economic system and the social elites that benefit most from it. The job of government is to organise public services and manage the population to the same end, but the relationship between the field of government and politics is generally, although not always, a hierarchical one, with politics framing what government officers can do.

The relationship between fields is not necessarily contiguous, and there may well be continuing or sporadic tensions between them. And fields are not all equal in status. Some are subordinate to others. Bourdieu argued that the field of education was a subordinate field because other fields were interested in its practices – the education field not only produces the people qualified to work at all levels in all other fields but also (re)produces the kinds of knowledge, skills and dispositions already possessed and valued by the social elites and managerial elites in all other fields. Because of the interest that other fields have in it, the education field is often subject to actions initiated outside it, usually mediated through the political and government fields. Bourdieu noted that

> [b]ecause it concentrates an ensemble of material and symbolic resources, the state is in a position to regulate the functioning of different fields, whether through financial intervention (such as public support of investment in the economic field, or, in the cultural field, support for one kind of education or another) or through juridicial intervention (such as the different regulations covering organisations or the behaviour of individual agents.)
>
> (Bourdieu, 1998b, p. 32)

The role of the state in relation to the education field is of course a crucial concern for those who are charged with leading/managing/administering educational institutions.

A field is populated by positions – positions are occupied both by institutions (schools, colleges, universities, nurseries, community education centres) and by people, or *agents*, as Bourdieu called them. A position might for example be headteacher, university student, primary school teacher, or nursery nurse. An individual headteacher is an agent who occupies the headteacher position.

Positions are not evenly distributed in a field. Fields are not equitable spaces – they are not, as the common saying has it, level playing fields. They consist of status and power hierarchies of positions, and there are both horizontal and vertical hierarchical distributions of positions. We can easily recognise a vertical hierarchy in the field of education based on the levels of education – nursery, primary, secondary, tertiary education – with greater social value attached to each level the further 'up' we go. The qualifications attached to each level also have different kinds of status and value attached to them – the qualifications can do different

10 *Introducing Pierre Bourdieu*

things within the education field and beyond. The 'highest level' of education, a university degree, not only has more occupation-getting capacity for its holder but also more social status than a school certificate gained at the end of compulsory schooling, while no qualifications at all are a serious and ongoing problem for many young people and adults (Maguire & Robinson, 2006; Simmons & Thompson, 2011).

It is also not too hard to see some horizontal divisions in the field of education – Vicki went to a state primary school but was going to a fee-paying girls' secondary school. An 'independent' school generally has more cachet than a state secondary school like the one Thanh was destined to attend. The higher education sector is highly horizontally differentiated and the status of the university – derived from age, size, a range of audit measures and self-organised groups (the Russell group in the UK, the G8 in Australia) – is often used as a proxy for the quality of the education on offer, evidence notwithstanding (McLean & Abbas, 2011). It is not too hard to imagine circumstances in which horizontal divisions matter a great deal – employment for example can depend on employer perceptions of schools, what they apparently offer and who is enrolled. Horizontal differentiation, manifest as a perception–opportunity connection, also makes a real difference at the university level; there is some research (e.g. Chevalier & Conlon, 2003; Triventi, 2013) which shows that employers *do* favour graduates from elite universities. And 'truths' about differently positioned universities play out in the ways that school students are counselled about higher education choices too, with teachers often urging an elite institution over one that is more modest, for little reason other than reputation (Byrom, Thomson, & Gates, 2007).

According to Bourdieu, institutions can be understood not only as positions but also as little fields in themselves. We might therefore think of a school with an internal hierarchy of vertical and horizontal positions, with the headteacher at the vertical pinnacle. Other leaders might have status related to their seniority, or to their job description; sometimes for example timetablers and those responsible for student discipline have more status and power than a peer whose job is to look after the professional development of staff. Horizontally, some subjects and specialisations may be seen as 'better' than others. There are even more obvious hierarchies of disciplines in universities, with horizontal positions in Science, Technology and Mathematics usually seen as more substantial and significant than for example Cultural and Media Studies.

Gender and race also play out in the ways in which positions are hierarchically distributed within institutions and fields (Blackmore & Sachs, 2007; Deem & Morley, 2006). In the contemporary university, white men hold the vast majority of professorial positions, except in female-dominated professions and disciplines such as nursing and education, where women are more likely to be promoted. In 2015, the Runnymede Trust revealed that there were only 17 black female professors in the UK across all disciplines (http://www.independent.co.uk/student/news/uk-study-finds-just-17-black-female-professors-10019201.html). Most universities struggle to meet apparent policy expectations that leadership

Introducing Pierre Bourdieu   11

positions will be equitably distributed – although a Bourdieusian analysis would suggest that disrupting the status quo will be a significant struggle.

So how do fields work? Bourdieu used the metaphor of a game to describe field practices. A game has players who take particular positions in the field, and where and how they move depends on the position they hold and its relationship to other positions. Bourdieu argued that similarly, the actions taken by players in a social field operate according to predetermined rules – fields are governed by their own logics of practice (Bourdieu, 1990b) – *practice* is a term I come back to later. Fields are, unlike an actual game, always in tension because the game is ongoing. There is always a game afoot. So fields are sites of continual contestation and internal schism, of agents jockeying for better positions and struggling to maintain their own ground. Fields are agonistic.

For now, it is important simply to note that each field has its own play, its own logic, its own tensions and its own specific practices. In order to explain this further I must go onto Bourdieu's next key idea.

Capitals

Every game has a point, a purpose. While the game in any field is to produce and reproduce the broader field of power, each field also has a specific game. The game can be understood by focusing on the capitals that are at stake in each field. Capital is most often understood as money. But Bourdieu's use of the notion of capitals was much broader than this.

Bourdieu (1986) proposed two general kinds of capitals:

Economic capital – as it is commonly understood, namely, money, assets and the capacity to access and use financial resources. Money is always a means to an end. It is 'cashed in' for example in exchange for goods, experiences, positions and influence. Economic capital has extrinsic value.

Symbolic capital – capital which is perceived as having intrinsic, as well as extrinsic, worth. Bourdieu suggested that symbolic capital was not a homogeneous category. He often wrote about the symbolic as both cultural capital and social capital, proposing that cultural capital took three major forms:

1   Embodied cultural capitals – knowledge – such as linguistic or scientific or management know how and know what expressed as long-lasting behaviours and preferences. These capitals are 'performed' through for example actions, utterances, lifestyle choices and taste in food, clothes, music or art.

2   Objectified cultural capitals – material artefacts, such as art works, books, furniture, property, writings, which are able to be bought and sold, collected, displayed, bequeathed and inherited.

3   Institutionalised cultural capitals – qualifications, awards, honours, titles and the like which are conferred by an institution to stand in the place of other cultural capitals; these could for example be knowledges demonstrated in exam results or publications produced for academic promotion or audit purposes.

12   *Introducing Pierre Bourdieu*

Bourdieu saw symbolic capital as:

- having both use and exchange value. Capitals have value within and between the relationships and practices of fields.
- able to be converted. In other words, capitals can be transformed from one kind to another as they are used or exchanged within or between fields
- part of the 'being' of the agent possessing it. People embody the kinds of capitals they possess.
- objects of desire. People often see capitals as something to aspire to, or in some cases, to resist and reject.

And what is valued capital in one context may not be valued in another – Lisa McKenzie (2014) for example talks about the ways in which residents in St Annes, a council estate in Nottingham, develop distinctive forms of local cultural capital which accrue status on the estate, but not outside it.

Bourdieu suggested that under certain conditions both social and cultural capitals can be used to gain economic capital, and vice versa. He argued that the kinds of capitals that agents already possess dispose them to acquire and accumulate more of the same:

> [D]epending on their trajectory and on the positon they occupy in the field by virtue of their endowment (volume and structure) in capital, they have a propensity to orient themselves actively either toward the preservation of the distribution of capital or toward the subversion of this distribution.
>
> (Bourdieu & Wacquant, 1992, pp. 108–109)

We can see in the story of Vicki and Thanh that Vicki had particular kinds of cultural capital – knowledge of books, computers and of the kinds of behaviour valuable in school settings. Thanh had cultural capitals which were less easy to 'cash in' in his school context and which made it less easy to acquire the capitals in which he was deficient – his knowledge of arithmetic was recognised and did lead to school success, whereas his knowledge of languages other than English did him no good at all. It is not the case that Thanh had no cultural capitals; rather, those that he had were not of equal status or exchange value to those held by Vicki – in the current school system. We can imagine the ways in which both Thanh's and Vicki's capitals might accumulate throughout schooling and the various possibilities that they might have, post school, to 'trade in', and on, their qualifications, social networks, and know-how.

Bourdieu specifically addressed the significance of **social capital**, the (dis) advantageous membership of social groups. In common parlance, social capital is about who you know. Social capital is often accompanied by collective cultural capital which is maintained though social exchange – participation in similar activities, living in similar neighbourhoods, attending similar events, going to the same school and/or university. Significant social capital may be accrued through family membership and through marriage. I referred at the beginning

Introducing Pierre Bourdieu 13

of this chapter to Bourdieu's own family conflicts caused by his mother's marriage to someone with lesser social capital. She married 'beneath her station' – this common expression encapsulates a vertical hierarchy of social status and the importance of the quantum and nature of social, as well as economic and cultural capitals. Vicki's and Thanh's families also had different kinds of social capitals, with Thanh's family potentially well networked into a South-East Asian business community which might eventually result in a substantive amount of economic capital. However, the family occupied a different part of the overall societal field than Vicki's middle-class family, who possessed school-friendly cultural capital – university qualifications and the social networks congruent with Vicki's future enrolment in private schooling.

Bourdieu's notion of capitals, in particular social capital, often gets conflated with another sociological use of the same term, that popularised by Robert Putnam (1993, 2000). Putnam proposed social capital as a kind of 'glue' that held societies together. Nations could be judged on the quantity of 'bridging' (vertical ties between social strata) and 'bonding' (horizontal ties between the same social strata) social capital that existed. This version of social capital is a normative concept amenable to quantification and comparison between locations, as well as to deliberate policy interventions designed to build bonds and networks (Baum, Palmer, Modra, Murray, & Bush, 2000; Sirianni & Friedland, 1995; World Bank Social Capital Initiative, 1999). It is important to distinguish this view of social capital from the Bourdieusian concept (see Edwards, 2004; and Portes, 1998, for further explanation). Bourdieu's social capital denotes the use and exchange of associational ties between positions in fields. Social capital is variously advantageous in field 'games' depending on its volume and type and on the specific game being played.

Bourdieu proposed that the game in each field was to acquire the capitals that are specific to it. At stake in the field of education are institutionalised symbolic capitals, specific knowledges which take the form of hierarchically organised qualifications. School certificates and university degrees are a proxy for cultural capital, and they can be converted in markets into economic capital and in networks to social capital. But there is more at stake in education than just qualifications. Educational institutions do more than impart knowledge. They offer various opportunities for students to be and become particular kinds of people, agents possessed of embodied cultural capital and immersed in particular social settings. The kinds of institutionalised and embodied cultural and social capital accrued in the field of education are, of course, not evenly or equitably distributed.

To take this a little further, we need to address another of Bourdieu's key concepts.

Habitus

Habitus is a difficult concept to both grasp and explain. If fields and capital are Bourdieu's way of discussing what many other social scientists called social structures, habitus is his approach to reconciling the structure-agency quandary. As a social scientist, Bourdieu did not believe in free will. He believed that social

14 *Introducing Pierre Bourdieu*

processes, institutions and thought systems framed what people did (Bourdieu, 1984). But he did not accept an explanation popular with many of his French peers, namely that what people did was ultimately dictated by the needs of the economic system, and their belief in free will and choice was simply a false consciousness inculcated and supported by various cultural and social apparatus (e.g. Althusser, 1971). Bourdieu did not accept that society was made possible through dominant ideologies which worked hegemonically to maintain control (Eagleton, 1991). He rejected this structuralist view, as did his contemporary Michel Foucault. Both Bourdieu and Foucault sought to explain how 'the social' worked through persons and institutions in ways that were not inexorably predetermined but that were nevertheless framed in space/time (see Murphy, 2013).

Bourdieu argued that 'the social' was embedded and embodied in people (agents) through their immersion in social fields and in the overall field of power. When an individual enters a field, playing the game specific to the field, they take up and take on its rules, beliefs and moves – in other words, they become a player. Much of what players initially have to consciously learn soon becomes almost automatic and taken for granted. Bourdieu often used sporting analogies to make this point. He suggested that learning how to be in a field is the same as how football players learn to play. As we learn the ways of the fields we are in, key aspects of it become second nature to us. Just as football players eventually (appear to) instinctively sense where a ball is heading and position themselves accordingly, we too become more skilful field players.

How does this happen? Learning to play in a field is about the acquisitions of dispositions, Bourdieu argued. That is, individuals are disposed to act, speak and think in particular ways because of their location in a field. And constellations of field dispositions come together to form the 'habitus'.

Neither the term nor the idea of 'habitus' was invented by Bourdieu (see Bourdieu, 1993b, for his tracking of the concept), but it is his use of habitus with which most current education researchers are familiar. In a much-quoted definition, Bourdieu explained habitus as

> systems of durable, transposable dispositions, structured structures predisposed to function as structuring structures, that is, as principles which generate and organize practices and representations that can be objectively adapted to their outcomes without presupposing a conscious aiming at ends or an express mastery of the operations necessary in order to attain them.
>
> (Bourdieu, 1990b, p. 53)

This definition alerts us to the ways in which habitus operates below the level of consciousness – an individual is predisposed to act in particular ways. On the basis of a particular arrangement of dispositions derived from participating in a particular set of fields, a person will:

- take particular things for granted,
- believe that particular things are important,

Introducing Pierre Bourdieu 15

- aspire to particular things,
- admire and want to possess particular kinds of objects and
- want to participate in particular kinds of social, cultural and political events and processes.

Habitus frames and often strongly shapes human actions. Habitus

> implies a sense of one's place' but also 'a sense of the space of others'. For example, we say of a piece of clothing, a piece of furniture, or a book: 'that looks petty-bourgeois or 'that's intellectual. What are the social conditions of possibility of such a judgment? First, it presupposes that taste (of habitus) as a system of schemata of classification, is objectively referred, via the social conditionings that produce it, to a social condition: agents classify themselves, expose themselves to classification, by choosing, in conformity with their taste, different attributes (clothes, types of food, drinks, sports, friends) that go well together and go well with them, or more exactly, suit their position. To be more precise they choose, in the space of available goods and services, goods that occupy a position in this space homologous to the position they themselves occupy in this space.
>
> (Wacquant, 2004)

These actions/emotions/beliefs seem completely natural, as noted earlier. They 'feel right'. When we are habituated to behaving in particular ways we feel 'like fish in water' (Bourdieu, 1990a, p. 131). We 'fit', or not, in the field(s) we are in; we desire more of the capitals that we possess; we value particular kinds of relationships and seek more of them out. Habitus is embedded in the practices of bodies and psyches living/working/playing in particular social worlds.

Bourdieu suggested that the habitus of agents are far from identical, although there are definable patterns amongst agents in similar field positions. Dispositional patterns are produced through the social/positional relations of class, gender ethnicity and race, ableness, geographical and historical locations. It is helpful to recall Vicki and Thanh at this point. Vicki felt at home in the classroom, just like a fish in water. Because of the way she had grown up (being read to at night and doing particular kinds of activities with her mother and father), she felt at ease. Thanh had almost the opposite experience – he felt out of place a lot of the time. He stood out because of his poor English. But perhaps because of the things he was accustomed to doing, such as chores in his family restaurant where he was a productive member of a working team, he may also have found it unfamiliar to become a child in a permanent subservient relationship to an adult teacher. Learning to 'do school' was a specific task for Thanh whereas Vicki came to school already disposed to it – she was ready for the educational environment.

Revisiting the notion of habitus after Bourdieu's death, Wacquant (2016) stresses that habitus is not static nor singular – it is he says, a "multilayered and dynamic set of schemata" which "records, stores, and prolongs the influence of the diverse environments successfully traversed during one's existence" (p. 68).

16 *Introducing Pierre Bourdieu*

There is a primary habitus acquired early in life through the family, and a secondary habitus grafted on through schooling. The lamination of additional dispositions continues through life. Because of the ongoing formation of dispositions and various field-specific accumulation of capitals, the habitus is neither coherent nor unified. Because individual people occupy more than one field at a time and they move through different fields during their lives, none of us is likely to have exactly the same habitus – the same set of dispositions. Growing up an Asian boy in a family struggling with poverty, living in social housing and going to a comprehensive school will produce a very different set of dispositions to a life growing up white Anglo girl in a rural village and going to the village school but living in public housing and on benefits. While both might at some point be counted as much the same in 'class' surveys and school statistics, their capitals and habitus (dispositions) will have some similarities but also important differences.

The experiences we have, when growing up, form our 'primary habitus' and, as we can see from Bourdieu's own life sketch, may lead us to feel like fish out of water in many places and for all of our lives. This is the case for academics who have working class origins, it is argued, where the dispositions formed in higher education sit uneasily with those from childhood (Reay, 2001a; Reay, Crozier, & Clayton, 2009). Some (e.g. Ingram & Abrahams, 2016) argue that a 'cleft' habitus, that is a habitus where the primary dispositions are at odds with those subsequently produced through the life trajectory through different fields, is especially conducive to reflexivity (Bennett, 2007). That is because dispositional contradictions are often located and experienced as emotional sore points: they can thus be held up to conscious scrutiny, a point I return to in Chapters 3 and 7.

Cleft habitus also explains the ambivalence of many working-class students towards the achievement of educational success (Stahl, 2013, 2015). There is now quite a bit of research about young people who are the first in their family to have a university education (Bourdieu & Wacquant, 1992, p. 127). They often feel uncomfortable and out of place with peers who seem to intuitively understand what to do. Sometimes their primary habitus is highly influential in their choice of university; they want to go somewhere where there are other people like them, not where the majority has been to a higher status ('posh') school (Cole & Gunter, 2010; Mahony & Zmroczek, 1997; Plummer, 2000; Reay, 2001a). This research evidence support suspicions towards higher education access policies which suggest that *all* that needs to happen to increase equity in higher education is that schools and universities must work harder at it. If habitus frames university choice, then it is clear that additional and different kinds of strategies from open days and summer schools might be required in order to make the 'non-traditional' student feel at home.

Habitus is not to be confused with individualism; it is not self-sufficient. As Wacquant (2016) puts it, "like a spring, it (habitus) needs an external trigger and so it cannot be considered in isolation from the definite social worlds (and eventually fields) within which it operates" (p. 69). The same habitus may support different kinds of conduct according to the state of the game and the strategic opportunities that are available. And sometimes field conditions are such that the

actions that arise from the habitus are not assimilative or adaptive but oppositional. As Bourdieu wrote

> a habitus continuously thwarted by the situation can be the site of explosive
> forces (as with ressentiment) that may await (nay look out for) the opportu-
> nity to exercise themselves and express themselves as soon as those objective
> conditions are offered (e.g., the position of a petty boss).
>
> (Bourdieu, 1993b, p. 87)

Bourdieu has been criticised for being unable to theorise change, for relying too
much on reflexivity caused by tension between dispositions and field position,
and for underplaying the ongoing intra-habitus practice of "reflexive accounting,
conscious strategising, and rational calculation" (Mouzelis, 2010). This is just
one of the many debates that surround interpretations of Bourdieu's work (these
debates are addressed more comprehensively in Chapter 7). However, Bourdieu
did imagine change as possible and likely via the interaction between habitus and
field.

Understanding the habitus of individual agents is complex. It is integral to
the ways in which we might understand careers. For example, a female primary
teacher from humble origins might work in a high-status school and have a
degree from a 'good university' but at a lower qualification level than that which
is currently considered necessary for promotion in the system. But because the
female primary teacher works in a particular institutional position, the ways in
which she plays the game will have strong commonalities with other primary
teachers, even if what she does is inflected with other dispositions related to the
social and cultural capital she has at her disposal. The social and cultural capital
she accrued at the high-status university might be advantageous, but her gender
and primary habitus might, however, dispose her to play the game and be played
against, in ways which are unlikely to advance her position.

To complete this explanation of Bourdieu's framework it is necessary to go to
additional, related concepts.

Logic of practice, doxa, illusio and misrecognition

First of all – a brief recap of the key concepts. I have already established that
Bourdieu argued that social life could be understood as consisting of a series
of overlapping and interrelated fields. He suggested that each field is relatively
autonomous, but all social fields work to produce and reproduce the status quo
of the broader society-wide field of power. One such field is education. The field
of education is organised according to vertical and horizontal status hierarchies;
different kinds of symbolic capitals are accrued according to the positions in the
field. In the field of education, the game concerns the distribution of capitals such
as qualifications and ways of being and becoming, the production of particular
kinds of dispositions and schooled habitus. And the cultural capitals at stake in
the field of education are not distributed evenly. Bourdieu argued that this was so

18 *Introducing Pierre Bourdieu*

because the education game is a highly competitive one. Its *logic of practice*, the underpinning way in which it works, is that of sorting and selecting.

As the story of Vicki and Thanh illustrates, some children enter the field of education already advantaged. Because they know how to play the game they are able to be, and be seen by their teachers as being 'good students'. By and large they behave appropriately. They speak school and book language. The vast majority of them want to succeed, or at the very least, they expect to succeed. Their families have social, cultural and economic capitals to provide them with the kinds of home experiences that are valued by the school game – this ranges from trips to museums to intensive tutoring and expensive grooming (Reay, David, & Ball, 2005). Middle-class children generally do better on tests and assignments and exams than other children who come in and have to learn the particular game of school. As each school year progresses, the gap between the advantaged children and the rest widens (Lareau, 2003; Reay, 1998b). Some children from 'non-traditional' backgrounds do, of course, succeed – they are 'selected out' through the everyday processes of schooling and the rituals of examination, just as Bourdieu was himself.

A 2016 headline in *The Guardian* newspaper in the UK recently reported "Decades of investments in education have not improved social mobility" (http://www.theguardian.com/commentisfree/2016/mar/13/decades-of-educational-reform-no-social-mobility) as if this were new news. The report, based on scholarly research, offered no explanation for the phenomenon of stagnant social mobility other than policy failure. But Bourdieu's notion of the schooling game – primarily one of sorting and selecting on the basis of particular cultural and social capitals and habitus – explains the persistent nexus between parental education, social class, and education so carefully documented by researchers (see for instance the longitudinal study by Comber & Hill, 2000; Hill, Comber, Louden, Reid, & Rivalland, 1998). However, very few people who work in the education field discuss, or indeed believe, that the school system works as a practice of sorting and selecting. Bourdieu's argument does not sit comfortably with many who work in education and beyond. Why is this so?

Bourdieu has an explanation for the lack of acceptance of the overwhelming evidence for the reproductive effects of schooling. This explanation was developed from his systematic studies of schooling and higher education (Bourdieu, 1988;Bourdieu & Passeron, 1977, 1979; Bourdieu, Passeron, & de Saint Martin, 1995). Bourdieu suggests that each field has its own set of beliefs – he calls this *doxa*. The doxa justifies and legitimates the game in the field. In the field of education the doxa is that of meritocracy. The notion of meritocracy implies that students advance in and through education, as do teachers, based on their merit. If you have what it takes – you have 'ability' and work hard – you succeed at the game. By definition then, those who fail must be less able and/or not work as much as they ought. They perhaps lack ambition or have important deficiencies in linguistic capital because their parents did not read to them (as did Vicki's parents).

Bourdieu argued that meritocracy was a myth. The schooling game was rigged at the outset in favour of people with particular dispositions and capitals – those with 'inherited' capitals were positioned to be successful at the game of education right from the moment they walked through the nursery gates (Bourdieu, 1977). The doxa of meritocracy, the myth held to be true, hides the inequitable nature of the game and conveniently sidelines the issue of what counts as merit, and who decides that this form of merit is the one to be recognised, used and rewarded.

Merit, and its fellow traveller ability, are not uncontested notions; see for instance the school-based reform in England where some schools abandoned ability grouping in primary classrooms on the grounds that it unfairly stigmatised some children and kept them in their place (Hart, Dixon, Drummond, & McIntyre, 2004; Hart, Drummond, Swann, & Peacock, 2012). Another site for doxic contestation is situated in the debates about vocational versus university-oriented curriculum and whether 'doing' is of lesser importance than 'thinking'. The mental/manual divide is tied into notions of superior/inferior intellect as well as the relative value of qualifications for work/university entrance. Debates about what kinds of assessment regimes produce higher or lower 'standards' are also about the efficacy of various sorting and selecting processes and the doxa of merit. If exams are 'too easy' they are thought to fail to select on the basis of merit. Policy rows over university entrance, which usually are conducted via a doxic rhetoric of standards and fairness, are always disputes about changing the capitals at stake in the field, thus allowing different players to advance (Bourdieu & Passeron, 1979).

Taking a Bourdieusian stance means not only understanding what doxic contests are being waged but also where the moves for and against policy changes come from: this is a sure indication of the positions whose agents feel they have something to gain and lose from proposed changes. It is not too far a stretch to suggest that almost any area in which there is ongoing policy debate is likely to be centred on the potential for shifting the distribution of capitals and hierarchical positions in the field. Those agents with something to lose are always vocal and active in such situations as they seek to shore up their position and protect their interests.

It is worth noting that the doxa of meritocracy is not confined to the education field. Although it is not a major logic in other fields as it is in education, it does form part of the doxa of many others. For example a major site in the struggles for equal opportunity in the public sector was and continues to be about what counts as merit (Thomson, 2010a). The battle for equal pay was and is about whether different kinds of work can be seen as having equal value (Bacchi, 1999, 2009; Eisenstein, 1984; Yeatman, 1990). This gendered doxic employment struggle also plays out in the education field, in the promotion and reward systems for the educational workforce, as in other areas of the labour market. This is one of the homologies across fields. Thus, the question of who gets to be a school headteacher, or a professor, and on what basis, is knotted into the doxa of merit and what capitals and dispositions are counted as meritorious enough for an agent to 'rise' to a leading position in the field.

Bourdieu argues that field doxa are so taken for granted that they appear to be unassailable 'truths' (Bourdieu, 1990b). They are embodied in the habitus – those

20 *Introducing Pierre Bourdieu*

who are successful in the field and who thus have a stake in doxa perpetuity are disposed to act to preserve the doxa and their position as if they were one. The embodiment and embeddedness of capitals produce dispositional allegiance to protect and produce that same capital. Doxa and disposition work together as a form of self-deception, which Bourdieu describes as *illusio*. Bourdieu argues that when we take up, and take on, the doxa of a field, and its illusio, we also take up ways of being and becoming that are 'appropriate' to our position. We have a sense of our place in the field/world. We know what is expected of us and what it is morally 'right' to be/do/say. We know what is 'not for people like us'. This sense of what it is right to do, and what is wrong, frames the kinds of choices that we make, including the kinds of schools at which we might want to teach or to lead.

The sense of 'belonging' to a particular social and field position is, according to Bourdieu, why some working-class students reject opportunities presented to them. Bourdieu suggests that it is not only through the practices of the education system that inequitable school outcomes are produced but that adherence to the doxa is also important. Students may be disposed to aim for particular kinds of life options and to frame their hopes and aspirations according to what feels natural to them. Writ large, this self-limitation also contributes to social stasis, working against social mobility (Bourdieu & Passeron, 1977).

However, Bourdieu did not see this adherence to a particular position and doxa as a lack, as a false consciousness. He argued that

> [p]eople are not fools; they are much less bizarre or deluded than we would spontaneously believe, precisely because they have internalized, through a protracted and multisided process of conditioning, the objective chances they face. They know how to 'read' the future that fits them, which is made for them and for which they are made . . . through practical anticipations that grasp, at the very surface of the present, what unquestionably imposes itself as that which 'has' to be done or said (and which will retrospectively appear as the 'only' thing to do or say).
>
> (Bourdieu, 1984, p. 130)

In other words, students from 'non-traditional' backgrounds and their families understand their probabilities of success in the education field – very low – as well as their actual costs – moving away from home, becoming somebody different from everyone else in the family (Bourdieu & Wacquant, 1992, p. 130).

Bourdieu took one more step in this argument. He suggested that when students are failed in the game of school or choose not to compete, they are then blamed. This was, he said, a *misrecognition* – the doxa is taken to be what actually happens in the field. Blame ignores the selective logic of practice in schooling and constitutes, Bourdieu argued, *symbolic violence* – those with the symbolic capitals that count in the field disrespect, dismiss, pity and abuse those who 'fail' simply because the field is working according to its selective logics.

The policy discourse of aspiration and raising aspirations in those who are deemed to have a lack of it, is a clear example of misrecognition and symbolic violence. Young people and their families are blamed for not 'wanting' to go into higher education' (McDowell, 2000; Stahl, 2015), rather than the workings of the system itself being seen as the issue. And to go back to our story, it is not too hard to see the symbolic violence that Thanh might attract – he needed to work more on his English, he needed to gain confidence, he had ability but is not applying himself, his outstanding work in math shows he is capable of more if he just spent more time on homework and less on working in the restaurant . . . These kinds of educational comments – not unfamiliar – are classic instances of what Bourdieu designates as misrecognition and symbolic violence. The child is blamed for having capitals that do not fit in the school rather than the classroom and curriculum being systemically ill designed, unaccustomed/unable/unwilling to deal with difference and favouring those who most easily fit in.

Crucially, Bourdieu does not blame individuals or institutions for these toxic doxic practices. The lack of recognition of what is actually happening is, he says, indicative of the ways in which the doxa of merit has become so much part and parcel of the habituated and taken for granted ways of doing things in the field of education.

Is it all just reproduction?

Bourdieu's social theory addresses one of the questions that he pursued through his long career – whether the French school system operated democratically and equitably in the ways that it proclaimed and if not, why not. He argued that it did not; it actually operated to hierarchise positions, to distribute capitals unevenly and inequitably, to sort and select. Bourdieu saw education as implicated heavily in the *reproduction* of society rather than its transformation. However, Bourdieu did not preclude change. In fact, it is quite the reverse. Bourdieu held that the education field was a site for change.

Bourdieu reasoned that fields are constantly adapting. He offered two propositions which go to the potential for significant field change as opposed to the maintenance of the status quo. He suggested that:

1 all fields are inherently unstable, as noted earlier. A field is always fundamentally in tension. At any one time, various positions and practices are being contested; multiple tensions are derived from positions with different doxic interpretations, subtexts, capitals and dispositions. These positions are constantly jostling up against each other. Just as in a real game, Bourdieu suggests, once an agent begins to play, they either have to maintain or improve their position in the field. Refusal to play the game results in failure of some kind – the non-award of symbolic capital, being positioned at a horizontal extreme, not being able to advance further through the vertical levels of positions. All of this continued play creates the possibility for change.

Furthermore, changes in the broader field of power and/or in dominant fields can produce changes in other fields, changes in capitals, dispositions and positions. This is not automatically about maintenance of the status

22   *Introducing Pierre Bourdieu*

quo. In the case of the education field, change might be produced when the political and economic fields to which it is subordinate, responds to shifts in the wider field of power – such as those produced through globalisation – and agents press the subordinate field and its agents for new formations of embodied capitals. And opposition in the political field might lead to changes in the education field, opposition in the education field might destabilise the political field and so on. When there is instability in the societal field, such as occurs at times of social/economic crisis, there is an opportunity for agents in individual fields to join together and act in their own and the political field to bring about reform.

2   agents (people) are possessed of reflexivity. It is possible, according to Bourdieu, for people to interrogate their own dispositions and their doxic assumptions and actions and to do something other than that which 'feels natural'. Individuals and groups can continually ask themselves for example who benefits from their actions – are they simply advancing their position in the field at others' expense? Agents can use their reasoning capacity to hold their own embodied social learning to account. Reflexivity goes beyond a counteraction generated from habitus conflict with the field – it is what enables the counteraction to become conscious opposition.

This combination of broad social change and the reflexive reasoning by agents was Bourdieu's answer to the possibility of making society more just. But in later years Bourdieu was also highly politically active, extending his own activities from the higher education to the political field. He was a significant figure in French anti-globalisation campaigns and also addressed the question of globalisation and its consequences in highly accessible academic publications (Bourdieu, 1990a, 2004). Bourdieu must be understood as developing not only his theory over time, through empirical investigations, but also his (dis)position for/in political action.

Where next?

This chapter has introduced Bourdieu and key elements of his social theory. The next chapter considers the field of educational leadership, management and administration (ELMA) and what Bourdieu might bring to it.

2 Introducing ELMA – educational leadership, management and administration

In this chapter I situate scholarship in educational leadership, management and administration (ELMA) in its wider policy, professional and academic field. My goal is to show the ways in which ELMA scholarship, policy and practice are mutually constituted and (re)productive. The second part of the chapter focuses specifically on the kinds of research projects that are undertaken by ELMA scholars. My intention is not to offer an intellectual history of the field per se but, rather, to sketch out the kinds of research questions and agendas that dominate, and that are marginal to, ELMA. I begin, as is congruent with a Bourdieusian approach, by considering changes in the education field writ large.

Education – a global/local affair

The vast majority of education systems now measure their success on interlocking national and international benchmarks and league tables. Some majority-world countries work to achieve universal access to education and see their success and/or failure reported by bodies such as the United Nations. Those nations that have already achieved universal access to schooling strive to move up the international rankings generated by PISA and various Organisation for Economic Co-operation and Development (OECD) score sheets (Grek, 2009; Henry, Lingard, Rizvi, & Taylor, 2001; Rizvi & Lingard, 2009). Majority-world nations may find that a condition of loans from bodies such as the World Bank requires them to institute particular kinds of policy initiatives; in education these may well include: quality measures such as performance management and systemic approaches for producing and evaluating effectiveness, for example, common planning and audit processes. While there is no similar external financial encouragement/coercion for the 'advanced' nations per se, the vast majority has moved to adopt the same approach to managing improvement in education systems. Performance management, audit and measurement and particular kinds of planning processes are now used worldwide.

There are, of course, distinctive national agendas and thus considerable local variations in education policy and practice. It would be a mistake to suggest that there is one way in which education systems are governed, regulated and managed around the world. Nevertheless, there is sufficient take-up of an overall

24   *Introducing ELMA*

agenda, and evidence of interlocking global policy networks (Ball, 2012a), for the general trend to measurement, audit and comparison to be worth signposting. It is important to understand these macro pressures in order to not only see the demands placed on local contemporary educational leaders but also to understand why it is this way.

The changes described – a focus on performance and measurable outcomes which can be compared at various scales – is often described as a shift from government to governance (Kooiman, 2003). The pro-capitalist nation-building states of the early and mid-20th century practised 'government' – they assumed responsibility for the provision of a range of services to citizens (Piven, 1992; Pusey, 1991). The most extended versions of government were to be found in the welfare states of Europe (Offe, 1996), where there were not only nationalised utilities – transport, water, power and the like – but also other services – health, education, wage substitute payments and other safety net benefits such as subsidised public housing and transport. The shift to governance is explained as a move from command and control government to 'steering not rowing' (Osborne & Gaebler, 1993). Nation-building governments typically heavily regulated currency, trade and employment (Cerny, 2000). Loosening and reframing these controls was integral to becoming a 'competition state', set 'free' in a world market (Sorens, 2000). The cause of this shift is often sheeted home to the set of political beliefs collectively known as neo-liberalism (Cahill, Edwards, & Stilwell, 2012; Harvey, 2005) or advanced liberalism (Dean, 1999; Rose, 1993), although this is arguably a largely empty label which fails to account for the wide variety of practices and beliefs that exist in so-called neo-liberal states (Barnett, 2010; Venugopal, 2015).

Stoker (1998) defines governance as a capacity (to get things done) which rests neither on the power of government for command nor on the use of its authority. Governments which engage in governance develop and use new tools and techniques to navigate, direct and guide. This requires a set of institutions and actors that are drawn from but that are also beyond government. These are not autonomous self-governing networks of actors but are tied, via new tools and techniques (see the following discussion), to centrally determined goals and practices. Governance blurs the boundaries and responsibilities for tackling social issues across public, private and third sectors and ensures that the relationships involved in collective policy action are dependent on each other, as well as on the power derived from being part of governing. The move to governance is sometimes described as a hollowing out of the state (Rhodes, 1994) but is more often seen as creeping centralism (Newman, 2001) through which top-down power is diffused but is paradoxically enlarged and augmented rather than diminished or diluted.

It is worth noting, before moving on, that the theory of governance outlined earlier is not without critique. Pierre (1999; Pierre & Peters, 2000) for example argues that there are different modes of governance – managerial, corporatist, pro-growth and welfare – which reflect different orientations (values, traditions, norms and practices) between and within cities and these can produce 'governance gaps' in which citizens can act. Stenson and Watt (1999) suggest that

Introducing ELMA 25

governance has not lead to the death of, but, rather, to the reformulation of, the social. It certainly seems that tensions 'between universalist principles and service provision and logic requiring the state and local to concentrate on narrowly targeted interventions' (p. 190) are played out differently in different local jurisdictions. Organisational actors in specific locations are also variously capable of mobilising support around civic ideas and goals (Raco, 2002). (In a similar vein, Rawolle and colleagues [Rawolle, Rowlands, & Blackmore, 2015] unpack the practices of contractualism, one of the tools of governance, and suggest that it is more complex than often suggested). It also seems that, while governments have incorporated many of the technologies of governance, they have not given up direct service provision or hefty, highly centralised regulation. Most contemporary nation states are engaged in forms of governing in which there are continuous tensions and contradictions between ongoing forms of 'government' and newer versions of 'governance'. For the remainder of this book, the term *governing* is thus used to describe current nation-state practice.

The policy strategy of school 'self-management'/'local school management' – or 'devolution 'as it was once known in Australia and now school 'autonomy' – was integral to the changes in modes of governing (Avis, 2002; Whitty, Power, & Halpin, 1998). This is because 'self-managing' schools and further education colleges, rather than the nation state, can be held accountable for what they do. Self-managing institutions can be inspected and compared with each other. Their performances can be league tabled. They can be severed from local and district authorities, as is now the case in England, even go private and/or be taken over by any kind of not-for-profit or for-profit provider, as is the case in some parts of the US. Self-managing schools and chains of schools operate more like independent schools and universities. However, even though not all national education systems have devolved particular operational responsibilities to schools; many others (e.g. some Australian states and Canadian provinces) have nevertheless adopted other elements of the governance agenda.

In sum, the tools and techniques used in contemporary governing include:

1   establishing a central policy framework which in part delineates service standards – in education this includes a national curriculum with target attainment levels, 'standards' for teacher and headteacher performance and benchmarks of school and service delivery effectiveness.

2   contracting out of responsibility for the delivery of formerly central services to a range of providers (Burch, 2009; Thomson, 1998; Yeatman, 1993). New Zealand was an early adopter of wholesale contracted-out public services (Kelsey, 1999). In schooling, contracting out has led an increase in a range of school 'owners' (Kachur, 1999; Lubienski & Weitzel, 2010): in England, those under contract to 'deliver' an educational service now include academies and free schools, where the high degree of autonomy academy and academy trust executive leaders have is similar to that of the 'public' schools (Beckett, 2007; Woods, Woods, & Gunter, 2007). There has also been a wholesale contracting out of services such as school cleaning, building

26 *Introducing ELMA*

maintenance, information technology provision and maintenance, transport, payroll and so on. There are now highly complex networks of business and entrepreneurial involvement in former state school provision (see the careful analysis of this in the UK by Ball, 2007, 2012b). Contractors are generally believed to be able to be held accountable for their performance, although there are clear cases where this has not happened easily (e.g. UK rail systems and US power providers). Consultants thrive on and in this environment (Gunter, 2015).

3   developing a system of audit to track the performance of providers, be they government or other agencies. This is sometimes called governing by numbers (Grek & Ozga, 2008; Rose, 1991). In education, audit mechanisms include school and university inspection systems, as well as school examinations and standardised tests which offer a whole system-wide view of performance. The move to self-evaluation is also significant as the means of individual sites and their leaders taking responsibility for meeting centrally determined standards (Ozga, 2009).

4   introducing market principles believed to encourage better performance (Cutler & Waine, 1997; Gewirtz & Ball, 2000). Marketisation requires providers to sell themselves, and potentially to work against each other or to form strategic alliances to garner more resources and esteem. In schooling, this involves for example de-zoning schools and introducing a policy of parental choice and the use of school and university league tables to encourage 'informed choice' (Marginson, 1997; Ravitch, 2011; Taylor, 2000; Woodrow & Brennan, 1999). Markets are notoriously poor at ensuring equity. The provision of alternative education in England, for instance, is a relatively unregulated contractualised market which cannot guarantee its students an educational entitlement (Thomson & Russell, 2009).

5   implementing a clear programme of leadership training for providers which mobilises the principles of New Public Management (Hood, 1998; Pollitt, 2011) and its variants. This form of public managerialism (Dixon, Kouzmin, & Karac-Kakabadse, 1998) is data driven, performance target–oriented and corporatised via mission and vision statements, glossy brochures and other public relations strategies. It also produces leaders and managers who are wedded to its practices (Hall, Gunter, & Bragg, 2012).

These technologies of governing, mediated through local differences and inflections, become important when considering the current responsibilities and practices of designated educational leaders.

Educational leadership and governing

As changes in governing were and are effected, they bring about changes in what is expected of those responsible for schools, colleges and universities. What 'leaders' do each day and the ways in which they allocate priorities and time are altered. Indeed, who is considered a leader is one of the interesting shifts in the field.

Introducing ELMA   27

These days it seems almost everyone is a leader – heads, students, parents, teachers and administrative staff. At the same time as leading has become ubiquitous, there have been other associated changes in 'who does what'. It is worth considering the English case as an example of shifts in role and nomenclature. In England, headteachers have in some instances become principals; most schools now have SLTs – School Leadership Teams, consisting of those in formal positions of responsibility; and the SLT may well include the school business manager and possibly the site manager or human relations manager. There are extended middle leadership teams (formerly heads of department), strongly differentiated in role from the teachers they line manage. Schools have extended teams of administrative and technical support, some of which may well be contractualised (payroll and temporary cover for instance). There are numerous teaching assistants, some of whom are able to teach in their own right. The principal or executive or CEO of a school, academy or academy trust may no longer have a teaching background, and in some schools, many of the teachers hold no formal teaching qualification. These changes in the names and positions within schools indicate an evisceration of the 'educational' and an expansion of the managerial. (This change is explored further in Chapters 4 through 7)

How did this change in the school workforce and its naming come about? I will recap and expand some of the key governing interventions:

- Devolution/self-management in schools (a similar move has occurred in further education) brought with it requirements that heads take responsibility for hiring, firing and staff management; the maintenance and development of buildings, plant and equipment; and the management of finances (Codd, 1993; Smyth, 1993; Whitty et al., 1998). In some locations, additional tasks such as the management of school buses and dinners also became part of the headteacher's lot. These additional responsibilities often led to administrative staff with higher levels of experience and qualifications being employed to support this side of school and college operations, as noted earlier (Gunter et al., 2007). In England, radical self-management also created a new brand of 'leader', the executive head, who is responsible for several sites. Despite the push to local management, self-management means that lines of accountability are actually directed away from local communities towards systemic requirements. Decentralisation is a re-centralisation, with centrally determined frameworks prescribing what must be accomplished locally to meet the needs of globalising nation states (Popkewitz, 1996; Seddon, 1997). In England, recentralisation has increasingly meant the elimination of local democratic processes for schooling – local authorities have been stripped of educational decision-making powers, and most recently, the legal requirement for parental membership of school governing bodies has been dropped.
- The development of audit regimes such as inspection, self-evaluation and performance management required heads to interact with staff in changed ways (Case, Case, & Catling, 2000; Macbeath, 2006; Thrupp, 1998). Heads had to show that they could 'deliver' centrally determined policy agendas

28   *Introducing ELMA*

to a satisfactory standard, better still to 'good' or 'outstanding' (Cullingford, 1999; Penn, 2002). Heads and other senior staff thus instituted regular observations of teachers geared to externally determined criteria, and spent (and still do) significant amounts of time documenting the minutiae of policies, procedures and plans. Ensuring the existence of paper trails available for audit changed, and continues to change, the work of everyone in the institution as they work to internal systems for 'self-evaluation' (Hall & Noyes, 2009; Perryman, 2005). Schools are generally legislatively more accountable than universities; universities have always had greater autonomy than any other educational sector, although this is arguably lessened.

- Almost all schools, colleges and universities in, inter alia, the UK, the US, Canada, the Nordic region, Australia and New Zealand, now have much greater focus on their public image (Symes, 1998), devote administrative time to managing selection and enrolment processes, and spend school funds on promotional material and sometimes staff (Ball, Maguire, & Braun, 2012; Wilkins, 2011). The introduction of choice policies and removal of de-zoning forces school heads to focus on how they are seen and on how they present themselves. This is not necessarily a bad thing. But it seems that marketisation produces paradoxical effects. While schools seek to differentiate themselves in their public relations materials in order to attract enrolments, they actually reproduce more standardised and normative views of what counts as a 'good education' (Savage, 2012). The public gaze on schools is potentially problematic too. Media must be managed, all parent queries and complaints are potential risks and frank discussions with neighbouring competitors are often casualties of competition for enrolments (Thomson, 2009). Universities now 'enjoy' regular league tables of almost all of their operations, and these operate both nationally and internationally. These are a significant driver for the allocation of resources and attention.
- In some locations, school curriculum and pedagogical responsibilities can become very focused on the production of the kinds of exam and test results that matter in league tables (Gillborn & Youdell, 2000; Thomson, Hall, & Jones, 2010). Schools positioned further up the league tables are able to focus on innovation; for some this means developing their 'unique selling points' while for others it means working towards goals of a more equitable and socially just education (Jones & Thomson, 2008). For schools on the cusp of 'failure' benchmarks, it means the introduction of coaching and booster classes combined with far greater scrutiny of classroom teaching. The consequences of not living up to systemic expectations can be severe for individual leaders.

There is general agreement that these kinds of changes require the designated managers/administrators – the head and other SLT members in schools – to acquire new constellations of knowledge and skills. They must be good managers and understand in great detail the legislative, audit and risk frameworks within which they operate. They must also have finely honed communication

Introducing ELMA 29

competencies since they have to speak regularly with a wide range of people, not just students and their parents but also media, community organisations, business leaders, government officers, peers and educators from other sectors. But the area which has become key to government policy is that of leadership. Management is now seen as insufficient for running self-managing educational institutions. Educational heads must now demonstrate that they can *lead* not simply manage. They must for example generate a vision and get staff and their community to sign up to it and develop a realistic but inspirational plan for continuous improvement that can be marketed to prospective 'investors and customers' (Courtney & Gunter, 2015).

Of course, in this sketch I have produced a highly generalised picture. It is certainly one which has multiple variations, produced not simply by different national policy regimes but also by virtue of the specific location, type and size of schools, colleges and universities; the uniqueness of each institution; and the very particular individuals in leadership posts. Nevertheless, as a description of a trend, it has sufficient traction to use as the basis for thinking about how ELMA as a discipline has responded to these changes in governing practice.

Before doing this, I want to pause to briefly signal how the phenomena described above might be re-explained using a Bourdieusian framing.

Bringing Bourdieu to the changes in the education field

I do not have the space here to undertake a detailed analysis of the changes I have outlined earlier. I therefore simply signpost some of the most important points using a Bourdieusian perspective. Chapters 4, 5 and 6 offer examples of more extended Bourdieusian analysis of these shifts and the following can be read as a kind of 'advance warning' of arguments to come.

The shift in governing practice can be understood as:

1   the education field becoming more subordinate to the economic, political and government fields (see Thomson, 2005, for a full elaboration of this argument). What happens in education is now germane to the standing of nation states relative to each other, as expressed in international league tables of educational performance.
2   there is a tighter suture between the education and political and government fields. This has not only reduced the autonomy of the education field but also created a bigger overlap between the educational and the political. Senior educational public servants who hold a position straddling the education and government fields – they are situated at a point where the two are conjoined – must work strongly to the political field (a process sometimes called the ministerialisation of decision-making; Knight & Lingard, 1996) – or alternatively the eradication of the Westminster system with its impartial bureau and focus on public good rather than ministerial accountability (Du Gay, 2000).
3   the elevation of the doxa of the superior efficiency and effectiveness of a small state, marketisation, contractualism, privatisation and devolution. This

30   *Introducing ELMA*

is supported by the introduction of new positions and new capitals in the field – advisers, think tanks, consultants and corporate partners.

4   new dominant practices in the field – particularly notable are those of audit and the wholesale shift to regulation by data (accompanied by a 'support' doxa of evidence).

5   new assemblages of agents and positions working to agendas determined in the political field – public, philanthropic third-sector and private agents/positions are tied, often legally via contracts, to political logics.

As a result, in the education field we see that:

6   there are renewed and explicit statements of the symbolic capitals that are at stake in the field; these are articulated through various 'standards' – national curriculum, school effectiveness, leadership profiles, quality teaching rubrics and so on.

7   as always, students are sorted and selected on their capacity to reproduce particular linguistic and disciplinary knowledge capitals via tests and exams. But teachers and leaders are now judged on their students' performance in this game through inspection (and the use of evaluative 'cause and effect' algorithms).

8   heads are judged for their managerial practice and knowledge capitals, that is for the practice of getting teachers to 'deliver' the prestigious symbolic capitals.

9   new hierarchies of position are created around the reworked game of schooling with for example executive heads in a vertically superior position to former colleagues; and schools that have 'good results' and 'good image' in horizontally dominant positions characterised by more autonomy from external perusal. In England there is a vertical elevation of those who inspect and regulate to the point where a chief inspector can undermine the position of a government minister – and the reduced status of a previously powerful position in the field – that of the local authority.

10   local community members and parents have considerably reduced strategic moves available to them as they can make far fewer local decisions; they are consigned to play the schooling game as customers and clients. Teachers have very little power and capacity to play the game differently within their schools if their headteachers do not 'lead the way'.

None of these changes has happened in isolation. They have occurred together through contestation – the ecology of countless moves and countermoves of agents and positions.

Mobilising Bourdieu's toolkit allows us to see the *relationships* between the changes in the education field – the position of schools and their designated leaders has changed, new and old forms of capital are at stake in the field, new 'leader' dispositions are produced and there are new games afoot – as well as their legitimation and the consequences for equity. Here, I focus on what they mean for the ELMA field.

The ELMA field

It is important to start the discussion of ELMA as a field by noting three important aspects of it.

First, a key characteristic of the ELMA field is that it encompasses both theory and practice. Professionals in the field, policymakers and academics all have an interest in ELMA, and something to offer. Knowledge about and interest in ELMA is dispersed across a wide range of people and organisations, including nurseries, schools, universities and colleges; university schools of business and education; a range of consultancy businesses; third-sector non-profit organisations; international policy–generating organisations; government at national and local levels; non-government systems; think tanks; media; and religious and ethnic organisations. This list would not have been so extensive two or three decades ago, and the expansion is indicative of some of the significant changes that have occurred around the very idea of educational leadership.

Second, the elements of ELMA – leadership, management and administration – are not clearly delineated. What each of them means has been subject to considerable debate and discussion over time (e.g. see the differences between Bates, 1987; Bennis, 1993; Bush, Bell, Bolam, Glatter, & Ribbins, 1999). As policy has moved from favouring administration to management to leadership, the ELMA field has responded variously. The three terms are used differently in different locations and literature. In this book, management is taken to be the practice of *systems* which keep the organisation functioning and leadership the practice associated with organisational improvement (Brighouse & Woods, 1999). While these two are generally mutually dependent, some aspects may be emphasised more than others in particular positions and by different agents. Management and leadership may be associated with different positions in the school. Managerialism is taken to be a practice which relies primarily on control systems such as executive decision-making, data monitoring and performance management (Hartley, 1997).

Third, educational leaders and those who write about them have enjoyed a protracted moment in the sun. Policymakers from almost all jurisdictions see those who are the designated titular head of educational institutions – be they vice chancellors or school headteachers – as the key to the implementation of their policy agendas. There is recognition that delegated leadership and management needs to reside with others lower down the 'org-chart' to ensure ownership and implementation within the institution (Harris, 2008; Spillane, 2006). In some jurisdictions, educational systems have decided that teaching aspiring and current leaders cannot be left to higher education, and have set up their own professional development agencies, qualification structures and approaches – the National College in England was one such example and the Bastow Institute of Educational Leadership in Victoria, Australia another. Some ELMA scholars have seen their work taken up by these government agencies and quangos. Others have not; not all those who study educational leadership have benefited from an elevation in esteem, as I now explore in more detail.

32   *Introducing ELMA*

Governing and ELMA scholarship

The changed role for educational leaders and the funding of specialised leadership institutes and training bodies have had particular effects in the ELMA field. Policymakers involved in field changes (described in the first part of this chapter) were particularly interested in what knowledge could be brought to bear on one key issue, namely how leaders could do their jobs 'better'. They focused on what they could do via training to make sure that leaders would support and work for governance-oriented changes in the field.

In some locations such as in England, Australia and the US, policymakers' interest produced increased funding for leadership research (as noted). This was sometimes channelled via leadership training institutions (as noted). Policymakers and those responsible for leadership training provision also sought out particular leading practitioners and academics deemed to have work pertinent to systemic change and improvement questions. The series introduction to this book designates the group of texts and people who travel the world advising governments and keynoting leadership conferences on educational improvement and reform as the Transnational Leadership Package (TLP). The TLP is neither homogenous nor static. It has shifted and developed, and some members are openly critical of governments that have opted for name and shame rather 'capacity-building' approaches (e.g. Fink, 1999; Hargreaves, 2004). Still, they remain popular with system leaders. Why is this so?

ELMA concerns and questions

ELMA is a distinctive area of knowledge production and can be seen, following Bourdieu, as a field in its own right. There are departments in universities around the world devoted to it. Government-sponsored bodies deal with it, as do organisations which bring together practitioners and academics (e.g. BELMAS, ACEA, CCEAM, UCEA) to discuss questions of mutual interest. There are also charities and for-profit companies engaged in leadership training and research.

The actual origins of the ELMA field vary from country to country, but in every case it has strong connections with practitioners as well as with scholars. ELMA is also an internationally well-networked field. I do not intend to trace the history of the ELMA field here, as there are entire texts devoted to the topic (e.g. Bush et al., 1999; Donmoyer, 1999; Gunter, 2012b; Murphy & Louis, 1999); Helen Gunter's (2016) recent intellectual history offers a detailed Bourdieuisan analysis of the development of the ELMA field in the UK in particular. Here, I want to focus on practices on the kinds of questions that ELMA scholars most commonly ask, the methods that they use and the kinds of uses to which their knowledge is put.

ELMA is not a field in which 'blue sky' research is generally practised. It is not surprising, given its origins and composition, that the ELMA field was and is dominated by questions designed to have an impact on practice. The area was always, and still is, profoundly directed to the world of schools, colleges and universities.

It is also important to note that ELMA is a field where many, such as myself, claim only partial involvement. Many ELMA scholars also research in associated fields such as urban school reform, educational change, effectiveness and improvement, policy, curriculum development, teachers and teaching and so on. When I write here of ELMA scholars I include those who usually work in the field and those who work in it but who also work in other areas. My interest in this section is the focus of the ELMA study, not the allegiances of the scholars, as well as the epistemic resources that are dominant and those that are imported from other associated fields. Please also note that all citations used below are indicative and not exhaustive!

ELMA scholars generally have an interest in the questions that follow.

1. What educational leaders do

ELMA scholars might simply seek to understand the job of a school head (Ribbins, 1999; Southworth, 1999; Wolcott, 1973). They might want to know which are the head's most and least important tasks. They might be concerned with documenting changes in the field and how designated leaders feel about them (Foster, 2004; Starr, 2001). Not so long ago, ELMA scholars wanted to develop a comprehensive set of characteristics of the job of leading and managing, but they are now more likely to engage in studies of 'best practice' and the development of standards and rubrics of effectiveness (e.g. Blatchford, 2015; Leithwood, Day, Sammons, Harris, & Hopkins, 2006). This kind of scholarship makes explicit the capitals and dispositions that leaders use to play the game to maximum 'effect'; the field reproductive practice of this kind of ELMA research can be seen in the use, inter alia, of student test and exam outcomes as the measure of leadership effectiveness and success (e.g. Day et al., 2007, 2009; Day, Sammons, Hopkins, Leithwood, & Kington, 2008).

Researchers interested in what leaders do sometimes adopt an additive genre – just add an adjective in front of the word leader to distinguish this particular piece of research from others in the field. ELMA has spawned a large number of these additive leadership categories – my google search yielded transactional, transformative, situational, servant, distributed, dispersed, entrepreneurial, caring, autocratic, laissez-faire, participatory, primal, constructivist, benevolent, pace-setting, coaching, charismatic, affiliative, authentic, emotional, empathetic, bureaucratic, inclusive . . . An outsider looking at the seemingly never-ending production of adjectival leader studies might harbour a suspicion that something else is going on here. A Bourdieusian perspective would suggest that the writers of additive leader studies seek to gain some benefit for themselves – as a scholar one must contribute knowledge and an adjectival contribution shows distinctiveness which, if it is much cited, may assure field status or approval for its proponent.

There is a small literature around leaders' work written by headteachers themselves. It is perhaps more a tradition in the great public schools for heads to write a memoir on retirement (Loader, 1997; Rae, 2009), but heads in the state sector have also joined in penning an autobiographical reflection (Hebert, 2006; Winkley, 2002).

34   *Introducing ELMA*

2. How leaders might do the job better

ELMA scholars seek to build diverse models achieved through transformational/ servant/transactional/strategic/etc. leadership (see for instance the review of the history of transformational leadership research in Leithwood & Jantzi, 2005). Scholars might also generate specific tools that leaders can use to plan, develop strategic directions, develop visions, develop staff, build relationships with the community, develop student leaders, work on school culture and ethos and so on (Davies & Ellison, 2003; West-Burnham, 2005). This corpus of ELMA research spells out the practices which are now valued in the field, and which are required to maintain position (e.g. Robinson, 2007). The ELMA work by Australian Brian Caldwell (1998), Caldwell & Hayward (1997b), Caldwell & Spinks (1988, 1992, 1998) focused on school self-management and was used by policymakers internationally to justify shifts in governing practice; it is particularly of note here. Based initially on a single case, that of Alberta, and a single school experience in Tasmania, Caldwell's work has legitimated changes in the wider field of education.

School change researchers and entrepreneurial policy consultants (e.g. Elmore, 2004; Fullan, 2005, 2006) are located around the question of better leadership too. They are sometimes very critical of aspects of the dominant game in the field, for example the counterproductive political use of naming and shaming tactics (Hargreaves, 2004) and the folly of the 'quick fix' (Stoll & Myers, 1998). Change researchers advocate paying more attention to teachers (Hargreaves & Fullan, 2012) and argue for a curriculum for '21st century' society (Hargreaves, 2003). Despite these contrary notions, some change scholarship also supports key dominant field practices – for example data used for systemic audit are also used to generate school change, a field reproductive strategy (e.g. Earl & Katz, 2006). And few change scholars challenge the fundamental premise of the schooling game, namely the production and reproduction of the status quo and particular elite capitals and habitus.

Surprisingly little around leaders' change practice has been written by leaders themselves. Notably, as for question 1, there are near-retirement narratives about 'turning failing schools around' (e.g. Coates, 2015; Hampton & Jones, 2000; Monroe, 1997; Stubbs, 2003) – or almost (Tompkins, 1998). There are also heads' accounts of generating new models of schooling (e.g. Meier, 1995, 2002; Meier, Sizer, & Sizer, 2004). Much of the formal research undertaken by practising school leaders into their change work – usually as postgraduate study – is not published. However, some heads have engaged in educational journalism, and the advent of social media and 'edublogging' has seen a rapid increase in the number of practising heads writing for each other and for the wider profession.

Questions 1 and 2 are primarily where school effectiveness and school improvement (SESI) scholarship is located and it is this area of inquiry which has grown most significantly in the shifts in governing practice. SESI have recently renamed themselves Educational Effectiveness and Improvement Research (EEIR) and are now known by both acronyms. EEIR uses field logics of cause and effect, of measurement and audit, as well as using dominant field symbolic capitals as measures of success. It is this field homology, combined with EEIR's explicit production of field strategies, dispositions and capitals, that creates the 'fit' between the overall field game and EEIR work in ELMA. The 'fit', that is the logic served, can be seen in the ways in which those who excel at the explicit game of valued EEIR leadership practice – as explained by EEIR scholars and advocates – achieve either vertical or horizontal distinction, or both, in the field (Blackmore & Thomson, 2004; Thomson, 2014).

I return to EEIR in the final section of the chapter.

The ELMA field is also concerned with the following questions.

3. How leaders do what they do

This ELMA research interest may well be married with both questions 1 and 3. It might involve looking at issues such as time, networks, roles, communication patterns and decision-making (Evans, 1999; Loader, 1997; Smulyan, 2000; Whitaker, 2003). It might extend to questions of identity formation (Bloom & Erlandson, 2003; Whitehead, 1998). It can encompass questions about doing the work of leadership differently, as in the research into co-principalship (Court, 2003a, 2003b). However, the question of how leaders work is also amenable to critical research, as I show in the next chapter.

4. How leaders can be taught to do the job

ELMA scholars interested in this question might investigate the balance of theory and practice in leadership learning (e.g. Eraut, 1999), experiment with various forms of learning including via web technologies, develop sets of cases for use in leadership education (e.g. SAGE's *Journal of Cases in Educational Leadership* and *Journal of Research on Leadership Education*) or generate texts for use in courses (e.g. Hallinger, 2003; Hallinger & Bridges, 2007). Researchers might be concerned with developing standards for preparation of leaders (see the literature review by Ingvarson, Anderson, Gronn, & Jackson, 2006). Scholarship around this question might be reproductive of the field game or contest some of its doxa and practices.

5. Leading understood as a profession

ELMA researchers might seek to demonstrate how leaders are different from other educators in their institutions and have particular responsibilities (Murphy, 2002). This line of inquiry has been linked to work on standards and to moves by some headteacher organisations for increased salary and conditions (e.g. see the debates in and around Murphy, 2005). Sometimes a more moral approach to the idea of leader as professional is taken (Beck, 1994). Research around this question may be linked to questions 6 and 8 discussed next.

To a lesser extent, the ELMA field has also been concerned with other questions such as these:

36   *Introducing ELMA*

6. Who gets to be a leader

Practices related to training, selection and promotion are central to this research. Feminist, urban, queer and postcolonial research, relatively sparse in the field, is often concerned with this question and mobilises additional theoretical resources around identity, pedagogy and life history in order to investigate it thoroughly (e.g. Addi-Raccah & Ayalon, 2002; Coleman, 2005; Fuller, 2013; Hall, 1999).

7. How leading and managing relates to other forms of work and professions

As opposed to question 5, this question focuses on similarities, rather than distinctiveness, between educational leadership and other forms of work (see for instance the special issue of the *Journal of Educational Administration and History*, 45[4], on New Public Management). Some ELMA scholarship on gender and race can be found around this question too, on work/non-work balance and on what the governing practice changes have meant generally for 'leaders' (e.g. Blackmore, 1999; Blackmore & Sachs, 2007; Chapman & Gunter, 2009).

8. Why the job of leading is the way that it is

This body of ELMA work often seeks to situate the work of designated educational leaders in a wider context, and with more general understandings of education, of public policy and of more macro social changes. It often takes a historical turn. Scholars interested in this question might examine the same practices as in questions 1 and 2 but place them in a broad sociopolitical context (Niesche, 2011). Concerns about the supply and retention of school leaders (Blackmore, Thomson, & Barty, 2006; Thomson, Blackmore, Sachs, & Tregenza, 2003; Walker, Stott, & Cheng, 2003) sit here but are also strongly connected to questions 6 and 7.

9. How knowledge about ELMA is generated

This question interests only a minority of ELMA scholars and practitioners who are concerned to see what knowledge is included and excluded in leadership training and education and why (Bates, 1993; Bates & Eacott, 2008; Eacott, 2011b). Histories of the field often address this issue (Crow, 2001; Gunter, 2016; Ribbins & Gunter, 2002).

10. How educational leaders might contribute to social justice

There is a range of ELMA scholars and practitioners interested in this question and a substantial set of literature (e.g. Frattura & Capper, 2007; Morrison, 2009; Normore, 2008; Ryan, 2005; Shields & Edwards, 2005; Skrla & Scheurich, 2003; Tillman & Scheurich, 2013). Social justice oriented research has

Introducing ELMA 37

strong connections with ELMA literature which focus on the moral and ethical dimensions of leading schools (Barth, 1990; Sergiovanni, 1992; Starratt, 2003). Scholars committed to social justice usually bring an explicit commitment and philosophy to question 3 and are often interested in questions 4 and 8.

It is important to note that this latter set of questions – 6 through 10 – are where the focus is less on questions that might reproduce the educational field and more on questions that go to its change. It is hardly surprising then that the ELMA scholars who address these questions are less likely to be TLP members and often locate their work within critical and post critical epistemological traditions.

All ten questions can, of course, be researched using various methodological approaches and methods. In the last section of the chapter I therefore consider some dominant methodological trends in the ELMA field.

ELMA and its methodological bases

Like educational research more generally, the ELMA field contains within it mixed influences (in the form of doxa, capitals, dispositions and strategies) from different disciplines – psychology, anthropology, sociology, history and philosophy. Different horizontal positions in the ELMA field are loosely associated with different knowledge-producing traditions (see Wang & Bowers, 2016, for a study of citations in major ELMA journals).

There is arguably a dominant epistemology – the underpinning assumptions about the knowledge being produced through research – in the ELMA field. It is a loose form of post-positivism, that is, research is conducted in and with the belief that there is an external reality which can be observed, measured and described. In quantitative ELMA work, researcher influences on the generation of definition, the choice of sample and the use of particular statistical techniques to generalise and 'round up' are generally addressed through a discussion of research 'limitations'. Nevertheless, the graphs, tables and diagrams of correlations are taken as the best 'truth' we can produce at present (see Brundrett & Rhodes, 2014). When a post-positivist stance underpins qualitative research it is often with an intention to understand participants' perspectives and their contexts (Gronn & Ribbins, 1996). There is generally an acknowledgement that the researcher is heavily implicated in the production of words, their transcription, thematisation and coding and that people's understandings are socially constructed (e.g. see A. R. Briggs, Morrison, & Coleman, 2012). Nevertheless, participants' words are surprisingly often taken as 'authentic'.

ELMA does host scholars from other epistemological traditions. These can be broadly designated as critical and post-critical (see for instance collections edited by English, 2011; Portelli & Foreman, 2015; Samier & Bates, 2006; Tillman & Scheurich, 2013). Critical and post-critical scholars work within a variety of traditions – feminist, queer, decolonising and postcolonial, to name some of the more obvious. Post-critical scholars mobilise understandings from poststructural theories, and often deconstructive approaches are integral to their methodologies

38 *Introducing ELMA*

(Lather, 2007). Scholars in these minority ELMA epistemological traditions share the view that there is no 'outside'; 'the social', including the researcher, is implicated in how a phenomenon is produced and understood. While there is a material reality, it is not neutral (Archer, 2007). Knowledge always works in particular interests, and all research is situated somewhere, at a particular time. Thus, a researcher is never able to 'see' or represent the totality of an event, utterance or phenomenon. Nevertheless, community scholarly practices make it possible to judge the relative rigour and merit of different kinds of research (Harding, 1993).

Many in the ELMA field maintain an axiological commitment to social justice and equity, as noted earlier. However, this plays out in very different ways depending on the researcher's epistemological position, their disciplinary basis and their chosen methodology and methods. An interest in equity and/or social justice is not necessarily sociological and may, as I argue through this book, lack some of the analytic tools necessary to see beyond the phenomena under investigation. In order to illustrate this contention, I now circle back on some of the preceding discussion.

I re-consider two dominant strands of contemporary post-positivist ELMA scholarship, which focused on developing understandings of leadership and that which looks at school effectiveness and improvement (EEIR). My aim is to tease out some of the key methodological elements of each so that, in the following chapter, these can be contrasted with a Bourdieusian methodological approach.

Leadership studies

Recent changes in governing practice brought, as argued earlier, a new interest in leadership. Governments wanted to ensure that heads would be able to meet, inter alia, the new accountabilities, financial and audit requirements and the public relations expectations of self-managing schools. A new grouping of researchers was drawn to this agenda. ELMA, change and EEIR scholars in particular, formed a loose network of 'expertise' able to work in, with and on this governing agenda.

Many focused overtly on leaders and leadership (see the previous section). They had a particular cluster of concerns. The kinds of questions asked often included, as outlined above: what do leaders (however defined) do, what are the characteristics of good/bad/ordinary leaders, what factors make leaders effective/good/ineffective, what do parents/teachers/students think good/bad/ordinary leaders do, what different kinds of leadership are there, what kinds of training do leaders need and what are the experiences of leaders in particular sites and times.

The notion of leadership was stretched. While leaders were historically often understood as those in formal leadership/management positions in schools, the notion of who can be a leader has recently come under pressure. It is not at all uncommon now to see the definition of leader extended to designated middle managers, teachers and, less frequently, students and parents, as argued for by the new coalition of leadership researchers (Harris, 2008; Spillane & Diamond, 2007; York-Barr & Duke, 2004).

Introducing ELMA   39

Leadership studies typically have an institutional focus. However, organisational and institutional theory are rarely mobilised. Instead, the school is made the unit of analysis together with (whoever is) the leader. Many leadership studies that were commissioned by government as part of the shift in governing practice were particularly oriented to generate:

1   an understanding of leadership actions which could be codified and named and potentially ranked according to their in/effectiveness, or
2   a taxonomy of effective leadership 'styles' or
3   the factors which contribute to (in)effective leadership.
    (e.g. Coleman, undated; CUREE, 2003; Gold, Earley, & Evans, undated; Harris & Chapman, 2002; National College for School Leadership, 2002, 2005).

Leadership studies take many forms. My review of four major ELMA journals suggests that ELMA qualitative methods are often confined to individual interviews and life histories, case studies and 360-degree interviews in the institution. 'Multi-method' approaches to leadership are also common; surveys are variously subject to simple or highly complex statistical procedures, particularly if the focus is on leaders' (in)effectiveness (see the next section). Image-based research, ethnography and language-based approaches, such as discourse analysis and conversation analysis, are far less common, although these are suggested in one of the very few specific leadership methods texts available (Briggs, Coleman, & Morrison, 2012).

These research methods applied to ELMA questions do yield a range of results and reports – from narrative accounts of personal experience to heuristics, models, lists of actions that are significant to 'good' leadership and descriptions of 'best practice' to elaborated manuals of 'how to do' leadership. Diagnostic tools used in leadership training usually draw on these kinds of leadership studies in order to help/train/instruct people to examine their own behavioural repertoires and to consider what behaviours are appropriate for what situations and with whom.

There are some taken-for-granted assumptions in many leadership studies. Leadership studies very often separate the leaders out from others in the same organisation through the binary of leader/follower (e.g. Hadfield, 2007; Skorobohacz, Billiot, Murray, & Khong, 2016). This is a revealing sleight of hand since the binary other of leader is not follower; it is a not-leader. Someone who is a not-leader includes not only those who follow but also those who resist both passively and overtly. And leader-follower is not the only doxic categorisation generated through leadership scholarship – one has only to think of the ubiquitous notion that all leaders must have a vision (e.g. Deal & Peterson, 1999; Leithwood & Reihl, 2003) to see a 'truth' which is widely taken up in the professional field – see for instance these blog posts on vision from the extremely popular blogger headguruteacher (http://headguruteacher.com//?s=vision).

Many leadership studies draw on the broad field of psychology and necessarily centre on individual development and/or cognitive and emotional behaviours.

40   *Introducing ELMA*

This disciplinary leaning is not surprising, given the history of the ELMA field and its initial strong connections with organisational studies in the field of business. Organisational psychologists produced, and still do produce, accounts of management strategies around the pattern and flow of work or the relationships with people, to aid productivity (Bates, 1993). A psychological ELMA leaning in leadership studies, combined with an individualised focus, stands in contrast to the minority of leadership studies that draw on sociology and anthropology (beginning with the classic Wolcott, 1973).

The different disciplinary bases of ELMA leadership studies play out in different approaches to the same phenomena. While the vast majority of leadership studies include the policy context in which leaders are situated, psychology-influenced scholars usually examine the ways in which leaders respond to particular policies and/or their work are framed, enabled or constrained by policy. Their focus is on the individual, their feelings and their actions. These actions and feeling can be aggregated and codified to show generalised behaviours and activities (e.g. Day, Harris, Hadfield, Tolley, & Beresford, 2000; Southworth, 1995). Social science–located researchers by contrast investigate the relationships among individuals, groups, institutions, and larger social relations and structures. In critical social sciences in particular, the 'little picture' of leader and school is always connected to a 'big picture' of the wider society and its unevenness, inequalities, histories and habituated practices (Gunter, 2016).

Critical ELMA researchers often focus on investigating the production, patterning and functioning of leaders and their work. They see an individual leader as a window to the ways in which the work of leaders more generally is constructed, and while individual idiosyncrasies of person and location must be taken into account in any study, it is the socially produced patterning of leadership actions, emotions and relations that are the object of study, as well as the purposes and outcomes (e.g. Lingard, Christie, Hayes, & Mills, 2003; Morrison, 2009). For social scientists, the social is not a contextual container, but at once a complex (re)productive set of relations and practices as well as a 'pincushion of stories' (http://www.socialsciencespace.com/2013/02/podcastdoreen-massey-on-space/).

The purpose of a critical sociological ELMA study is not to produce generalised accounts of individual behaviours/feelings, but to explain how those patterns come to be, and thus why leaders act and feel as they do. While psychologically based studies might examine the personal life histories of leaders and generate heuristics which show the connections among context, biography and location, these are different from sociological studies which focus on the ways in which an individual is always social – as allowed through for example Bourdieu's notion of habitus, field and capitals.

Before I go on, it is important to note that I have so far constructed a simple oppositional binary between psychology and sociology. This is, of course, inaccurate both in disciplinary terms and in relation to the ELMA field. Social psychologists for example do have a strong interest in social patterns – see for instance the work of feminist social psychologists whose concerns with gender see them share with sociologists a desire to understand and explain broader social phenomena through their focus on individual actions, identities and feelings (e.g. Walkerdine, Lucey, & Melody, 2001). Some feminist ELMA scholars also take this approach (e.g.Lyman, Strachan, & Lazaridou, 2012; Strachan, 1993). So, rather than thinking of psychology and sociology as a binary it is more helpful to think of them as ends of a continuum with various hybrid forms in-between (the collection of 24 international case studies in Arlestig, Day, & Johansson, 2016 shows this spread; the sociological end point is a minority of one, Normaud). Arguably, the less sociological and post-positivist forms of psychology have been particularly influential in the ELMA field.

I now turn to another highly influential strand of research that is both part of ELMA, but which also sees itself as a separate field of study in its own right. EEIR has become an integral part of ELMA in the change in governing practice.

Educational effectiveness and improvement – EEIR

EEIR research straddles the ELMA field, as one of its foci is on leadership.

School effectiveness research arose from a concern with social justice. Early studies sought to understand the different influences of schooling and society on educational achievement. By using combinations of case study and statistical surveys linked to test data, school effectiveness scholars were primarily concerned with the school as the unit of analysis and as site of action (e.g. Rutter et al., 1979). Arguing that schools had no purchase on the rest of the society, early SESI scholars sought to find the key factors/actions/foci that would give some traction on what schools might do to maximise the influence that they did have on students' learning. They were interested in the *what* of school change, what needed to be done and what could be done, in the interests of greater equity (Teddlie & Reynolds, 2000).

School improvement sought to deal with the *how*. Working with understandings generated through school effectiveness research – the importance of capacity building/professional development for teachers, good leadership and good relations with families for example – SI scholars worked to demonstrate the best and worst processes of reform (see discussion of the relationship between SE and SI in Stoll & Fink, 1996). SI work took two major directions:

1   Hands on. Researchers worked with schools as critical friends (now increasingly as paid consultants) to develop sustainable processes of change. They might for example work with a 'cadre' of insiders who conducted school-based inquiries, develop and trial new approaches to teaching and lead professional development. Practitioner and action research were often key to this approach, as well as the promotion of learning communities and learning networks (Harris, James, Gunraj, Clarke, & Harris, 2006; Hopkins, 2001; Hopkins, Ainscow, & West, 1994).

2   Hands off. Researchers investigated how schools had changed, often using mixed methods approaches. Typologies were often developed to assist others to follow the best practice that was identified. For example schools and

42   *Introducing ELMA*

leaders that were 'successful', 'coasting' or 'failing' were deemed able to yield useful information about what all schools, and their leaders, should do (Day et al., 2011; Mitchell & Sackney, 2000).

There is considerable debate between EEIR and critical ELMA scholars about the importance or otherwise of educational and wider sociopolitical contexts (see Slee, Weiner, & Tomlinson, 1998; Wrigley, 2004, 2006). Some critical scholars do not take account of the serious differences within SI, in particular, and its more democratically inclined practitioners (e.g. Gray, 2004; Macbeath & Mortimore, 2001; Moos & Macbeath, 2004; West, Ainscow, & Stanford, 2006). Nevertheless, the critical sociological critique of all EEIR scholarship is that:

1 the initial move – to separate out the 'internal' school from 'external' context, to statistically eliminate the social from the school or to confine it to context – is untenable and does not stand up to scrutiny (see Lupton, 2004; Thomson, 2000, 2002), and
2 the measure of effectiveness and improvement – the use of student test and examination data – is reductive and ignores the ways in which curriculum, assessment, school organisation and teaching practices are themselves implicated in the production of inequalities. In short, the argument is that the measure used to test effect is part of the problem, and is not a 'neutral factor'.

These critical responses to EEIR are as much methodological as they are theoretical. They are not only to do with the purposes of the ELMA research but also with the questions asked and with the ways in which the research is designed and the analysis conducted. However, the response from EEIR to these critiques is to suggest that the approach taken by critical scholars is paralysing and offers nothing practical to schools. Critical ELMA scholars reject this response, arguing that the work of change must always be both theoretical and practical and that the two are mutually informing and generative.

The take-up of EEIR and leadership studies as part of governing

The ELMA field has been troubled by government interest in particular kinds of ELMA research and people. On one hand, it seems undeniably positive to have ELMA research make a difference. But what kind of differences does it make? Furthermore, has government interest skewed the work undertaken within the field?

In England, Weindling (2004) suggested that the National College for School Leadership not only invested heavily in ELMA but also narrowed its focus to concentrate on research pertinent to processes of improvement. This highly particular investment, he argued, had been a disincentive to other funders who had largely withdrawn from the field. Thrupp (2005a, 2005b, 2003) has been particularly vocal about the ways in which particular ELMA scholars actively worked for government agendas: he dubbed them 'textual apologists'. In the US there has been strenuous internal debate about ELMA academics' involvement in the development of leadership 'standards' (Anderson, 2001; English, 2000, 2006; Murphy, 2005). And there is also, as noted, ongoing debate between EEIR and critical ELMA scholars about a governing-friendly, devolved school-focused lens (Slee et al., 1998; Wrigley, 2004, 2006).

It is important to note that the interest taken by the government in ELMA not only provided a focus for academics and practitioners favoured by policy; it also took up a lot of critical attention too. A great deal of critical ELMA work has been devoted to interrogating the official government leadership agenda (e.g. Blackmore, 1999; Gronn, 2003; Gunter, 2005; Lumby & English, 2010; Niesche, 2011; Thomson, 2009), and to trialling, documenting, theorising and advocating for alternative approaches (e.g. Anderson, 2009; Lingard, Christie, Hayes, & Mills, 2003; Morrison, 2009; Ryan, 2005; Shields & Edwards, 2005). This book series sits with this critical position in the ELMA field, arguing that the tasks of critique and reconstruction of schooling can be greatly assisted when social theory is brought to bear.

But it is interesting for critical scholars to speculate on what else we might have done in the ELMA field if policy shifts had not taken such a dominant role in our work. Would we have spent more time on thinking and doing other things? If so what? Would we have generated more practical alternatives, thus answering the charge of EEIR scholars?

Where next?

In the next chapter the debates and tensions with ELMA, as well as the changes in governing outlined in this chapter, are brought into conversation with a Bourdieusian approach to ELMA research.

3 Bringing Bourdieu to ELMA

Because Bourdieu was one of the most significant scholars of the late 20th century, it is hardly surprising that there is a substantial extant educational literature which is Bourdieusian in orientation. In this chapter I canvass some of this territory. I argue that Bourdieu is most helpful when used methodologically and then survey of some of the ways his theoretical toolkit, outlined in the first chapter, that has been applied in educational research generally. I then propose some specific ELMA questions that arise from taking a Bourdieusian approach.

Using and misusing Bourdieu

It may seem odd to begin with a discussion of how not to use Bourdieu. The need to approach Bourdieusian research from the negative arises from the widespread, common-sense use that is made of his work. Understanding what not to do situates the subsequent discussion of the ways in which Bourdieu might be helpful. Knowing what constitutes a misuse sets boundaries around reading/writing about generative use.

Some of Bourdieu's key concepts – capitals and habitus in particular – are frequently mobilised in educational research. My mid-2015 search of Taylor and Francis online journals, using the search terms (school) + (Bourdieu), produced 334 results. Searching for (school) + (habitus) yielded 216 results. This perhaps suggests that many educational researchers are interested in understanding the individual as a social actor. (School) + (Bourdieu) + (capital) produced 165 results, raising the question of whether habitus is sometimes discussed without reference to other key concepts. But my relatively random scan of journal papers was hardly a scientific exercise – it could not be taken at all seriously, were it not for more substantive expressions of concern about the ways in which Bourdieu's work is mobilised.

Habitus and capitals are an important nexus. Indeed, Bourdieu once wrote "[(habitus) (capital)] + field = practice" (Bourdieu, 1984, p. 101), suggesting that it was not possible to understand strategic action in a field without mobilising both habitus and capital. Reay (2004) argues that habitus has been taken up as a singular and ubiquitous explanation within educational research, an intellectual habit which runs counter to Bourdieu's work.

Bringing Bourdieu to ELMA 45

Michael Grenfell (2010) lists eight ways in which Bourdieu's oeuvre has been misused:

1 Bourdieu is partially and/or superficially read, 'falsely accused' – of being deterministic/structuralist/lacking a theory of resistance – and then summarily dismissed. (I discuss this in more detail in the Chapter 7.)
2 Bourdieu is set up as a straw person to be demolished. A partial reading leads to the allegation of gaps in the work which the critical reader is keen to fill.
3 Bourdieu's conceptual toolkit is reduced – habitus becomes agency, field becomes context and so on, and the argument is made that this is same-old-same-old dressed up in fancy terminology.
4 Bourdieu's work is read out of its time and place and is judged against contemporary literature to which, of course, his scholarship has contributed.
5 The key concepts are laid over a set of data in order to give apparent depth.
6 An additive approach is adopted – particular kinds of capitals for instance are listed. The point seems to be the development of new subcategories of one term rather than using the concepts together as a lens to open inquiry.
7 Bourdieu is added in a footnote to add an aura of scholarship.
8 Bourdieu is ossified, and an orthodoxy is developed about correct/incorrect readings.

Grenfell argues that such misuses result from common academic argumentative ploys which are themselves part and parcel of the scholarly game, the ways in which academics advance their own position in the field. Finding gaps, false accusations, simply adding new subcategories and so on, he says, are integral to advancing in the academy.

Armed then with some caveats about the pitfalls of bringing Bourdieu to educational leadership management and administration, what might we do instead? What does Bourdieu have to offer ELMA? I suggested in Chapter 1 that Bourdieu's conceptual frame requires empirical research, and this chapter elaborates what this means for ELMA scholarship and scholars.

Educational researchers can gain from Bourdieu at least four things: (1) an ontological orientation, (2) a commitment to rigour, (3) reflexivity and (4) a broad methodological approach. I discuss each in turn.

1. An ontological orientation

The term *ontology* refers to the ways in which we understand reality, the world and ourselves within it. Bourdieu's ontological stance was social and relational. Bourdieu's work began with the premise that society is what happens between people – interactions, social bonds, exchange, activities, conversations and so on. He rejected the idea that society is a separate entity, a container for human activity, and the corollary that individuals are separate from society. Instead, he sought to theorise the relationships between the macro scale, which might be called society, and the micro level of the individual. His toolkit of habitus, capitals and

46   *Bringing Bourdieu to ELMA*

field is his way of getting beyond the sociological structure–agency impasse to examine the relational. Bourdieu understood the social world to be dynamic and agonistic, amenable to change through continual contestation. His toolkit is not a way to generate 'laws' which govern social relations but, rather, to see the logics of (inter- and intra-)action which are heterogeneous and particular but also patterned.

Bourdieu can be seen as an epistemological relativist (Maton, 2014). He maintained that knowledge was a social construction, specific to time and place. Bourdieu was also oriented, via his axiological commitment to equality and democracy, to see that different knowledge practices work in different ways to either advantage or disadvantage those who possess and use them (Bourdieu, Chamberon, & Passeron, 1991). Rejecting universalism and ahistorical scholarship does not, however, mean that there is no basis for deciding on truth claims – decisions about what constitute truth emerge through, and as, a relational, intersubjective practice. The understanding that truth practices are socially produced is congruent with Bourdieusian social ontology.

2. Commitment to rigour

Bourdieu had a strong belief in the importance of dispassionate scholarship. He argued that the autonomy of the scholarly field was simultaneously a strength and problematic (Bourdieu, 1993b). He was adamant that social scientists should not allow their scholarly work to be subject to political interference. In order for their scholarship to be 'legitimate', he wrote, scholars must conduct their work according to the principle of separation from the political and economic fields. Social scientists were to observe social, political, economic and cultural phenomena and then investigate them with fearless methodological neutrality, prepared for surprises and contrary 'results'.

Unlike those who argued for the conduct of science for its own sake, Bourdieu saw field-specific 'neutrality' not as a practice carried out for its own sake but, rather, as the means of ensuring that knowledge could be used to effect in other fields. Bourdieu argued that the authority of social scientists to speak in public about inequality, as he did vociferously later in his career, rested on their capacity to do their work according to (socially produced) scholarly norms of validity and rigour (Bourdieu & Wacquant, 1992). Later in his career, Bourdieu suggested that there was no difficulty in reconciling the autonomy of the scholarly field with political engagement or with maintaining distance from the topics under investigation in the scholarly field while also collaborating with social movements (Wacquant, 2005). Bourdieu's position might be seen as a gloss over a fundamental tension around the potential for the scholar to produce research results that fit their pre-existing political understandings – policy-informed evidence making as we might put it today (see the next section for more on this). However, this argument is refuted by many Bourdieusian scholars, who suggest that Bourdieu's position was not unlike his contemporary Michel Foucault. Both argued for a 'specific intellectual' who "intervene(d) in the public arena only on those issues that his [*sic*] specialised knowledge permits him to speak about with authority" (Swartz, 2010, p. 54).

In Chapter 2 I suggested that, within the ELMA field, the tension around the scientific nature of research and political skewing emerges in relation to the ways in which the research agenda around leadership and reform has been shaped. A significant corpus of 'hands on' ELMA work *is* the result of consultancies with, and commissions from, school authorities and sectional groups, such as principals' associations, and is geared to instituting particular forms of policy-directed school change (Thrupp & Wilmott, 2003). This is work where Bourdieu's basic tenet of scholarly autonomy has not been adhered to. A Bourdieusian approach has such 'hands on' work as lacking in sufficient scholarly detachment and rigour.

The inherently policy-associated (commissioned and/or promoted) body of ELMA work does stand in contrast to other strands of ELMA scholarship, where the principles of field autonomy and scholarly distance are held as crucial. But some of this 'hands off' ELMA work has *also* been appropriated by policymakers, often selectively, to support agendas that are doxic in the political field – privatisation, contractualism, audits and the like. It is important not to conflate ELMA as a field of knowledge production with the way that ELMA knowledge has been selected, taken up and used in policymaking. While some ELMA scholars *are* implicated *directly* in governing activities, many are not. Some of those who are not may, of course, still want to be!

3. Reflexivity

Bourdieu argued that knowledge is symbolic capital. It has a use and an exchange value. Some knowledge is more valued than others and all knowledge and know-how works to particular ends and in particular interests. Conducting research then means that no knowledge, no know-how and no 'truth' – however 'scientifically' produced – can be taken for granted, including the researcher's own knowledge. Reflexivity is essential.

Bourdieusian reflexivity is not a one-off event. It is not a ritual reflection at the end of a research project. Working with Bourdieu means that the questions – 'How might this knowledge I am producing and/or using either advance or reduce social inequality and injustice?' and 'How might this research advantage me, rather than those that I hope it will?' – is always at the forefront of the researcher's mind. A Bourdieusian-inspired self-interrogation demonstrates more than a concern for epistemology, the basis on which a researcher claims to know things. Reflexivity is also ontological – it refers to the world of social relations that are produced and reproduced through scholarship, to the ways that researchers and teachers act in concert with or against others. Reflexivity is also axiological and works as a practice with an ethical frame, against which researchers can make decisions and measure the effects of actions. Bourdieu suggests that taking account of, and interrogating the ways in which we as researchers are disposed to know and act, must become an embodied and embedded scholarly disposition.

48   *Bringing Bourdieu to ELMA*

In the ELMA field, Bourdieusian reflexivity has different resonances, depending whether we are researchers or practising leaders, or both. Practising leaders must account for the consequences of their leadership practice but also be cognisant of the ways in which being a leader and 'doing' leadership might perpetuate practices which reproduce the status quo. This means working with the uncomfortable recognition of the ways in which leaders might benefit from their leadership, using their practice to advance their own careers rather than more socially just ends. Even activities which apparently run counter to dominant doxa in the field can bring distinction to an individual agent. This is particularly the case when the doxa of governing suggests that process does not matter as long as designated outcomes are met. Headteachers adopting progressive pedagogical approaches while maintaining test results may thus find themselves lauded for their initiative and leadership and used by agents in the political field to demonstrate the benefits of school autonomy (see Thomson, 2014, and the next chapter).

Reflexivity implies that the ways in which our work is 'social' is always under scrutiny. Following Bourdieu, reflexivity is a necessary habituated scholarly self-analysis: ideally, it is dispositional and integral to the academic habitus.

4. Bourdieu as methodology

Bourdieu's interest was in understanding the ways in which the world worked. Bourdieu's research addressed a diverse range of topics. He looked for example at the ways in which the art world operated (Bourdieu, 1991), the development and uses of photography (Bourdieu et al., 1990), the housing market (Bourdieu, 2005), gender (Bourdieu, 2001), journalism (Bourdieu, 1996) and French elites (Bourdieu, 1998c). However, this did not mean that the theoretical toolkit he developed was an overlay, something that could be brought to data generated using any old approach, answering any kind of question. His thinking tools were specifically designed *through*, and *for* research which aimed to see the ways in which the social, institutional and individual are mutually constructed. It is helpful to look at Bourdieu's own work to begin to see what this actually means.

Bourdieu's *The Weight of the World: Social suffering in contemporary societies* (Bourdieu et al., 1999) investigated the ways in which changes in the French economy, political regime and demography played out in geographical locations, and the everyday life of particular classed, gendered and raced social groups. His initial starting point was a 'big question'. The empirical research was both a comprehensive survey of the actual changes at a large scale (the field), combined with a large corpus of interviews undertaken with a carefully designed sample of people, a sample designed to represent different 'positions'. The questions that were asked in semi-structured interviews were constructed to focus on the field in which individuals were positioned, the logics of the game in which they were imbricated, and the various 'plays' that they had available to them and those that they wanted to make. Interview questions were designed to allow people to talk in ways that would illuminate their dispositions and capitals, highlight doxa and reveal any symbolic violence to which they were subject. The interview transcripts are presented in full in the book, accompanied by an analysis which deploys the thinking tools in order to show the habitus and habitat of the various individuals/positions.

The research in *The Weight of the World* was constructed according to Bourdieu's sociological stance. He advocated always starting from the macro – the wider society, the field of power. This beginning point stands in contrast to ELMA research which often starts with a position, either a particular kind of school – successful, failing or coasting for example – or with a particular person – the headteacher, the bursar, the head of department (see questions 1–6 in Chapter 2). Beginning reflexively by considering their own positioning and doxa, Bourdieu and his team investigated their question through three explicit steps:

1   analyse the position of the field(s) vis-à-vis the field of power,
2   map out the objective structures of relations between the positions occupied by the agents or institutions who compete for the legitimate forms of specific authority of which this field is a site and
3   analyse the habitus of agents, the different the systems of dispositions they have acquired by internalising a determinate type of social and economic condition, and which find in a definite trajectory within the field . . . a more or less favorable opportunity to become actualized. (Bourdieu & Wacquant, 1992, pp. 104–105).

This three-step approach allows a researcher to reveal the *correspondences* or 'fit' between a position in the field and the 'stance' or position-taking of the agent occupying that position (see Grenfell, 1996; Grenfell & Hardy, 2007; Grenfell & James, 1998, 2010). In *The Weight of the World*, these correspondences were made discursively, through the juxtaposition of the interview with analytic texts in which the 'funnel' of field, positional relations and habitus were documented. Because the focus in this book was on explaining the experiences of suffering, the analysis was slanted to the habitus clearly in active relationships with position and field. It was a relational analysis.

An earlier book undertook a similar ambitious mapping of French society. *Distinction: A social critique of the judgment of taste* (Bourdieu, 1984) addressed the question of 'high and low' culture and the status attached to groups who shared particularly proclivities and activities – sport, food, the arts and so on. Bourdieu was concerned to show the ways in which social status and accompanying lifestyle choices and tastes were not individual but produced hierarchically and in relation to other social, economic and political practices. He sought to show the cultural and social capitals associated with various positions in the general field of power.

Bourdieu used mixed methods in order to undertake this research. His empirical work followed the three steps outlined earlier and used a particular kind of geometric mathematical modelling, called multiple correspondence analysis (Grenfell & Lebaron, 2014; Lebaron, 2009), to plot the association of

50   *Bringing Bourdieu to ELMA*

socioeconomic position with taste. Step 3 – understanding the habitus of particular positions and the capitals associated with various positions in the field sought, from a carefully selected sample determined through step 2, the following positional information:

- basic biographical information – place and date of birth, number of children, location of home;
- family background – profession of parents;
- educational trajectory;
- career progression;
- specific positions in the field such as membership of councils, boards etc
- indicators of symbolic capital e.g. prizes, awards, decorations;
- indicators of social capital membership of groups such as professional associations. (Lebaron, 2009, p. 17).

In *Distinction*, interview questions were asked about music, art, sport, food, clothing, housing and so on. Photographs were taken to demonstrate the differences between, for example, the objects which decorate the living spaces of dominant, middle and working classes. Interviews were semi-structured, and this allowed Bourdieu to record and analyse the ways in which 'taste' was discussed; this in turn allowed him to elaborate doxa and illusio, as well the strategies and logics of the 'taste' game.

A further elaboration of statistical position plotting can be seen in *Homo Academicus* (Bourdieu, 1988) a study of the production of the French university scholar, in which the first step of field analysis led to Bourdieu representing the scholarly field as divided by fundamental tensions, or axes. Bourdieu plotted scholarly positions around (a) academics' political positions in relation to their response to May 1986 on one axis and (b) traditional versus modernist approaches to disciplinary knowledge and academic practice on the other (p. 19). It was not possible to understand the French academy (at the time), Bourdieu argued, without recognising these chiasmatic divisions.

Homo Academicus, Distinction and *The Weight of the World* are helpful exemplars of the ways in which Bourdieusian thinking tools can be used to *construct* research projects. The conceptual frame is a set of thinking tools, used methodologically.

Bourdieu and educational research

Bourdieu has been used extensively within educational research, and I now point to some of the relevant literature before going on to look at the way his toolkit has been specifically used in ELMA.

Bourdieu has been typically brought to bear on educational problems that require a social explanation. Educational researchers pose a question that requires making connections between the broader social world, a particular institutional, policy or local setting and the actions of individuals.

Bringing Bourdieu to ELMA 51

This Bourdieusian educational research shares a common approach and analysis, despite having different foci. Education is typically seen as a boundaried field, with subfields of schooling and further and higher education. However, the borders of the educational field are loose and permeable and can encompass informal learning and even forms of 'public pedagogy' (Sandlin, Schultz, & Burdick, 2010) such as television and the web. The education field is generally understood as in a subservient position to a number of other fields, including the economy and the political field. Key players from outside the field – political and business leaders for instance – are seen as having steadily gained in influence and their doxa – human capital formation, entrepreneurialism, the benefits of competition, the inevitability of globalisation – as expressing the currency of the educational game, the capitals that are most effective for exchange and advancement (Addison, 2009; Lingard & Rawolle, 2013; Lingard, Sellar, & Baroutsis, 2015; Thomson, 2005). Within the field, educational sites are distributed in vertical and horizontal arrangements – these show the status of levels of education vis-à-vis each other and of types of institutions against each other. Not only is secondary schooling positioned vertically above primary and below further and higher education; it is also differentiated via horizontal status with high-fee, high-cultural-capital schools on one side and alternative vocational provision for excluded young people on the other.

Beyond this, researchers then define a particular interest which focuses their research on specific positions, capitals, doxa and aspects of the game. So for example there is Bourdieusian research which examines:

- the practices of school choice, an important aspect of the shift in governing practice. This research seeks to explain the ways in which choices are framed and delimited, as well as the social effects of choice (e.g. Ball, Bowe, & Gewirtz, 1996; Ball, Macrae, & Maguire, 1999; Ball, Maguire, & Macrae, 2000; Reay, 1998a; Reay & Lucey, 2000a; Reay & Wiliam, 1999).
- classed and gendered behaviours related to education, for example, mothers' attitudes to schooling (Reay, 1998b, 1998c, 1999), family behaviours in relation to schooling (Lareau, 2000, 2003), the attitudes of children from city estates toward their class position and education (Reay & Lucey, 2000b) and non-traditional students in higher education (Archer, Hutchings, & Ross, 2003; Reay, 1998d; Thomas, 2002).
- the ways in which education success and failure is distributed via, inter alia, types of schools, subjects and geographies (Teese, 2000; Teese & Polesal, 2003; Teese, Davies, Charlton, & Polesel, 1995), higher education institutions (Marginson, 2008; Naidoo, 2004) and disciplines (Ladwig, 1996).
- language and literacy practices in educational settings (Albright & Luke, 2008; Carrington & Luke, 1997; Grenfell, Bloome, et al., 2011; Luke, 1992). Bourdieu understood language to be a key to the process of educational social selection, and this body of work continues and updates that of Bourdieu.

52   *Bringing Bourdieu to ELMA*

- the workings of specific particular policy and practice contexts – for instance, higher education (Maton, 2005), languages (Grenfell, Blackledge, Hardy, May, & Vann, 2011), education policy in globalising and mediatised times (Lingard & Rawolle, 2004a, 2004b; Lingard, Rawolle, & Taylor, 2005; Lingard, et al., 2015), vocational education (Colley, James, Diment, & Tedder, 2007) and physical education (Gorely, Holroyd, & Kirk, 2003).

It can be seen from this very indicative list that educational research mobilising Bourdieu's thinking tools has a variety of foci. Common to all of them is the way researchers have worked with Bourdieu to develop sociological explanations of educational phenomena. Furthermore, Bourdieu's thinking tools have been used to develop research questions which take equity and social justice as their axiological norm.

And there is some educational scholarship which discusses Bourdieu as methodology, as is the case in this book. Mark Murphy and Cristina Costa have focused on the ways in which Bourdieusian thinking tools can be applied to questions of equity and social justice (Murphy & Costa, 2016), and on habitus focused research, where the primary lens is the particular position and dispositions (Murphy & Costa, 2015). Rawolle and Lingard (2013) have also written about Bourdieu and research practice, bringing to the fore Bourdieu's rejection of epistemological innocence, his insistence on the interrogation of familiar ways of understanding problems and his advocacy of 'intellectual love' for research participants.

However, Bourdieu has had much less uptake in ELMA than in other areas of educational research. The next section of the chapter considers some Bourdieusian ELMA literature and then speculates on what might be fruitful ELMA areas to pursue with Bourdieu as a companion.

ELMA and Bourdieu

There is already a small body of work in ELMA which uses Bourdieu.

ELMA studies which work with Bourdieu's thinking tools usually begin by mapping the field of education broadly, as suggested above. However, the specific field of ELMA itself is also plotted. ELMA Bourdieusian researchers map field positions, the relations between them and the agents that occupy them. The nature of vertical and horizontal positioning within ELMA is specifically examined. Educational 'leaders' are attached to particular positions (groups of sites), with their 'agent' position homologous with the position of the organisation to which they are attached. So for instance an executive head usually has a higher vertical status than does a head responsible for a similar but single school. A head who is under less scrutiny, that is has more autonomy, is generally of horizontally higher status than one whose 'failing' school is heavily steered.

ELMA Bourdieusian scholars are particularly concerned to analyse the dispositions, capitals and strategies of leaders. Leaders can acquire status in the field by changing positions horizontally or sometimes vertically. Field-specific capitals are required to move from one leadership position to another. If a leader moves horizontally from a state comprehensive to a high-fee 'public school', he or she does so by mobilising embedded and embodied cultural and social capitals. A vertical move from the school sector to higher education requires overlapping but also different embedded social and cultural capitals. However, leaders can also change the position of their particular site through their own field activities. 'Star' leaders, those who play the game par excellence, can elevate their schools within their area of the field. It is possible for example to achieve distinction in the field from a special or alternative school and to have a positional advantage not only over other special or alternative schools but also schools in adjacent areas of the field, such as vocationally oriented secondary schools (Thomson, 2014).

It is also important to situate this kind of analysis historically and to track the ways in which the game is changing. Schools, colleges and universities now require particular kinds of leaders with particular capitals – managerial and marketing knowledge and entrepreneurial dispositions for instance (Courtney, 2015).

What ELMA scholars research

The take-up of Bourdieu within ELMA is limited but also diverse. For example a special issue of the *International Journal of Leadership in Education* (vol 6, issue 4, 2003) was the first collection of peer-reviewed articles which brought Bourdieu into conversation with leadership. It is worth looking at the journal's contents because they indicate some major themes in the use of Bourdieu in ELMA. An introductory essay (Lingard & Christie, 2003) suggested that Bourdieu's thinking tools might be used to understand both the field of leadership and the practices of leading. The issue contained a paper on the intellectual history of ELMA as a field of knowledge production (Gunter, 2003); an examination of changing dispositions of middle leaders in managerialising universities (Zipin & Brennan, 2003); an elaboration of the ways in which field changes, the massification of secondary schooling, supported more democratic processes of student leadership (Thomson & Holdsworth, 2003); the organisational theory of loose coupling as misrecognition (Edward & Green, 2003); and the rhetoric of 'violent schools' with which leaders have to contend, as symbolic violence (Anderson & Herr, 2003). These kinds of themes have continued to be of concern and interest within critical ELMA scholarship.

ELMA Scholars often have an overarching concern about the formation and maintenance of the field itself. Bourdieu discriminates between fields in which practices of (re)production are dominant and those devoted to production and diffusion. The purpose of a field of production and diffusion, and ELMA is a quintessential example, is one devoted to knowledge work, generating and conserving 'consecrated' capitals as well as agents who specialise in the work of cultivating and legitimating the symbolic goods – in this case the leadership knowledge and know how – required in the field for its (re)production (Bourdieu, 1993a, Ch. 3).

54 *Bringing Bourdieu to ELMA*

Some ELMA Bourdieusian scholars thus begin from the position that the field itself is a little social world, constructed through the strategic coming together of agents in the higher education field and agents within the schooling field. The very notion of educational leadership is understood as a doxa, an underlying truth which holds the field together: the majority within the ELMA field hold that the practice of some agents in the field is best understood as leadership. Some scholars, as is the case here, seek to interrogate the ELMA field – and this book and the wider critical leadership series must be understood as being inside the field, and part of its internal contestation.

Scholars might seek to document the history of the ELMA field and its key agents and positions with different knowledge and knowers distributed according to position (school or university) with different capitals attached to each position (Gunter, 2016). They might investigate how field specific and field valued ways of knowing, being and acting are inculcated, required, produced and rewarded through leadership training and formal qualifications (Eacott, 2011b). Highly specific management knowledges are dominant in the ELMA field – Chapter 2 discussed leadership studies and school effectiveness and improvement (see Gunter, 2000, 2004, 2010a) – but these are not static. They change over time because they are an integral part of field games. Different knowledge and agents are taken up in and by policy at different times (Forrester & Gunter, 2009; Gunter & Forrester, 2008, 2009, 2010b). Systemic agents' development of leadership standards for example is seen as strategies to support particular doxa, capitals and habitus (English, 2012). ELMA scholars pursue these changes.

A variant of the critical scholarly move to understand fields might not only involve tracking the ongoing relational strategies which maintain and develop ELMA as a field; this work might seek to establish a counter, alternative approach (e.g. Eacott, 2015). And ELMA scholars could, although we are yet to see this work emerge in any quantity, examine the idea and rhetoric of leadership as a misrecognition which enacts symbolic violence in order to maintain the status quo of existing field relations. Perhaps the closest we get to this is in studies which examine who gets to be a leader (Eacott, 2010b; Grant, 2011) and explanations of the consequences of the changes in the game and current field formation – the shift in governing practice (e.g. Thomson, 2009).

Related ELMA scholarship tracks the logic of leader moves – why leaders behave as they do in current circumstances. Leadership is seen as a practice (Eacott, 2011a; Gunter, 2001) and as social action (Eacott, 2010a). Researchers analyse horizontal and vertical field positions of leaders (Gunter, 2000; Thomson, 2005) in order to understand the logics that produce and reproduce leadership practice. The actions of leaders might be understood as a leadership habitus (Lingard et al., 2003; Reay & Ball, 2000) or as a set of field-specific dispositions (Thomson, 2010b). Bourdieu's key concepts are used to deconstruct current expectations of school leaders (Hatcher, 2005), changes in the workforce and thus who is and can be seen as a leader (Gunter et al., 2005), the professional development offered by leaders to teachers (Hardy, 2010) and the stresses experienced by school leaders (Thomson, 2008a).

The sequestration of ELMA from other fields of educational research – there are separate organisations, separate special interest groups, specialist journals within the field – means that relevant 'leader' research outside of the ELMA field may not penetrate far into it. There are for example studies of leaders in elite schools (Koh & Kenway, 2012), leadership as subject to 'gendered games' (Acker, 2010) and documentation of the challenges for school leaders in newly multi-ethnic schools (Devine, 2013). Some educational researchers use Bourdieu to develop strategies for change, for example critical leadership in the physical educational field (Fitzpatrick & Santamaria, 2014) and leading mathematics teaching reform (Melville, Hardy, Weinburgh, & Bartley, 2014). Many critical scholars straddle the ELMA field, as already noted, engaging actively with wider sociological scholarship. They may be aware of and use these studies for their complementarity with research within ELMA.

Designing a Bourdieusian ELMA study: a hypothetical proposal

Because Bourdieu is relatively infrequently used in the ELMA field, there are topics which could benefit from the methodological approach his thinking tools afford. There are numerous ELMA sites and foci to which Bourdieu might usefully be brought. For example there is still only a little Bourdieusian research into processes of recruitment, selection and promotion of leaders. There are relatively few Bourdieusian projects which examine the commonalities between educational leaders and those in other fields. There is more Bourdieusian work on leaders in schools than in colleges and universities, and the homologies between different sector positions is a potentially fruitful area for further analysis. Analyses of the field of ELMA knowledge production might further interrogate doxic taken-for-granted terms and practices including the notion of leadership itself, as already noted.

Therefore, to conclude this chapter, I want to consider a possible research question and use it to think about the various ways in which a project might take a Bourdieusian approach. I must note at the start of this hypothetical exercise that I cannot avoid thinking about where research questions come from – Bourdieu has us remember that research questions are integral to their field and cannot be separated from it. Research questions may appear to be related simply to curiosities and puzzles and from observations we have made about the field. However, they not only arise from the field but may well be connected with the researcher's (agent's) own habitus as well. I suspect that this is probably the case with my hypothetical project, as it reflects my own trajectory through a history of struggling for, and about, more democratic and socially just forms of schooling, much of it as a practising school headteacher. For the time being, I proceed as if my hypothetical project comes from something I have been musing about.

My hypothetical project is to investigate what is happening to leaders of 'teaching schools'.

In England, there has been a steady shift of teacher education out of universities into schools. There are now 'teaching schools' which are contracted by the

56 *Bringing Bourdieu to ELMA*

government to provide initial teacher education as well as training and development to experienced teachers. Teaching schools are those that:

- have an outstanding rating from Ofsted;
- provide evidence of successful partnerships;
- show excellent leadership with a proven track record of school improvement;
- have an outstanding headteacher with at least 3 years' experience;
- have a leadership team with the capacity to lead the 6 core areas of the teaching school role (https://www.gov.uk/guidance/teaching-schools-a-guide-for-potential-applicants).

'Teaching schools' make strategic alliances with other schools, dioceses, local authorities and private-sector organisations, as well as universities. Teaching-school arrangements bring new legal and audit requirements and responsibilities that their leaders must address.

How might leading a teaching school be researched? A leadership study might focus on the layers of senior and middle leaders, using perhaps a survey and follow-up interviews, looking for descriptions of work patterns, descriptions of change and opinions about opportunities and difficulties. A researcher might use comparison cases so that leaders in non-teaching schools as well as teaching schools could be compared against a general leadership rubric. A 360-degree study could engage other (lower status) staff members to get their views on what the leaders in teaching schools do and how it affects them and their work.

An EEIR study might look to gauge what effective leaders of teaching schools do. In addition to leader interviews and surveys (as described earlier) the EEIR researcher might examine the employment statistics, experiences and performance assessments of cohorts of teaching school 'students'. Student results on tests and exams could also be factored into using quantitative measures (multi-level modelling). Criteria for effective leaders would be used as a guide but might also be modified as a result of finding which key activities were more strongly statistically associated with outstanding teacher performance (cf. Gu et al., 2015).

A Bourdieusian study would begin with the field, looking at changes. As this is *my* hypothetical study, I would, in addition to a general field analysis (see Chapter 2), also want to think about what appear to be field changes in relation to teaching and teachers' work. For example:

(1) there is recently much more discussion about teachers and their crucial importance to student learning. Bullet-point lists handed out at leadership conferences, and downloadable online, frequently refer to Finland and the ways in which teachers are educated to a master's level, and are expected to innovate and adapt curriculum to suit their students (Sahlberg, 2006, 2012). Trust in teachers and the comparative absence of audit are also frequently mentioned. Teachers are said to have 'professional capital' (Hargreaves & Fullan, 2012) which is the basis for sustainable changes in curriculum and assessment and thus student learning. Leaders must now nurture 'professional capital'.

Bringing Bourdieu to ELMA 57

(2) there is now a strong push from some in the profession, some academics and some policymakers towards using 'what works' in classrooms (see Whitty, Anders, Hayton, Tang, & Wisby, 2016, for a detailed discussion). Randomised control trials and other forms of intervention studies are promoted in both the US and the UK as the way to find 'what works'. EEIR scholars (e.g. Robinson, 2007; Robinson & Hargreaves, 2011) now point to instructional leadership as the key to school improvement – this brings meta-studies and evidence reviews, or their translations, into school. There are frequent references to blockbuster books of meta-studies (Hattie, 2008, 2011; Hattie & Rates, 2015) and to 'evidence-based' reviews. Teachers can then discuss and adapt the 'evidence' and use local attainment data as their measure of success.

Both of these phenomena point to a change in capitals in the field – knowledge about EEIR is important, there are new positions in the hierarchy of knowledge production and new positions in schools where at least one member of the senior leadership team is the curriculum leader/head data analyst. This is rarely the head. There are also changes in the relative positions of teacher educators and education departments in universities and new players in the field.

There is a question about how responsibility for a teaching schools might change the capitals, game strategies and everyday practices of school leaders. Up until the advent of the teaching schools there was a surface 'pedagogisation' (or what Biesta (2006) calls learnification) of leadership via the focus on test data. However, ELMA and other critical scholars have documented the ways in which deep educational expertise has in reality been stripped out of the official discussion of leadership (Blackmore & Sachs, 2007; Court & O'Neill, 2011; Gunter, 1997; Hall, 2013) and of its practice. Many senior leaders express deep regret that they are not able to spend more time on educational matters (Thomson, 2008a). Heads in particular do not have to have any particular pedagogical expertise but mainly manage and monitor so that teachers can address learning improvements (Thomson, 2011a; Thomson, Jones, & Hall, 2009). What does the doxa of 'professional capital' achieve in these circumstances?

And how might this be researched? The empirical methods used to garner information about what is happening in teacher training and non-teacher training schools – interviews and examination of texts, analysis of current policy for instance – might appear to be the same as a leadership study. However, the questions asked would be different. A Bourdieusian ELMA scholar would not ask,

> What has happened to educational leadership, why can leaders not spend any time on educational leadership, how do leaders do educational leadership?

Rather, he or she asks,

> What kinds of educational leadership are now being promoted via teaching schools, and how do these differ from what has gone before? Have we gone

58 *Bringing Bourdieu to ELMA*

from one educational leadership game to another? And how is this push for educational leadership happening on the ground, as practice? How do 'what works' and 'professional capital' rhetoric and practice sit alongside each other, and alongside those other games in the field which require school leaders to maintain their focus on management and competition for enrolments and reputation in local and national markets? And how does this affect the relative vertical positions of schools and the horizontal status differentials between schools and universities? What is changing in the capitals, habitus and the game of teacher education? What strategies are being used in teacher training positions to maintain or change positions?

A Bourdieusian study would work to get a firm grasp on the situated and historical dimensions of the kinds of educational leadership practices under investigation, the habitus, logics of practice and the capitals involved. It would get purchase on the social relations, practices and representations that produce the differing practices of particular agents in particular positions. This example tangibly illustrates the argument made in Chapter 2 about the differences between a sociological and a more psychologically oriented approach to studying leaders work.

My hypothetical study might however not be entirely palatable to ELMA scholars and other educational researchers. David James (2015) helpfully points to four tensions that are inherent to working with Bourdieu within the educational field:

1) Tensions around 'interests and proximity'. Many educational researchers, including those in ELMA, may find it "difficult and quite possibly perverse" (p. 107) to be reflexively asking how they might be implicated in the production of educational inequality, when they experience what they do as working in a committed, positive and proactive way *for* teachers and schools.
2) Tensions around the unit of analysis. The shift – from an individual or site focus to that of agents embroiled in practices which (re)produce fields, capitals, dispositions and positions and relationships – will not be comfortable. James observes that some educational researchers will

    > find it disrespectful . . . that social researchers do not always take the testimony of participants at face value or impute motives to them that the people themselves do not directly express, acknowledge or even recognise. (p. 107)

    However, as Bourdieu points out, interpreting participants' words does not mean knowing better than participants; it means knowing differently and with different intent (Wacquant, 1989).
3) Tensions around 'compass or scale'. Because the unit of analysis is not the individual or school, the boundaries of the research are necessarily broad, and this can make getting a purchase on action and intervention difficult and the resulting discussion often abstract and lacking in fine and recognisable

detail. This is, of course, not always the case, and many Bourdieusian studies are based in ethnographic traditions where rich description is the norm.

4) Tensions around 'tenor', that is the balance of hope to pessimism. James (2015) notes that educational systems consistently urge innovation and change but a Bourdieusian approach suggests that such rhetoric and the resulting initiatives consistently overestimate the possibilities for change. Bourdieu reminds us of the magnitude of the task of working against the odds (pp.107–109). This is not very cheerful news for those who seek to retain an 'improvement' focus.

So would my hypothetical study of educational leadership indeed offer any hope for change? Perhaps, possibly, maybe.

In analysing the kind of 'educational leadership' now expected in the field, other possible practices of educational leadership are also made visible. Once the overall game and its stakes are brought centre stage, and tensions in the field elaborated, potential countermoves and strategic alliances with other agents in the field also become much more obvious. In other words, if, as I strongly suspect, my hypothetical study of the move to teaching schools reveals that what is meant by 'educational leadership' in current times remains an instrumental and narrow version of education, then the research provides a way to show this to others, and to explain why it is so. This then opens up the question of what a broader view of education and educational leadership might be, what practices heads and other 'leaders' might take up and what they might avoid.

And it is, of course, also integral to the process of research that the researcher themselves – that is the hypothetical me designing the hypothetical project – analyses the potential benefits and distinction that they might accrue through this work. The pretend me cannot simply assert the benefits for those in whose interests I might claim, and hope, to work for. Reflexively examining my own positions says a great deal about the ways in which I not only conduct the research but also communicate the results and with whom I choose to engage in conversations. If *all* I do is publish some obscure papers in journals, then I have largely served my own interests.

Where next?

Chapter 3 argued that Bourdieu could be helpful in ELMA studies primarily as a methodology. It concluded with a 'made up' exercise for the purpose of indicating how Bourdieu as methodology might be taken up. The next three chapters demonstrate doing Bourdieusian ELMA studies 'for real'. Chapters 4, 5 and 6 all track the ways in which the field, capitals, habitus and position are integral to the ways in which leaders (agents) make decisions (play the game).

4 Why do headteachers want autonomy?

This chapter can be seen as a precursor to a larger study. It uses Bourdieu's thinking tools to unpack a particular problem in order to orient further empirical work. The chapter uses some empirical data, primary historical in nature. It also draws on a selection of literature, on other published research. It is a partial realisation of Bourdieu's first step (see p. 49) of analysing the field and changes within the field.

In this chapter I focus on an important aspect of my own past professional life, that of the position of the headteacher. In particular, I am concerned with the ways in which I acted to support more autonomy for myself and my colleagues. In beginning from the apparently personal my goal is, following Bourdieu, to locate the social. I therefore use my own experiences as 'pointers' to readings of the field and an analysis of the headteachers' 'game', attempting to understand why headteachers continue to not only support but also actively lobby for more and more autonomy. The chapter traces autonomy as a field strategy and doxa. In conclusion, I offer some speculation about the reasons for this play in the schooling field.

I begin in part A with the 'evidence' that headteachers desire and work for an apparent ever-increasing autonomy.

Part A: the phenomenon of headteacher desire for autonomy

In this first section I present evidence that policy shifts to extend school autonomy have been accompanied by expressions of headteacher satisfaction and also the desire for still further extension of apparent freedoms. I suggest that these headteacher behaviours are relatively constant over a relatively long time, across school sectors and in several different places (although I mainly discuss Australia and England). In making this generalisation, I do not want to suggest that this means that there are no differences among sectors, systems and times. Rather, I want to argue, after Bourdieu, that headteachers are disposed, by virtue of the game they are in, to press for more authority and that this has been a relative constant in the field over the last forty years, despite the relative autonomies of time/space. This desire, I suggest in conclusion, is important to understanding

Why do headteachers want autonomy? 61

the *logic* of much of their practice. I thus present a selection of evidence, spread over time, space and sectors to illustrate this point. I also indicate a potential research agenda.

Local autonomies – new Australian freedoms and new English ambiguities

The early 1970s in Australia were heady with student protests, community activism, the election of more progressive (national and state) governments, and a general sense of optimism and possibility. My first headship was in 1975 in South Australia, a state generally acknowledged as one of the places in which the process of changing the balances of central and local school leadership/management began.

In 1970, the then director general of the South Australian Education Department, Alby Jones, sent to schools the *Freedom and Authority Memorandum* which stated that headteachers had the legitimate power to make number of important decisions about their schools – school rules, how curriculum guidelines were to be implemented and organisational and school ethos issues, including student groupings, setting and streaming, length of school day and timetables (see Jones, 1978, 1980). On the back of this memorandum, local School Councils were established and non-salary school budgets were devolved. There was debate about whether or not this move constituted a shift away from authoritarian modes of school leadership/management to more democratic forms (Kaminsky, 1981; Smithson, 1983). However, the first response of school principals, no matter how much or how little they were democratically inclined, was to welcome their new powers.

One principal from that time, Les Kemp, remembers the memorandum as a professional landmark and it is worth quoting his memories at some length, since they illustrate the feelings and beliefs that accompany a desire for and realisation of 'autonomy'.

> Before he retired John Walker (director general in the 1960s) spoke to principals at a dinner held in his honour by the principals of high and technical high schools at the North Adelaide Hotel. It was planned, he said, to give more freedom to principals to run their schools on their own lines. I remember these particular words: 'We are going to give you freedom – freedom till it hurts'. He thus foreshadowed the *Freedom and Authority Memorandum* which was later issued by Alby Jones. It was certainly a **breath of fresh sea air** for schools.
>
> The *Freedom and Authority Memorandum* was a fine document for principals. It **gave them their heads**. Some principals **took advantage of the memorandum** to immediately **restructure their schools**. Some of the officers of the Education Department did not like the memorandum. It reduced their former authority which was in my view open to abuse. The 'department' was not democratically included. Disagreement with departmental decisions was seen as disloyalty to the department. This was a peculiar point

62   *Why do headteachers want autonomy?*

of view as most teachers **put loyalty to their students, their colleagues and their own educational and moral stands**, well ahead of the department.

As a principal, on at least three occasions, I **had to remind** a **departmental officer** of the existence of the memorandum. On each occasion **an officer sought to interfere** in an internal matter. On one of those occasions the Director General of Education stepped in to support me. The memorandum did not give licence. Principals had to **act within the lines** set down by the Education Act and the regulations under the Act. Beyond that, **the internal affairs of the school were in the hands of the principal**.

(Kemp, undated, my emphases here and in following quotes)

This extract demonstrates several components of the autonomy narrative construction. A set of binaries are created – us/them, inside/outside the school, local/central – within which the role of non-school agents and agencies is to set guidelines. Heads act; they do things; they have agency in their schools. Heads know best what the inside/local needs in order to meet the guidelines. Provided they follow the rules, their accountability is inside/local. The school is 'mine' to run. In this early articulation, the offer from the education system is clear; heads have autonomy *from* interference from central authorities in order to have the autonomy necessary *for* running their schools.

The shift to grant headteachers more authority and freedom was accomplished over time in all Australian states with some variations. Only South Australia and Victoria moved early to a system of School Councils, but all state systems moved away from centralised non-salary budgets and micromanagement of school routines. New South Wales, the largest of the state school systems, clung longest to 'command and control' organisational arrangements.

But in England, the authority in which South Australian heads rejoiced was taken for granted, with heads in the state system having an 'unusual degree of autonomy' most commonly exercised in 'an authoritarian way' (Peters, 1976a, p. 1). The 1944 Education Act made explicit that the head was responsible for internal organisation, management and discipline of the school and for supervision of all staff (p. 6). Jack Sheffield's bucolic Yorkshire memories (2007, 2008) are indicative of the comparative autonomy that heads enjoyed at the time, with only the occasional visit from them/the local office to be concerned about. John Watts, headteacher of Countesthorpe College in Leicester (England) and a renowned progressive educator, wrote at the time of the six powers of headteachers as:

1   defining the objectives and values of the school, operating within the limits of what governors set;
2   determining curriculum, what is taught;
3   control of internal organization of curriculum – timetabling, student grouping and allocation of teachers to classes;
4   distribution of available money;
5   choosing his [*sic*] own staff (within limits set by local authority);

Why do headteachers want autonomy? 63

6   control of the media of communication which regulates who knows what about what. (Watts, 1976, pp. 129–30).

However, the freedoms that heads had enjoyed were increasingly being questioned. Writing in the previous decade, Edmonds (1968, p. 1) had noted that

> [f]or at least a century and probably longer, it has been customary to speak with admiration of the Head of a school in this country being the captain of his [*sic*] ship. Heads themselves, however, have become increasingly skeptical about this; and for very good reasons. At least three other hands (central office, local authority, governors) are on the tiller as well as his own, all taking a curious mixture of language of persuasion, making suggestions, recommending for consideration etc., but leaving no doubt that **they expect** their wishes to be implemented.

Debates in England focused on the changing role of the head, with some arguing that heads ought to behave more democratically, while others were more concerned about how the head might respond to increasing pressures from Westminster, local authorities, parents and pupils. The focus of the debate was not just on role but also on the question of headteachers' agency, their freedom and autonomy. The Headteachers' Association of the day produced a pamphlet for new heads which stated that

> [t]he idea of freedom and wide discretion for the headmaster is one of the chief beneficial contributions made by the great public schools to the English tradition, and it is no accident that the schools which the public holds in highest esteem are those in which there is **least interference** with the headmaster [*sic*] in his conduct of the business of the school . . . he is **in charge of the school** and it is **for him to say** who may enter it . . . however carefully their respective functions are defined by prescription, there will remain a marginal and ambiguous area between the spheres of the headmaster and the chief education officer. It is in this area that the headmaster may have to **be vigilant to preserve his position**.
>
> (cited in Bernbaum, 1976, p. 23)

Here, too, is the inside/outside, us/them, local/central binary. In this case and at this time, the outside/them/central was both the local authority and Westminster.

Educational administration texts shifted from simply explaining school procedures and routines (e.g. Goodwin, 1968) to attempts to clarify what the headteacher must do (Cook & Mack, 1971; Peters, 1976b). Poster (1976) for example argued that the role of the head could only be understood by focusing on the nature of responsibility and decision-making; he explicated the pressures and responsibilities emanating from both inside and outside the school and detailed inside organisational responses. Subsequent work by Whitaker (1983)

64   *Why do headteachers want autonomy?*

took account of the growing move to spell out, and also change, the ways in which headteachers' authority and freedoms were to be organised and experienced. Whitaker described as a fascinating paradox the great freedom heads have, on one hand, to interpret their role, while also, on the other hand, having to match considerable and increasing policy expectations (e.g. the Taylor Report, DES, 1977). In the light of subsequent developments, the paradoxical freedom from direct central fiat and freedom for action in the school can be seen as a relative autonomy, one which is steered from outside rather than through direct micromanagement. Whitaker compared England to the US, where heads' powers were tightly defined and where autonomies were, in general, far more limited.

The slow progress to school-based management

Australia also moved relatively early to embrace the *idea* of 'self-management', defined by (possibly its most prolific) advocates as "significant and consistent delegation to the school level of authority to make decisions related to the allocation of resources (knowledge, technology, power, material, people, time and finance)" (Caldwell & Spinks, 1988, p. vii).

However, achievement of the Australian imaginary of self-management was relatively slowly realised. In Victoria, principals received charge of their non-staff school budgets in the late 1980s, but they only gained total control of staffing somewhat later (see Caldwell & Hayward, 1997a). In South Australia, where I was based, any move beyond non-staffing budgets were constantly stymied, not only by the need to staff schools in rural and isolated areas but also by fears that devolution would widen existing gaps between rich and poor schools, resulting in the ghettoisation of the schools in most need. There were nevertheless ongoing pressures for more autonomy from headteachers and advocates, which eventually saw something a little short of the full local hire and fire model established in the early years of the 21st century (Kilvert, 2001).

Across the world similar shifts were occurring, albeit at different rates and with local variations. Caldwell and Spinks (1998), key proponents of devolution, are worth tracking. They argued that school-based management provided the basis for a new professionalism and new forms of educational innovation (curriculum and school restructure) that would provide children and young people with an education fit for the future (see also Beare & Slaughter, 1993). This was an argument which resonated elsewhere. The 1988 Education Act in the UK saw schools in England move to self-managing status while school districts in the US began to experiment with forms of devolution from about the same time. Australia's immediate neighbour New Zealand energetically implemented a funder–purchaser–provider model, complete with purchase agreements and local charters (Thrupp, 1999; Wylie, 1999).

As the school system in England was de- and re-centralised, various policy initiatives achieved the clarification of roles and accountabilities that had previously been at issue. Much curricular decision-making was removed from headteachers' purview; school budgets, including responsibility for staffing and buildings were

Why do headteachers want autonomy? 65

devolved; and a new form of school inspection was introduced. New Labour continued on the Thatcherite track, tightening up even further on measurement of 'performance'. Over less than a decade, heads in England gained new freedoms and authorities to act within their schools, but there were also new audit and risk management procedures and new lines of accountability which delimited what they could do. This shift in governing local autonomy was accomplished at the same time as educational marketisation and privatisation were stimulated and promulgated (Ball, 2006, 2007, 2008a; Gewirtz, 2002; Tomlinson, 2001; Whitty, 2002).

Moves to local school management were met in each country by opposition, critiques and debates (e.g. Blackmore, 1998; Chitty, 1997; Smyth, 1993). The argument, in each case and despite national and local variations, was made that the state was wilfully withdrawing from its historical responsibility to ensure that quality education was an entitlement for all citizens. However, by and large, headteachers were enthusiastic about devolution. Some opposed but found it an unsustainable position (Grace, 1995):

> I would resign tomorrow if LMS (local school management, the term first used in England) disappeared. It used to drive me barmy having to telephone the eighty-ninth filing clerk to get permission to buy a stamp . . . One of the good things is that it gives **flexibility and makes you** a much better housekeeper in terms of accountability – in moral terms really . . . I am disappointed that the school is not GM (grant maintained, an extension of devolution) . . . would have **enjoyed the independence** of equals working together . . . there is a form of head's dependency on LEAs and I resent this . . . **I would have valued the additional flexibility** and opportunities to upgrade the school and enhance the low levels of confidence in the community.
>
> (Higham, 1995, pp. 61–62)

Heads' responses, as this quotation clearly illustrates, were framed strongly by the binary. They (outside – local authority, central office, politicians and policymakers) do not know what's best for us or if they do they can't deliver it (in here). If only they would give me/us the resources, stop interfering and leave me/us alone, we could just get on with it.

In Victoria, Australia, the vast majority of principals applauded the autonomy they had to determine staffing and expenditure. When there were debates about policies of devolution, it was principals who vociferously opposed the idea of limiting the new powers that they had on the grounds that 'going back' would produce more 'interference' in the running of the school. I can remember arguing with Brian Caldwell in the pages of *Principal Matters*, the journal of the Australian Secondary Principals Association of which I was an executive member, that there was more than one way forward and that going back was always impossible.

At the time, principals/heads who supported devolution were accused of 'selling out' and of only being concerned for their own power, prestige and influence.

66   *Why do headteachers want autonomy?*

When Victorian state school principals, who had broken away from the single teacher union to form their own separate association, accepted a clause in their salary agreement to allow School Councils to pay for private school fees for their children, there was widespread public outrage not only at what appeared to be a further shift to business models of leadership but also that this was a visible sign that principals thought the schools they ran were not good enough for their own offspring. In South Australia, by contrast, school principals stayed in the teacher union and argued for a way forward that would not result in exacerbating inequities in the system and which might enhance local participation and democratic practices (Dow, Jolliffe, Petherick, & O'Brien, 1996; Thomson, 1994). This is a line of argument that can be seen stretching from Kemp (undated) to the present day (e.g. Moos & Macbeath, 2004; Morgan, Hall, & Mackay, 1983; Waters, 1979; Watts, 1976; Woods, 2005). Indeed, some principals and heads in some localities did use the capacities of self-management to enhance local participation and achieve specific community goals (e.g. Jones, 1999; Strachan, 1999). In other words, in the hands of democratically committed headteachers, autonomy *for* local/inside change did have many positive benefits even if there was not the desired freedom *from* steerage from above/outside.

These positive benefits came at a cost; there were inside/local effects that were unappealing. In England heads rued the paperwork that self-management brought. In England a single school budget and new centralised demands often required unwelcome personal as well as professional adjustments and costs (Southworth, 1995; Thomson, 2009, Ch. 7):

> LMS has provided something of a mixed blessing. Under the LEA formula we are net losers . . . The net results . . . are significantly increased class sizes as well as increased staff loading . . . On the positive side we are able to establish priorities and attached resources . . . on a scale not possible before LMS . . . small but important improvements have to be paid for by savings to be located elsewhere in our budget. To this end we have found that by putting out to competitive tendering the bulk of our minor works and maintenance contracts we are able to make significant savings . . . The downside of dealing directly with contractors is the time that needs to be devoted (to it).
> (Atkinson, 1991, pp. 150–151)

In interview with BBC Radio 4, ex-headteacher John Illingworth relates the shift over his career, remembering with some pleasure the ambiguous days pre–self-management (see Thomson, 2008a, for an analysis):

> I was responsible for everything to do with teaching and learning and pupil welfare and I had a huge budget of three and a half thousand pounds to spend on books and equipment in the school each year. The most significant accountability measure in those days was **your link with your local education authority**. Each school would have a local inspector and advisor who did have a job which was related to monitoring but it was also about

Why do headteachers want autonomy? 67

supporting the school and looking at areas where the school needed to move on and develop . . .

Contra to writings at the time, Illingworth remembers the local authority as part of **us** while a distant office in London had become **them**. This may always have been his position, or it may be a revised memory – another aspect of the current policy agenda has been to systematically strip local authorities of their support roles and their capacity to mediate national priorities. As the game has changed, a head's view of who are his or her allies and 'in the same boat' as him- or herself may have shifted.

By contrast, Illingworth sees the increased budgets and clarified lines of accountability as an unacceptable intrusion by the outside on the inside:

> More and more there has to be very precise evidence and justification for eve-rything that's happening **in** a school and the introduction, this year, of the new Ofsted model where every year a head teacher is supposed to undertake this huge self-evaluation of the school. . . . I was spending my whole school holidays writing school stuff for evaluations; collecting evidence to support it all and at the same time **the government decided** that **they wanted** every school in the land to restructure their management responsibilities last year. Whether it was necessary or not **we all had to do it.** At the same time **the government rightly insisted** that all teachers needed some time outside the classroom for planning and preparation and assessment. A wonderful initia-tive but **they didn't** fund it **so we were then** looking at how we could work and cut other budgets to provide that.

Here again we get the beleaguered head who just wants to be left alone to exer-cise professional judgement.

Most heads in England do not wish to give up the autonomy that they have. Instead, they argue for a relaxation of testing and inspection and related audit requirements. They want less onerous accountabilities and less cut-throat conse-quences for apparent lack of progress against government targets. Principals in Aus-tralia, not (yet) subject to quite the same kinds of public league tables and regimes of inspection, voice concerns about other forms of accountability – risk manage-ment and paper-driven audits (e.g. Perry, 2006; Perry & McWilliam, 2007).

State school heads in England eye off what they see as the freedom from con-straints enjoyed by heads in the independent sector. Winkley (2002, p. 326) for example writes that

> [o]ne virtue of the best independent schools is **their ability to protect their teachers** from hassle that is unrelated to their work in the classroom, and to retain an emphatic emphasis on the quality of discourse between teachers and pupils.

This is a case now made in Australia by advocates of independent schools who argue that generous government funding does not mean curtailment of their

68 *Why do headteachers want autonomy?*

autonomy – they must remain free to make decisions as they see fit. The chair of one such school recently made this case to an OECD conference:

> The independent school sector, as one portion of non-government schools in Australia . . . is **not faced with the plethora of obstruction to innovation caused by centralized school management** because, apart from operating independently, each school of this type is connected with its customer base. If the educational product delivered by an independent school does not meet the expectations of its clients the school must eventually fail as the clients seek a better product elsewhere . . . For these reasons reformers of government schools must look to the successful independent schools as the benchmark by which devolutionary reforms must be measured and as the model by which they can be achieved.
>
> (Morgan, 2003)

In this example, freedom and autonomy equate to each school becoming a business, the other end of the continuum from local school management being a means of enhancing democracy and social justice.

But, even those heads in England who arguably do have almost complete freedom and authority – those who run the great public (the name given to independent) schools and who provided the model for the ambiguous pre-1980s headmaster tradition in England – also express the desire to be left alone. John Rae, headmaster of Westminster school in London, peppers his memoirs (2009) with tales of getting the right chair of the governing body in place and serial wranglings with governors over a variety of policies ranging from whether pupils beyond bona fide British nationals could be enrolled to whether the school would borrow money to extend its buildings. Rae also wanted unfettered exercise of both moral leadership and management decisions and fought hard to get his own way, grumbling about restrictions that **they** put on him (see also Hampton & Jones, 2000; Loader, 1997; Stubbs, 2003).

Recent changes in both England and Australia have shifted the educational landscape even further towards the imaginary of all schools, regardless of their funding and provenance, acting as independent 'autonomous' units.

While Australia constitutionally makes states the providers of schooling, the federal government has increasingly manipulated state activities through funding agreements and a council of education ministers. The introduction of national testing and a league table system is the policy 'lever' designed to bring schools into a more direct line of accountability to national policy. (Comber, 2012; Lingard, Thompson, & Sellar, 2015; Thompson & Cook, 2014). In Australia, the federal government now promotes the idea of 'independent' state schools, apparently autonomous and independent of state interference (Niesche & Thomson, in press).

In England, the Coalition (2010–2015) and now the Conservative government (from 2015) dramatically accelerated the academies programme and introduced 'free schools', a version of charter schools established by parents and funded by government (Gunter, 2011; Ranson, 2012). By 2015, academies made up nearly

Why do headteachers want autonomy? 69

half of the total number of schools; free schools, however, are small in number but big on symbolic value (Higham, 2013). The local authority is marginalised, budgets slashed and its powers reduced largely to monitoring and the provision of some safety net services (Hatcher, 2014; Thomson, 2011b). Headteachers in England are now more on their own than many of them ever envisaged. The growth of academy trusts substitutes in some way for the local authority, but these are secretive organisations with emerging anecdotal evidence of centralised control and budgetary top slicing, a far cry from the aspiration to democratic accountability via local governments. Heads now suggest that they have less freedom working for academy trusts than they had under local authorities.

The dominant political rhetoric however remains that of freedom from the bureaucratic impost of systems and public servants, despite burgeoning regulation and audit imposts (Niesche & Thomson, in press).

Part B: a Bourdieusian sketch

The puzzle

If then, the desire to be left alone, to have ever more freedom, power and authority, appears as a desire and as a rationale for various kinds of local school management forms and in various sectors, places and times, how is this to be explained?

This section sketches a possible way to understand the phenomena of headteacher autonomy. There is too little space to flesh this out in full, but this section does attempt to place some signposts to a further explication. It mobilises Bourdieu's work on fields, habitus and capitals. As suggested in previous chapters, using Bourdieu's toolkit affords an analytic focus on:

- the social production of individual behaviour. In this case it means moving beyond a view of headteachers as individually power hungry to an explanation which foregrounds the ways in which the position requires its occupants to act in the interests of retaining power and attempting to gain more.
- the logic of the practice. If the practice of heads can be understood as acting to gain more power for the position and to create further autonomies, then the question can be refocused to ask about the purposes of this practice. In whose interests does it work, defining interests as also socially (re)produced.

I address these two aspects of headteacher's quest for autonomy by examining the schooling field, the logic of actions in the field and then changes that relate to de and re-centralisations of the field. In making this explanation, I recap some of the details provided in Chapter 1 about Bourdieu's theoretical toolkit.

Understanding schooling as a field

Bourdieu argued that distinctive areas of social life could each be thought of metaphorically as a field chiasmatically divided by various kinds of cultural and

70 Why do headteachers want autonomy?

economic capitals (Bourdieu, 1990a, 1990b, 1996). The metaphorical field represents an actual social and material hierarchy in which some positions have much more status than others, or as Bourdieu has it, some have more 'distinction' (Bourdieu, 1984; Bourdieu & Wacquant, 1992). Positions in the field represent clusters of similar institutions, and the people (or agents) in them and the kind of economic and/or cultural capital that they possess (Bourdieu, 2005). The sums and nature of cultural and economic capital possessed by each position can be measured through complex calculations which show how highly the school, its head and its pupils are regarded and how well attending the school, obtaining qualifications and awards and entering and making new networks of associations can be 'cashed in' in work-related and other civic fields (Bourdieu, 1989).

According to Bourdieu, the object of the game played on any field is to maintain or advance position by multiplying the quantum of capitals which is at stake in the field possessed by each position. The game in the field is 'played' by agents. Bourdieu calls the intersections of structure and agency, embodied in a position/agent, a habitus, arguing that as agents advance through the field occupying position after position (here, student, teacher, middle manager, headteacher) they accrue a constellation of dispositions to act in ways to not only maintain the position but also to keep advancing. They are literally disposed to think in particular ways that (re)produce the field.

One of the key positions in the schooling field is that of principal/headteacher. Each school can be thought of as a subfield, and headteachers must act both within the school and without in the field in order to ensure that the institution thrives.

Headteachers are responsible for a school and occupy the same position in the field as their schools. They are disposed through their positions and their life histories of playing the educational game to act according to its rules and internal narratives of truth in order to protect the interests of their schools – that is to maintain its/their relative position in the field and to advance it if possible and to ensure that students can use the capitals accrued in the school to maintain their pre-existing social and economic positions if not advance them. The actions headteachers take – the strategies that they adopt feel completely natural to them.

What heads do can be understood as a practice – the logic of practice is to play the game, to maintain or advance relative positioning (the school, its students, themselves) in the field. Headteachers' practice falls into clusters of activities – organisation of systems, symbolic and rhetorical work, strategic development and planning, establishing governing systems that operate in harmony to the benefit of the school, pedagogical leadership, associational work with key allies and partners, promotional work and so on.

It can be argued, based on the phenomenological evidence presented in the first part of this chapter that the quest for autonomy is a disposition of headteachers, that it is integral to their habitus and that it is necessary for playing the game. But why is this so? Before continuing with the notion of field, I focus briefly on the concept of dispositions.

A disposition for autonomy?

The habitus, the embedded embodiment of social structures, consisting of constellations of dispositions, is produced through a life trajectory through specific, culturally and historically constituted social fields (Bourdieu, 1990a, 1990b, 1996). The relationship between habitus and field is complex, and there are considerable debates about its adequacy as a conceptual solution to the structure/agency conundrum. However, for the purpose of this sketch, it is the notion of dispositions that is important. I want to suggest that a disposition for autonomy is not simply that of the headteacher but is integral to the field of education.

Interestingly, the desire for autonomy is also one that is demonstrated by teachers. The iconic figure of the lone teacher with his or her class in a single classroom has been the target of considerable scholarly and policy attention in recent years. The quest to find the ways that he or she might become more cooperative, collaborative and less singular has generated policies (performance management and data-driven improvement) which 'get inside' professional autonomy. (These operate in the same manner as audit and risk-management requirements steer and open to scrutiny the operations of the school and its headteacher.) These steerage tactics evaluate individually but standardise behaviours across the same position in the field.

Furthermore, the figure of the individually striving but externally accountable teacher is reminiscent of those good students who are independent learners. The drive for autonomy is a disposition which is necessary for students to do well in school. The logic of 'studenting' (how to be a student) practice is to do your own work (not cheat) and to do more than is asked for. Successful students read more books, search the Internet more assiduously, make more connections and write better and more. They thrive in the individualised systems of testing and examinations since they have learnt that individual performance is how to succeed in the game. And they have learnt that education is a game in which they want to succeed. Some students are clearly advantaged in schooling, but even those without homes in tune with the knowledge required for educational success can do relatively well if they are disposed to act as striving and autonomous learners.

Finally, all successful graduates of the schooling field – professionals in law, medicine, engineering and so on – all hold autonomy as one of the doxa in their relative fields.

It may well be therefore that the disposition for headteacher autonomy I have described as a phenomenon draws on the same dispositional repertoire as that exhibited by teachers and by students and is one of the logics of practice not only within education but also that education inculcates within professions more generally.

However, Bourdieu argued against the idea of fixed dispositions and habitus. He stressed that habitus is produced/produces practice in relationship to the specificities of the field. According to Bourdieu, habitus is:

1   malleable. It is not only subject to experience, but also changed through experience.

72 Why do headteachers want autonomy?

2 responsive to experience. Bourdieu (in Bourdieu & Chartier, 2010/2015) says,

> It is in a relationship to something that habitus produces something. It is like a spring. It needs something to release it. (p. 57)

3 capable of different responses. Depending on the situation, 'habitus can do contrasting things'.
4 constitutive of a situation as well as being constituted by it – this may or may not be recognised. As Bourdieu puts it,

> [a]ccording to the habitus that I have, I either see or don't see certain things in a given situation. And depending on whether I see these things or not, I shall be incited by my habitus to do or not do certain things. (p. 58)

The habitus of the headteacher then may position them to act in particular ways, when in particular contexts, with consequences that they do not anticipate, or indeed even see. And what begins as a disposition for autonomy to meet the particular needs of the pupils in the school may also be the very same disposition triggered by different policy agendas for devolution/self-management.

I therefore now turn to consider further what those policy triggers might be.

The logic of actions in the schooling field

In order to make sense of the contemporary press for freedom and autonomy, it is necessary to venture outside of the field of schooling. Again, this is the sketch of an argument, a possible line of analysis.

Bourdieu was adamant that fields are not static. In reality they are amenable to change and are thus sites of intense contestation between and within fields. Often changes in one field are in response and in part generated by changes occurring outside of the field – demographic shifts, new economic demands and new political requirements. Sometimes they are a result of the operations of the field in concert with others, as Bourdieu illustrated in his study (1993a) of the ways in which avant-garde art became mainstream high cultural capital (Grenfell & Hardy, 2007).

In the countries under discussion (Australia and England) the post–World War II period to the present day has been one of the major changes, including:

- significant increases in population,
- significant migration creating ever more cultural diversity,
- technological advances, and
- significant shifts in the ways national economies are organised, finances are managed, manufacturing is undertaken and communications are effected.

These changes are often clumped together under the sociological/political terminology of globalisation. This is not the place to debate these events. It is sufficient to say that these are changes which have created profound challenges not simply for every nation state but also for the various fields which do the work of re-creating and creating the nation. Education is one such field. In conditions of instability traditional hierarchies are under threat. There is increased contestation over key aspects of the game as various agents in the field seek to retain or further position.

Since World War II the schooling field has been highly unstable with more students, new students and new demands for ever-higher levels of knowledge production. The mass level of education has risen. External agents in other structurally dominant fields (government, economy) act in order to harness the schooling field to their needs. It is possible to understand the trajectories of education policy and the frequency of adjustments as a series of moves through which government has attempted to de- and re-centralise aspects of the field in order to fulfil the needs of the nation state and cope with necessary changes. But in post–World War II Australia and England there have been potentially contradictory games at work (Thomson, 2005). The government and economic fields require higher levels of education for all, the nation-building functions of curriculum to be strengthened, and for the school system to demonstrate on a global scale the national 'capacity' and legitimacy of government. On the other hand, in the schooling field the game is not only to meet these demands but also to maintain existing advantages and hierarchies. By and large, the logic of the actions of agents in the schooling field is to ensure that both games remain compatible, although there are clearly some agents in all fields who work to change existing hierarchies.

I have argued elsewhere (Thomson, 2005) that managing uncertainties in the political field, viz. in the state, and in the broader economic field, required the development of an administrative mechanism through which to orchestrate activity in a number of fields and to ensure that agents act to ensure (re)production of the status quo continues. The administrative mechanism through which contradictory pressures are balanced was via the simultaneous development of new forms of governing across fields, generally known as NPM, marketisations, privatisations and performatisations (Boden, Gummett, Coz, & Barker, 1998; Common, 1998; Considine & Lewis, 1999; Vickers & Kouzmin, 2001). These new governing practices, contra to its new doxa of, and some material, networking, rely on each individual position (agent and subfield) not only following new codified rules but also competing to further or maintain itself within the field. And these new forms of field practices required different kinds of subfield autonomies which would operate within each field according its doxa(s), allow the reproduction of the capitals that count within each field, maintain the competition for those capitals and encourage play.

Thus, successful headteachers in new times must be expert not only at balancing competing demands arising from new pressures of massification and older games of distinction, but they must also be experts at playing according to the codified rules of audit, management and markets which individualise, through the use of data, the performance of each teacher, each head and each school. This

74 Why do headteachers want autonomy?

is not left entirely to chance. Heads of schools are now trained and selected for particular marketised managerial capitals (as I show in the next chapter). Practising heads are disposed to act (perform) in ways that advance the interests of the students, teachers and themselves within the wider field. This apparently new set of autonomy practices, I suggest, draws on pre-existing dispositions, produced and reproduced through the policy trajectory of changes in governing practice. Heads pre-academisation *and* pre–self-management also wanted autonomy and agency, and wanted to 'win' in the schooling game. Even if the game allowed them to work for more democratic and social just interests, the dispositional desire for autonomy was at its heart. Historically, the disposition was often explicated as a doxa of professional autonomy and the desire to be left alone.

This doxa has not been replaced by that of subsidiarity – the view that local autonomy leads to bespoke leadership and management and that this is a more efficient and effective way of achieving centrally determined outcomes. We must also not forget that there is a consequence for failing to adhere to the subsidiarity game – to live school autonomy as common sense – that of removal from the game. Failure in steered policy via data-driven performance brings a reduction in field freedoms: the school is literally taken over, and the headteacher, sacked.

However, if this sketch has traction it must address a further puzzle – exactly how the interpellation of particular heads and particular dispositions happens at the level of the position and the school. Empirical research, as Bourdieu would argue, is required in order to test out this sketch, to probe the specific ways in which the conditions of the field both incite headteacher's drive for autonomy, frame the ways in which this is negotiated with other actors within and without the school and build on historical constellations of embodied field practices. However, the notion of a disposition to autonomy triggered by its field and the ongoing logics of its practice seems to have considerable promise for empirical investigation.

Problems with a logic of autonomy practice

I conclude this chapter with three personally discomforting reasonings.

The first is that headteachers' desires for autonomy are logical. The quest for more and more freedom is a necessary positional disposition which drives agent's actions (their practice) to shore up position (school, self, students) and to play for the achievement of new distinctions and position. Thus, the ever-present sense – of wanting to be left alone and us against them – is not about the acquisition of power for its own sake but is, rather, both a product and a producer of the game of educational distinction. Quite literally the desire for autonomy and freedom comes with the contemporary headteacher's job. To refuse it is to refuse the game. This does not mean, of course, accepting the games as it is. The quest for freedom equally applies to those who resist, who have contrary beliefs and play counter-games, as to those who adhere religiously to its tenets and subsequent inequities.

Second, it is incumbent to note that scholars whose analysis of current policy intentions and headteacher responses suggest that headteachers are active agents

Why do headteachers want autonomy? 75

able to mediate policy are in one sense correct but in another are missing part of the point. Regardless of whether one is for or against policy, for or against the game, heads are key players, and while they work to advantage their school and students, what they do – their agency – is always framed by a decision about whether they are prepared to play to their own positional detriment. There is a research agenda here which is only in part taken up by advocates of networking and forms of collectivism but which would test out whether the sketch I have offered has merit. When do heads act collectively in all of their interests? When do heads of like-minded schools/positions work together to advance their collective interest? Under what circumstances are heads prepared to cede decisions to a networked organisation and which decisions do they hold as their own? What are the points at which collectivisms are abandoned?

Finally, it is important to note that this sketch for an analysis of headteacher autonomy does suffer from an apparent determinism. Despite stressing that agents do have the capacity to act, putting the micro analytic of dispositions together with the macro analytic of the field does present an inevitability. It almost seems as if the game is too big and too out of reach of any particular agent or set of agents. This pessimistic and structuralist tendency has long been a criticism of Bourdieusian analyses, and it is pertinent here. Perhaps the real question is not whether it is 'right' or 'depressing' but, rather, what explanatory power a Bourdieusian analysis does and does not afford. Other theoretical explorations of the headteachers' quest for autonomy might counter or affirm the picture created in this chapter. And fully fleshed-out empirical investigations might well modify a sketch which as preliminary thinking, finds the logic of reproduction more easily and finds less about contestation. Finding contestation requires on the ground investigation.

5 What do leaders need to know? The doxa of the thoroughly modern manager

There is a great deal of interest in the ELMA field in leadership training. Educating leaders was integral to the establishment of ELMA and there has been a significant corpus of research and professional practice dedicated to it. There is now a substantial archive of writing on the topic – there are actual teaching texts, research into leadership and management practice in order to draw out lessons for leadership preparation, and research into the training programmes themselves (Anderson & Bennett, 2003; Brundrett & Crawford, 2008; Huber & Hiltmann, 2010; Lumby, Crow, & Pashiardis, 2008; Robertson, 1999; Tomlinson, 2004).

As explained in Chapter 3, both critical and dominant ELMA scholars have an interest in what potential and current headteachers need to learn formally and informally. This chapter does not survey of all of this material. It focuses instead on the recent past and on some of the writings that have accompanied, and in some cases been implicated in, the shifts in governing. It looks particularly at England, where the national system for leadership training was one of the most comprehensive and expensive in the world. Now almost entirely abandoned as an initiative of a previous era, The National College for Teaching and Leadership, formerly the National College for School Leadership and then the National College (NC), is now an influence, if not a direct model for leadership initiatives in other locations. Throughout the chapter I refer to the NC to sidestep the various changing remits and labels.

The chapter proceeds in this way: there were concerns within the ELMA field about the NC before it was established, and I briefly canvass these. I then introduce the case, a document analysis which focuses on the current configuration of three major leadership training programmes. This NC framework has been designed to deal with a specific concern raised earlier by both practitioners and researchers – namely a tendency to promote leadership as one thing, and one thing which works in the same way, in all kinds of schools, and with all aspiring leaders, regardless of their prior knowledge and experiences and the changing leadership context. The texts are subject to critical discourse analysis (Chouliaraki & Fairclough, 1999; Fairclough, 2002, 2003). I then bring Bourdieu to the table – I look to see what kinds of education and educational leadership is being promoted in the framework, what kinds of capitals and practices of leadership are privileged. I relate this analysis to other critical literature which raises allied

What do leaders need to know? 77

questions about whether the current doxa of personalised leadership training is a misrecognition.

I begin by signalling some key features of the context in England and the development of the NC training programmes. This of necessity repeats some of the analysis from earlier chapters, but here I am more closely focused on the position of agents in the NC.

The context of the case study

England is arguably highly advanced in the shift to governing practice (Ball, 2008a; Gunter, 2012b; Thomson, 2009). Since the formation of the Conservative–Liberal Democrat Coalition in 2010 and its successor Conservative government in 2015, there has been an acceleration of the conversion of both primary and secondary schools to 'academies', schools which are privately administered and publicly funded. The government also introduced 'free' schools, the national term for publicly funded and parent-initiated and administered schools, the equivalent to early North American charter schools (Harrison & Kachur, 1999). In 2016, the Conservatives declared that they would like all schools to be academies by the end of their term of office. (Blair had also expressed this wish.) Academies do not have to adhere to the national curriculum, although most do. Academies are increasingly not stand-alone, but are part of 'chains' (a mini system of anywhere from 2 to 30 or so sites; see Adonis, 2012). Academies, and the newer free schools, are subject to the same regimes of testing, league tabling and inspection technologies as schools which remain part of local authorities. All schools, regardless of 'type' – and there are now somewhere between 70 and 90 types (Courtney, 2016) – are regularly externally inspected and graded as outstanding, good, satisfactory or failing. Failing schools, that is those which fail to meet national benchmarks, are liable to be closed and reopened, amalgamated or converted to academies, with a change of leadership and quite often staff (Gunter, 2011).

A Bourdieusian perspective on these changes suggests that the political field has acted on, and in, the schooling field to create new positions, that of academy and free school. Many academies are schools that were at the far end of horizontal hierarchies created through league tabling, inspection and target setting. The doxa offers academisation as the remedy for poor positioning (as measured by performance). By changing the name/type of the school and some of its internal agents, particularly the head and leadership teams, the school will be able to change its place in the hierarchy. This policy doxa seems to suggest that it is possible to reduce the horizontal hierarchy of schools. Whether this is possible or not, the creation of these new school positions and the ongoing scrutiny of their 'success' or otherwise does mean that there are committed leaders/players appointed to free schools and academies. As a result of these changes, there is intensified jostling for status and survival across the field.

But where did these new game players come from? How was a mass of new leaders able to play the governing game produced? Of course, many of the 'new

78 *What do leaders need to know?*

leaders' were, in fact, selected from the 'old' and chosen for their dispositional match with the new positions (see Chapter 4). As Bourdieu remarks, neo-liberalist governments generally depend on selected capitals and agents produced by, in and for earlier versions of the field game (Bourdieu, 1998a). The answer to the question, 'Where do the new school leaders come from?' is therefore complex, but part of it lies in the introduction of formal leadership training.

The National College

The NC was initially established as the National College for School Leadership (NCSL) in 2002. The NC was intended to be the primary structure through which leadership training was offered to aspiring English school leaders. The NC was legally a quasi-autonomous non-governmental public body in which central-ised control was exercised through the annual letter and funding regime (Gunter, 2012a). Situated in a new building on the newly established 'knowledge econ-omy' campus of the University of Nottingham (where I work), its new 'green' architecture symbolised the desire of the Blair New Labour government to be futures oriented, globally significant and thoroughly modern.

There was initial concern from higher education based leadership educators about the move to government-sponsored leadership training. Riley (1998) had already argued that government emphasis in more locally based leader train-ing was directed solidly to accountability. Bolam (1997) had suggested training courses had unhelpfully reanimated the separation of theory and practice. Before the NC had even begun to appoint staff, questions were raised about the research base being used to develop its courses, the potential for short-term policies to dominate the training agenda and the knowledge on offer, and the apparent determination to reject academic knowledge about scoping and sequencing lead-ership learning programmes (e.g. Bush, 1999, 2000; Bush et al., 1999). Initial ELMA responses to the NC saw these trends being strengthened. Critics were not entirely persuaded by government rhetoric of valuing research. However, the appointment of Geoff Southworth (1995, 1998), a respected leadership aca-demic, and former primary headteacher, as director of research in the NCSL, and the cross-accreditation of headteacher training and Master of Education pro-grammes, sent the message that university expertise and courses were still impor-tant. However, suspicion lingered – was the NC intended to be a rival to higher education ELMA in the field?

The NC was serious about ELMA research that would help it do its job. Along with a suite of leadership programmes (e.g. some inherited and some new, such as Leading from the Middle), it developed a two strand research approach: (1) a programme of commissioned research and (2) an offer for practising leaders to come out of their schools to undertake practitioner research. Some NC com-missioned research even examined the suite of NC training programmes, sug-gesting a degree of criticality that was welcomed by many within the ELMA field. And some of the commissioned research was indeed critical. Weindling (2004) for example argued that the NC had very substantially increased the amount of

What do leaders need to know? 79

funding available to researchers but this had caused a reduction in the variety of other funding and a narrowing of research topics. This made the research field, not only within the UK but also internationally, more tied to the NC agenda. Weindling noted the obvious danger of a potential lack of independent and critical ideas.

There was both a struggle over the horizontal positioning of university ELMA versus the NC and a contest about capitals. What knowledge about ELMA was to count most in the field? There were two dominant concerns voiced by ELMA researchers about the first wave of training offered by the NC. The first was a concern about the 'scripted' nature of the training on offer. Even though the courses were taught by different providers in different locations, the NC insisted on its training being standardised across the country. While the intention to provide a common approach was understood by university academics and practitioners alike, they argued that:

1   leadership training needed to have traction across a range of contexts, levels and challenges;
2   the needs of newly appointed heads needed to be taken into account;
3   there was an urgent need to focus on school-based succession planning;
4   aspirant leaders did not all have the same kind of backgrounds, prior knowledge, needs and current experience; and
5   the needs of women and minority and ethnic leaders needed special attention. (e.g. Bright & Ware, 2003; Castagnoli & Cook, 2004; Glatter & Kydd, 2003; Gold et al., undated; Hartley & Thomas, 2005; McKenley & Gordon, 2002; Tranter, undated)

Secondly, there were concerns from critical ELMA scholars about the NC privileging a particular version of educational leadership which focused largely on questions about 'what works' (see Chapter 2), ignoring the interrogation of policy and other traditions of thinking about schooling and its purposes and practices (Gunter, 2004; Thomson, 2008b; Thrupp, 2005a). But critical concerns – within ELMA and beyond – about universalisation and prescription about capitals and practice were more general and not just about the NC. They were directed to the overall government approach, the standardisation of students' learning in mandated literacy and numeracy hours and the four-part lesson formula. There was suspicion about the manipulation of national data which confirmed continued increases in student performance against national benchmarks and which acted as the measure of 'good leadership'. All of these concerns attest to ongoing field contestation over position, capitals and practices.

Nevertheless, critiques of the NC training and more general policy directions were apparently heard. New Labour policymakers argued, on the basis of 'objective evidence', that their first-term policy push to standardise had raised standards, and the way to continue to secure further improvement was to allow some degree of flexibility into the system. This was to be achieved by maintaining the requirement for outcomes and intervention in schools failing to achieve

80   *What do leaders need to know?*

national benchmarks but, otherwise, promoting variety in the process, the means of achieving those outcomes. Variety was also introduced into leadership training.

It is important to consider why the policy doxa apparently changed to allow more variety. Bourdieu can help us attend to its logic. When strategies in the field stagnate and the 'settlement' begins to run out of capacity to maintain the power hierarchy, dominant agents introduce new strategies, often by appropriating the rhetorical tactics of agonistic agents, the critics in the field. In its second term, New Labour did precisely this – education policy moved to apparently re-professionalise and re-localise curriculum development, to re-involve higher education in professional development through master's qualifications and to promote more innovation. This created some potential for higher education agents with contrary ideas to act anew to change the order of what counted in the field. Universities for example developed new academic programmes which brought teacher education programmes to master's level, offering incentives for beginning teachers to 'top up' their certificates to a full Master of Teaching and Learning.

Policy rhetoric swung heavily to 'personalisation' (Leadbetter, 2004; West-Burnham, 2005), the bespoke tailoring of 'delivery' (Barber & Moffit, 2010), matching courses and programmes to particular contexts, sites and learners. It did not matter how you got there, the story went, as long you reached your targets and test results in the end. The severing of means and ends appears to make sense. After all, one can take different roads to end up at the same destination. However, schooling is rather more complex than a simple journey metaphor suggests. The learning on offer to students (or indeed leaders) varies hugely, depending not only on the processes used but also on the assumed purpose for the learning activity and the different resources that are available, including those that learners and teachers bring to the process (Thomson, 2011c). The rhetoric of bespoke methods did not address this question at all. Nevertheless, the allied notions of personalisation and delivery, fitting neatly with the idea of autonomous sites able to determine their own ways of doing things, were rapidly taken up in schooling and in leadership training.

I now turn to the revised leadership training framework and the desired outcomes. It is important to note, however, before moving on how the position of the NC has changed over time.

The NC leadership training framework

Although established as a semi-independent organisation, a 'quango', the NC was fully integrated into national government when the Coalition came to power in 2010, becoming an 'Executive Agency', as part of what is locally known as the 'bonfire of the quangos' (e.g. Syal, 2012). The NC awards, intended to support leadership development in a college, school or children's centre, were, for a time, a compulsory prerequisite for new headteachers. This requirement was abolished by the Coalition government who declared, contra to the notion of standards and training for leaders, that anyone with any kind of background could lead a school. At the time of writing, leadership qualifications are still optional, although arguably they function as a measure of quality in the recruitment, selection and appointment process.

Changing the status of the NC and its courses was another instance of the political field acting on and in the schooling field to change a position and its agents. The re-location of the NC within the government system was legitimated in market terms – it was an expensive monopoly – and schools needed to be 'free' from government interference in their choice of leaders. The shift in the NC's position from provider to commissioner in the ELMA field opened possibilities to other providers, including higher education. Its star fading rapidly, there was and remains considerable pressure for the NC to maintain position by ensuring that its programmes are seen as saleable, valuable and worthwhile.

From 2012, the NC offered three qualifications intended to support people aspiring to leadership positions, although they were also open to some early in their tenure in these posts. They were: the National Professional Qualification for middle leaders (NPQML), senior leaders (NPQSL) and headteachers (NPQH). Details of these are, at the time of writing, still located on the government website (http://www.education.gov.uk/nationalcollege/index/professional-development/modularcurriculum/modularcurriculum-moduledescriptions.htm). Within this qualification framework, leaders are not necessarily equated with formal positions but, rather, with 'levels' of experience and responsibility. However, 'middle' is generally understood to be to heads of department and other positions such as year-level coordinator, 'senior' to mean assistant and deputy heads and some heads of department, and headteachers are both the head of the school and an executive head responsible for more than one site.

I have undertaken a semiotic content analysis (Hsieh & Shannon, 2005; Manning & Cullum-Swan, 1998) of the National College curriculum framework. I began by examining the titles and descriptors of each of the modules, asking questions drawn from a Bourdieusian framing, viz.

- What leader practices are being promoted?
- What leader capitals are valued?
- What hierarchies of leader are being imagined and created?
- What evidence is there of doxa related to leadership, equity and school effectiveness and improvement?

The following section shows my analysis. My goal in writing this account in some detail is to show the ways in which a Bourdieusian analysis unfolds.

A content analysis

No longer mandatory, NC programmes had to appeal, and sell, on the basis of relevance to a wider range of heads, prospective heads and schools. Programme 'delivery' had thus to demonstrably include elements of choice and negotiation, recognition of local context and the need to match the pressures of the job to

82   *What do leaders need to know?*

the approach to leadership being advocated. The qualification curriculum design recognised prior knowledge, emotions and the needs of newly appointed heads and encouraged more reflective practice. It allowed for personal coaching and for considerable variation in content and process within an overall framework. The framework specified the outcomes; the means of getting to the prescribed outcomes were variable. The NC programme itself was modular, consisting of core topics and options.

There are compulsory modules at each qualification level, as shown below. These are the core knowledge and practices that are required of all leaders.

NPQML: (a) Leading teaching; (b) Managing systems and processes.
NPQSL: (a) Succeeding in senior leadership, (b) Closing the gap
NPQH: (a) Leading and improving teaching, (b) Leading an effective school, (c) Succeeding in headship.

What can be interpreted from the titles and their synoptic course descriptors?

A middle leader is expected to get their team to perform 'high quality teaching' (NPQMLa). This is to be verified by headteachers who need to assess teachers' "subject knowledge, effective planning and accurate pupil assessment" (NPQHa) and to use "consistent and effective staff performance management" (NPQHb). Senior leaders contribute to this endeavour by being able to "identify gaps, diagnose causes, and address in school variation (e.g. differences in performance by teachers with similar groups of pupils") (NPQSHb). Senior leaders will in particular have to address the "needs of disadvantaged pupils" as their poor performance could prevent "closing the gap". A nested hierarchy of scrutiny and responsibility and the imagined vertical distribution of positions within the school (as a field in itself) is apparent.

There are different responsibilities attached to each hierarchical position within the school. These speak to the self-managing nature of the English school: the need for 'delivery' of system priorities, the risk-averse management of resources and demonstrable adherence to system frameworks and audit procedures. Middle leaders must know the importance of "effective management", implementing school policies "in a systematic and consistent way with their team" (NPQMLb). Senior leaders are expected to examine their own practices to see that their leadership is directed towards "school improvement priorities" (NPQSLa). Headteachers are expected to provide the necessary structures and cultures to support this improvement through the management of pupil's behavior, finances and the recruitment, employment and deployment of "human resources" within the required legislative frameworks (NPQHTb). They must conform to accountability regimes, work productively with the governing body and "manage relationships within and beyond the school" (NPQHc).

This hierarchy of responsibilities tells us something about the ways in which capitals are 'officially' valued. Everyone who is a leader, regardless of level, must line-manage people and work with data as the means of judging effectiveness and guiding improvement. This is knowledge capital associated with management. Additional capitals are required at different levels to manage the spread of responsibilities. In the case of the head, this extends to public relations and being the point of contact with the wider accountability systems. But again the required capitals are those associated with management, and with conforming and performing.

Back to the qualification structure. . . a further two elective modules can be added at each qualification level, and it is here where there are topics that appear to be more 'educational':

- leading for inclusion via raising expectations, improving tracking, intervention and assessment and working with parents (NPQML);
- school self-evaluation, understanding how to use evidence and evaluate the school's strengths and weaknesses to guide strategic planning and performance management (NPQSL);
- curriculum development – how to "design, develop and deliver" curriculum which encompasses and extends the National Curriculum and uses assessment to "monitor, support and improve' students' learning" (NPQH);
- leading in diverse contexts in which consideration must be given to how leadership and management must adapt to different contexts (NPQH); and
- improvement through effective partnership working – partnerships with chains of academies and the voluntary and business sector are to be directed to pupils' learning progress and school improvement priorities (NPQH).

The emphasis in these optional modules remains on practices which are audit oriented. Leaders are expected to acquire the valued managerial capital of data analysis and performative paperwork, as well as ensuring that there is no dip in performance attributed to diversity. This requires a practice of identifying potential problems, targeting support, designing interventions and monitoring teacher and student performance against standardised outcomes. There is little here of leadership.

In order to elaborate this analysis a little further I counted word frequencies in the synoptic course descriptors, the 'top level' of text.

Word counts of the online module descriptors show that, apart from the words *leading, leadership* and *leader* (31 mentions), the next most common word is *effective* (21 mentions) with *performance* (15 mentions) and *improvement* (13 mentions) next. *Implementation* (9 mentions) is also high on the list. This count supports my initial reading of leadership as a doxa of management, effectiveness and improvement, embedded in training materials to be transmitted to prospective leaders. Despite the apparent flexibility and choice involved in the NC qualifications, the dispositions attached to leadership at any level are largely to do with meeting system expectations and regulating and overseeing what other people do.

An examination of the verbs in the module descriptors shows that leaders do some of the same things at each vertical level, albeit at increasing scale; some new activities also accrue with seniority. There are also in module descriptors explicit

84   *What do leaders need to know?*

references to knowledge. There is for example a mention of research knowledge and two references to Michael Fullan (a key member of the TLP). Some of this knowledge is propositional, know what, while other knowledge is procedural, know-how. Following Bourdieu, we can see propositional knowledge as related to capitals, and procedural knowledge as related to dispositions. Both help to shape, and are shaped by, the logics of practice in the field. These actions and knowledge appear in Table 5.1.

The analysis shows that the 'core business' of leading schools is the production of student performance/progress. This requires effective teaching across the school. A leader's job at each hierarchical position is geared toward making sure that this occurs. Leaders are responsible for management systems – of people, money, plant and equipment image – to ensure that there is an efficient and seamless infrastructure set up to audit, intervene, support and develop. This is a quasi-scientific and highly rational model. It has at its heart a set of data about pupil's progress and it is this data set which guides what actions are to be taken.

The modules present leaders; actions as cause and effects; if the know-what and know-how are followed, then improvement will result. As will success, defined as monitorable, measurable improvement. But of course, the reverse is also true; if improvement does not occur, then it is because the know-what and know-how of the leader is deficient. Ergo, a leader is one who is dispositionally and positionally responsible. A leader takes on ownership of student/school success and failure with accompanying, ongoing anxieties about never-ending improvement. Their personal place in the hierarchy of the school is dependent on practices which 'show' how they have lead others. This is the logic which drives what leaders do, perhaps to the point where it becomes second nature; it is only natural and common sense to act as a leader in this way.

With any kind of content analysis, it is always important to consider things that are not explicitly mentioned and the things that are implied.

To this end, it is interesting to think about what room there is, in this imaginary of a school and its leaders, for innovation and for resistance:

- There is an implied space for additional curriculum offerings to be developed around the national curriculum. How much and what is developed obviously depend on the degree of mandated content, and the degree of effort the leaders/school must make in relation to the mandated outcomes.
- There is no prescription per se about pedagogies, and there is a clear steer towards the need to adapt the curriculum to particular groups of pupils who typically do less well. However, there is also a clear advocacy of Achievement for All, a programme developed by central government with Pricewater-houseCoopers to attend particularly to pupils with special needs. Achievement for All requires continuous tracking of pupil progress in English and Maths and intervention, termly conversations between parents and teachers about pupil progress and a 'commonsense' approach to negative influences such as bullying, truancy or "poor social skills" (see www.education.gov.uk/

Table 5.1 Qualification level, capitals and dispositions

	Practices	*Propositional (capitals)*	*Procedural (dispositions)*
NPQML	implement (3), develop, build, sustain, operate, adapt, work, improve, raise	The role of team leaders Models and theories of leadership The relationship between leading and managing The characteristics of highly effective teams Research evidence about how to build lead and sustain a team Leading and managing change for school improvement	How to develop a team How to develop individual team members (spot talent, grow potential, manage performance) How to respond to underperforming teachers How to develop own leadership capacity How to adapt leadership to different contexts How to work collaboratively with other team leaders
NPQSL	apply, close, identify, diagnose, improve, strengthen, design, implement, support, develop (2), capitalise on, promote (2), engage, explore, address, know, use	Research evidence about which pupils succeed and fail International research evidence about leading and improving teaching Critical issues in C21 teaching and learning and research about addressing them Essential knowledge about leading change in practice using Fullan's research and an analytic tool	How to understand self (motivations, values) How to apply leadership to address SI priorities How to close gaps, how to identify gaps, diagnose causes and address in school variation How to improve teaching and learning via policy, models of teaching and evaluating pupil progress How to strengthen management of key systems (curriculum, performance, behavior, finances, health, safety, welfare) How to undertake whole school self-evaluation, how to use evidence How to design and implement professional development How to develop successful partnership How to promote and lead research How context changes what leaders can do

(*Continued*)

Table 5.1 (Continued)

	Practices	Propositional (capitals)	Procedural (dispositions)
NPQH	develop, improve (2), sustain, implement, appraise, tackle, learn, lead, interrogate, work (2), close, know (4)	Know the importance of teachers' subject knowledge, effective planning and accurate teacher assessment Key management systems (teacher performance, pupil behavior and financial management) Essential legal and accountability components What successful heads do in practice (governors, key groups) International research about partnerships Cases of diverse schools Evidence from research about variations in pupil performance	How to develop, improve and sustain high quality teaching across the school How to implement staff performance management system, quickly tackle staff underperformance and address capability across school. How to led curriculum development (design, development and delivery including assessment to monitor, support and improve progress) How to analyse data How to interrogate research evidence and use discerningly How to work with different partners How to close gaps How to improve practice by implementing Achievement for All

What do leaders need to know? 87

schools/leadershipschoolperformance/a00199926/achievement-for-all).
This is a more intensive version of what is already the preferred model.

- There is perhaps some room for manoeuvre produced through partnerships with other schools and partners, although these too must be designed to improve performance.

It is equally interesting to see what is missing from this set of descriptors. The research literature (see Chapter 2) highlights the ways in which leaders' work is shaped by league tables, inspection, marketing and dealing with other public relations including media. However, the NC qualification framework says nothing explicit about the entrepreneurial activities leaders need to use to position their school within the local and national scene. On this, more later. And equity is equated with dealing with diversity. An equitable leader works to enable underperformers to step up to the expected norms rather than make changes to the content and organisation of knowledge, pedagogies and assessment.

Missing altogether from the framework are some things that leaders might be expected to know and do. There are no mentions of the ways in which priorities get decided and negotiated. Information distribution, communication and decision-making responsibilities seem to rest with positions – the headteacher and the governing body – rather than being presented as a more democratic practice. Teams appear largely in the work of middle leaders and collaboration only as something that occurs with others at the same level. The 'three major message systems of schooling' (Bernstein, 2000) – curriculum, pedagogy and assessment – are conflated, and there is an assumption that the same assessment practices serve to monitor overall outcomes and to support students' learning. There is no discussion at all of the purposes of schooling over and above performance data, although the optional curriculum development NPQH module does suggest that leaders must ensure that pupils enjoy "spiritual, moral, social and culture development".

Additionally, and of particular note, there seems to be a shift away in the NC framework from some deeply held views emanating from the TLP. While the NC framing elevates the rhetoric of school effectiveness and improvement, derived largely from some of the TLP, it doesn't adopt wholesale from the SESI (now EEIR) movement. There is for example no mention in the module outlines of developing a vision and getting staff and the community to sign on to it; this was a hallmark of New Labour NC prescription of best practice, and a feature of the first phase of the NPQH where aspiring heads had to prepare, for assessment, a talk that could be used with staff to get them to sign up to their vision. There is precious little about teacher learning and teacher expertise, held as crucial by SI scholars. And while there is continued mention of improvement throughout the framework, there is nothing in the qualification descriptors about transformation and transformational leadership arguably also at the core of much of the TLP work (see Chapter 3).

Furthermore, the data-driven processes that are central to the NC approach to schooling have been extensively critiqued by some of the TLP, particularly

88   *What do leaders need to know?*

advocates of the Finnish system (e.g. Sahlberg, 2012). Michael Fullan's (2011) change formulation – earn trust, fine-tune, fine focus, develop others, know your impact, embrace complexity, hope no matter what – is very different from the quasi-scientific model on offer in the National College modules – even if some of the same content is covered and his name is mentioned. The tone of Fullan's work is much more humanistic and draws on ecological approaches to organisations and to contemporary theorisations of social systems as 'complex'.

These shifts in the ways in which the TLP is drawn on – away from change theory and theorists to more exclusive use of effectiveness studies which are based on meta-analyses – suggests a re-hierarchisation of capitals in the schooling field in England. Management capitals count above all. The practice of monitoring to ensure conforming and performing counts above all. This content analysis of a leadership qualification framework begins to show how the ELMA game is now to be played, and the kinds of leader dispositions and capitals that are necessary when conservative politics dominate the political field.

Bringing Bourdieu to the qualification modules

Although I have been providing some Bourdieusian commentary throughout this content analysis, it is important to summarise the argument, and then see what else might be said. But first, a caveat. The outline of the qualification framework is not the same as a detailed syllabus or how these guidelines might be variously interpreted by the contracted providers, of which there are several scattered throughout the country. Nor should my analysis be taken for an empirical account of what actually happens in the field.

However, the modules do signify some things about what is officially said about the job and what capitals are being promoted as desirable.

1. *The capitals that are said to matter most*

There is an overwhelming emphasis on management capital, as noted. The framework is focused on a specific view of management, one concerned with the systems of planning, quality assurance and performance management, and capacity building. It uses a particular lexicon, with frequent use of terms such as *effective, improvement, performance, implementation, monitor, diagnose, intervene* and *evidence*. This is top-down management; there are references to lateral collaborations between middle leaders and references to internal and external partnerships, but this is not the same as an organisation in which collaboration is the modus operandi. This is management which draws both on 'scientific management' traditions, as well as New Public Management. Perversely, these capitals are actually not leadership, since most of the knowledge and lexicon associated with leadership – developing a vision, scanning trends in policy and practice, forming teams to design local innovations, acting in ways to transform the organisation – are missing from the NC qualification framework. We could guess at some discussion of forms of leadership and management in the compulsory module for middle leaders, but thereafter references to anything resembling a debate in the field is invisible.

And there is a marked lack of what we might call educational capitals. Teachers are required to have detailed knowledge of their own area of curriculum and they need to be inspected, but it appears to be a matter of personal choice whether headteachers develop knowledge of wider 'whole curriculum' issues and debates. Middle leaders don't need more knowledge than they have as teachers in order to do their job, and neither do senior leaders. There is thus a question about who in the school understands broader curriculum questions of the selection and organisation of knowledge, international debates about pedagogies, assessment practices and curriculum architecture (genres of instruction and student grouping practices for example). As well, knowledge primarily seems to come into the school from elsewhere. It resides in international evidence and research and in government interventions.

There is a shift in what counts as ELMA capitals from the New Labour period to the Conservative period.

2. The practices of leadership

Aspiring leaders must know the game of management and how to play it. They must be able to demonstrate that they have acquired desirable and approved management capital. They must make visible in their leadership training that they can plan, perform, interpret data, intervene and manage. When appointed to leadership positions they must do more than 'talk the talk', that is demonstrate that they have the preferred lexicon, the right linguistic capital. They must now play the game for real by producing tangible evidence of their learning in the form of student test and exam results and good inspection reports. The NC training modules act as a kind of rehearsal for this required practice and as such, they are geared to produce the necessary surveilling and calculating disposition before it is applied in the school. How well this occurs, of course, is a subsequent, and researchable, question.

3. Field position

The NC qualification framework is an imaginary of three different positions in the educational field: school middle leader, senior leader and headteacher. There is little explicit recognition that some leadership positions have more status than others by virtue of vertical and horizontal hierarchies of school type, of discipline, of location, of reputation, of size. The 'leader' is presented at the top level of the qualification framework as if the first and biggest differences between positions are those of seniority and influence within a school. Inter-school divisions are presented later as diverse contexts, with no reference to the power dimensions of hierarchies.

90 *What do leaders need to know?*

4. Doxa

Not surprisingly, my analysis of the training framework focused strongly on the doxa of leadership, the approved way of doing things. The NC leadership training framework suggests that:

- what happens in the school produces students' success in learning. This is inline with much of EEIR, but contrary not only to Bourdieu's analysis but also to *all* educational and sociological analyses of the significant influence of parent income, neighbourhood and parent education on learning;
- while context might change what leaders do, successful leadership should be always measured against universal criteria;
- that what leaders do via teacher performance development and monitoring, resource allocation and strategic partnerships will improve the school and students' learning;
- it is not essential for leaders to have expertise in change management or in curriculum; and
- professional titles have been replaced by generic leader labels, and sometimes it seems as if everyone is being spoken to as leaders or potential leaders.

As noted, the leadership doxa promotes leadership but is directed to management as a rational, calculable and calculating practice. It is at this point that it is helpful to go back to a history of the ELMA field. Doxa is always historically situated.

The approach taken to management in the qualification framework has deep historical roots in Taylorism (Taylor, 1911/1947). Taylor is generally known as one of the founders of the US 'efficiency movement'. The efficiency movement held that organisations must be managed in such a way as to minimise wasted effort; any enterprise or element of an organisation that fails to produce to the level required must be eliminated. Politically, the doctrine of efficiency legitimated free markets over cartels and monopolies on the grounds that inefficient business would simply 'go under'. Taylor held that efficiency and effectiveness (in production) depended on: breaking up large jobs into smaller separate tasks; and tasks organised as a linear progression performed as quickly as possible by different teams, under direct supervision (see Figure 5.1). The assembly line is quintessential Taylorism in practice.

In education, the post–World War I efficiency movement aligned with a vocational curriculum for those not destined to go onto to higher education (a cost-effective schooling) and the use of observable measurable teaching objectives (Bobbitt, 1924). The efficiency movement also supported the direct transfer of business methods into post–World War II school leadership and management (Callahan, 1962), arguably an ongoing practice in education systems (Berman, 1983).

The division of intellectual and physical labour that Taylorism fostered has often been sutured together in education policy with other similarly 'scientific'

First. They develop a science for each element of a man's work, which replaces the old rule of thumb method.

Second. They scientifically select and then train, teach and develop the workman, whereas in the past he chose his own work and trained himself as best he could

Third. They heartily cooperate with the man so as to insure all of the work being done in accordance with the principles of the science which has been developed

Fourth. There is an almost equal division of the work and the responsibility between the management and the workmen. The management take over all work for which they are better fitted than the workmen while in the past almost all of the work and the greater part of the responsibility were thrown upon the men (Taylor, 1911, p p. 25–26)

Figure 5.1 Taylorist principles of organisation

approaches – the application of extrinsic motivators (reward and punishment; Skinner, 1968) and the introduction of particular teaching methods, particularly in areas such as reading. But the influence of Taylor and the cult of efficiency (e.g. Callahan, 1962) can still be seen in contemporary educational practices, for example in a curriculum where there is lock-step progression through a series of very small, perhaps daily, targets or competency levels (Amin, 1994; Brown, 1994).

The foundational importance of Taylorism and efficiency to forms of scientific management doxa is not confined to the US. In England, Taylorism mapped onto traditional hierarchies of power and was inflected by existing classed, raced and gendered practices and relations (Grace, 1995). Taylorist approaches were taken up worldwide and have become a feature of many education systems and sectors (Welch, 1998) through the global interconnections formed by international policy networks. The Taylorist view sees work in a rational, machine-like way, separating the decisions about work (leadership) from the actual labour process.

Applied to education, a Taylorist perspective has the head acting as a kind of human calculator, always on the alert for inefficiencies and ways to make the machine run more cheaply and effectively. While the designated leader may have values which underpin their actions, the school itself and the wider education system are value-neutral. It is interesting to consider Taylor's four principles (Figure 5.2) as if they applied to current school leaders in England as expressed in the NC leader qualification framework:

One: a science for each element of work.
There is a distinct set of leadership tasks for each level and these have an 'evidence' base in (some) research and practice.
Two: scientific selection and training.
Applicants for leadership training must apply or are encouraged to apply as a result of having been 'talent spotted'. The NC courses are then undertaken to consolidate initial promise.
Three: ensure that the work undertaken is in accordance with the principles.
Once in the job leaders are responsible for outcomes which can be inspected, measured and evaluated

92 *What do leaders need to know?*

Four: responsibility is evenly divided between workers and management. Outcome frameworks, monitoring and inspection and resource allocation are decided away from the school, the school leader is responsible for 'delivery". Systemic bifurcation of conception and execution is mirrored in the school, where curriculum responsibility is devolved to teachers while leaders take responsibility for all the management tasks – planning, outcome frameworks, monitoring and resource allocation – that support teachers' 'delivery'.

But the NC framework also draws on another variant of efficiency, that of Total Quality Management (TQM). J. Edwards Deming (1992, 2000) is generally understood to be the 'father' of quality management. He applied his training as a statistician to the "production line" and its predetermined division of tasks. He rejected hierarchical command and control management and opted instead for a 'systems' approach which saw workers at each level delegated responsibility for making their own judgements about their own effectiveness and efficiency (Seddon, 2003). Deming moved away from highly atomised tasks to designate more holistic production and points of responsibility. He suggested that each production task, if defined broadly, could be understood and managed through the use of data which indicated how close or far 'the product' was from a prescribed standard. If those responsible for the task were able to monitor the data, then they could take responsibility for making any adjustments necessary to ensure greater 'product' consistency. Deming's work was famously taken up in Japan as Kaizen (Imai, 1997), a more holistic approach to manufacturing, in which those involved in production would not only become self-monitoring but also be able to develop strategies for improvement (see Figure 5.2).

It is both the congruence with calculation and a 'scientific' approach, combined with the shift from direct top-down control to management at a distance via regulation, that creates the rhetorical and strategic 'fit' between TQM and the move to new governing practice.

It is not too difficult to see some connections between Toyota's management emphases – continuous improvement via ongoing self-monitoring, making strategic partnerships, monitoring customer satisfaction and meeting expectations and developing leaders who are already part of the system and understand how it

---

The Toyota way
Foster an atmosphere of continuous improvement and learning
Create continuous process "flow" to unearth problems
Satisfy customers (and eliminate waste at the same time)
Grow your leaders rather than purchase them
Get quality right the first time
Grow together with your suppliers and partners for mutual benefit

---

Figure 5.2 Toyota management principles (Liker, 2004)

What do leaders need to know? 93

works – and the preferred mode of school management in England, as expressed in the NC leadership training framework. Both focus on the same kinds of issues. Car manufacturers place an emphasis on customers, as does a marketised schooling system. Car manufacturers develop and train their own leaders, as does a school system where the government sets training frameworks and contracts out the training. And is it too far a stretch to see a connection between car manufacturers fostering of relationships with suppliers to ensure that they get the best materials, and schools' offers of parenting classes and homework to address their apparent 'supply problem'?

While vertical hierarchies in the school and the linear nesting of responsibilities are linked with the history of Taylorism, the emphasis on calculation and devolved horizontal management sits with Total Quality Management. But before I go further, another caveat: I am not arguing that business influence is automatically 'A Bad Thing'. I am suggesting that there are management doxa commonalities between public and private sectors; these are based on their 'family trees' and to a shared 'root' system. This root system is located in organisational and human relations (psychology), as taken up in the field of business studies.

The family resemblance (the homology) between the current education field and the field of business can be seen very clearly in the doxa around equity. Deming and his inheritors have it that quality is improved by both eliminating the degree of variation in the system and incrementally raising the overall standard (Aguayo, 1990). In education this notion has been taken up as a 'quality and an equality' doxa – better results for students from particular social and cultural contexts are to be achieved by 'closing the gap and raising the bar' (see NPQSL: Closing the gap). It is this contention, perhaps better called a mantra, which leads to both the policy emphasis on getting more students across an arbitrary benchmark such as a C exam grade, and the EEIR interest in statistical measures, which establish what systems are most effective and efficient in achieving shifts in measurable outcomes.

Interestingly, and contra to the NC leadership qualifications framework and current policy and practice, Deming explicitly rejected the notion of individualised performance management and target setting, arguing that (1) individualised performance corrupted cooperation and (2) target setting meant a skewing of the system. One of his favourite examples was of insurance sales staff who were set sales targets rather than given the job of finding long-term customers. They unscrupulously sold numerous policies which customers then defaulted on; while there were quick gains in targets, there were long-term losses in profit. This seems to be a lesson which has fallen on deaf ears in the education field. Quick turnarounds in 'failing schools' in England are often promoted at the expense of more long-term, sustained change. Only *some* aspects of Deming's quality approach are embedded in the current governing policy doxa. Reducing variation and raising standards incrementally are taken from Deming and sutured together with older Taylorist hierarchical stick-and-carrot supervision and decision regimes.

Scientific management doxa operate as a kind of black box. Once inside the logic of its practices, it seems entirely reasonable. This is how doxa works; it

94   *What do leaders need to know?*

becomes 'the way we do things around here', part of our culture. It is only when one steps away from this logic to look critically at it from a distance that some of the workings of doxa can be seen. A Bourdieusian view facilitates getting such distance on everyday practice.

Outside the doxic black box: misrecognition

Bourdieu notes that the stance of scientificity, neutrality and rationality, such as that adopted by the national leadership training framework and found in Taylorism, the efficiency movement and TQM,

> is a fiction, an interested fiction which enables its authors to present a version of the dominant representation of the social world, neutralised and euphemized into a particularly misrecognisable and symbolically, therefore, particularly effective form.
>
> (Bourdieu, 1975, p. 18)

It is helpful to conclude a Bourdieuian analysis of the NC training framework by considering it as a fiction, looking for what is euphemised and misrecognised within it, considering the social consequences of this misrecognition.

My reading of the NC qualification framework, as suggested previously, shows that it misrecognises the following.

1. The reason for students' lack of success

The lack of student success in tests and exams is causally linked to teachers and heads, and as already noted, this ignores the mountain of evidence about the importance of material social conditions and relations. While schools can make some difference in students' learning, they cannot make all of the difference. Schools by themselves cannot redress profound social inequalities (Connell, Ashenden, Kessler, & Dowsett, 1982; Thomson, 2008b). Some recognition is given in the framework to home factors that might need intervention. While there is an acknowledgement that this might in an unspecified way be related to social conditions and even to social group membership (Harris et al., 2006), the connections to broader social economic and cultural processes is invisible. The lack of recognition of material reality in the framework thus gives leaders no help to think about the school and the complex interrelationship of processes and relationships that produce inequality, the necessity for public policy agendas to work together, the limits of public policy to address social and economic conditions and the ways in which these social economic cultural and political processes manifest themselves not only in students, but throughout every aspect of the school (e.g. see Gulson & Symes, 2007; Lupton, 2003, 2004; Thomson, 2002).

Equally, the role that the curriculum, pedagogy and assessment itself have in producing and reproducing uneven results is also ignored. The curriculum is taken for granted, as is the way in which the school works as a hierarchy. The ways in which the language of the classroom and the knowledge on offer are geared to favour some students and not others are ignored (Gonzales & Moll, 2002; Gonzales, Moll, & Amanti, 2005; Gruenewald & Smith, 2008; Janks, 2009; Thomson & Hall, 2008). The ways in which an individualising approach to managing student behaviour might ignore ongoing oppressive practices based on particular class, race, sexuality and gender relations are invisible (Archer & Francis, 2006; Arnot & Mac An Ghaill, 2006; Francis & Skelton, 2001; Slee, 1995; Smyth & Hattam, 2004). That the organisation of the school itself and the curriculum might actually *produce* both success and failure at the same time and through the very same processes is outside the logic of the model on offer (Connell, 1993; Gewirtz, 2002; McInerney, 2005).

Because the view of the school presented in the framework omits or reduces the view of the social and, indeed, potentially links to broader doxa which dismisses most discussion of the importance of the social as 'excuse making', it legitimates the doxa of meritocracy. 'Good' students do not need leadership intervention; they do well on their own, without special help. Those who do not do well lack 'aspiration' and need to have their aspirations raised. As long as teachers perform effectively then differences can only be created by the students' own 'innate ability' and their work habits variously acquired from 'supportive/unsupportive families'. There are no system-inherent or inherited advantages of capitals and habitus.

The politics of blame of students and their families are arguably a form of symbolic violence. While the training framework itself does not overtly perpetuate symbolic violence against students and their families it does, via its misrecognition of social relations and practice, provide the logic of practice for the sorting and selecting practices that do.

2. The power of headteachers and teachers

An important corollary of the disappearance of the social to focus on only on a stand-alone closed school system is that the capacities of teachers and headteachers to make a difference, as leaders doing leadership, is overstated and overemphasised. It is as if school staff's intentions to make a difference, by acquiring the necessary knowledge and the right rational practice, will lead automatically to improvement. The presence of some schools and leaders who have made considerable improvements as measured on tests and exams serves to reinforce the doxic point that all schools, leaders and teachers must be capable of the same – despite the reality that there may be other explanations for their change (Thomson, 2014). There is a nod to context in the NC training framework, but it is assumed that everything that counts as context is amenable to leadership action at the local level. This is patently not the case, as many issues that press on families, such as unemployment, lack of transport, cost of rent and cost of food for instance, are well beyond the reach of a local headteacher, a coalition of academies, even a local authority. The distribution of well-paid employment is, under globalising conditions, also apparently beyond the reach of national governments and public policy.

96 *What do leaders need to know?*

To establish a policy and a training framework which implies that leaders and teachers can make all of the difference in student learning is a grave misrecognition. It attributes more power to teachers and leaders than they actually have, particularly as they are also often not in a position to change the ways in which the structure and practices of the school itself might produce and reproduce inequalities – if they are in academy chains for example or under the watchful eye of an inspector. Subsequent blaming of teachers and leaders, via discourses of derision (Kenway, 1990), for failure to change outcomes sufficiently, is a form of symbolic violence which, when it is translated into practices of bullying, unreasonable workload and ultimately dismissal, becomes actual and material violence.

In conclusion: what does this example show us about what Bourdieusian thinking might offer to ELMA?

An evaluation of the NC qualification training framework I have examined was conducted and published (Crawford & Earley, 2012). It praised the flexible delivery mechanisms, the combination of coaching, choice of topics and materials and its more negotiated approach. The evaluators concluded that the new leadership-training modules had largely achieved their goal of personalisation, and the only problem with them was the lack of accommodation of the variation in learning styles and experiences that candidates brought to the learning experience. The evaluators suggest that the framework is still too narrow in its view of what aspiring leaders already know, what they want to know and how they want to learn. The evaluation is in part critical.

But bringing Bourdieu to an analysis of the training framework offers a much sharper focus on these issues. My analysis suggests that what appears to be personalisation in delivery is in reality the homogenisation of what knowledges and practices are considered important. The highly managerialist and scientised model on offer pays lip service to the notion of context, over-responsibilises leaders and teachers and reduces notions of equity to narrow measures. As I have suggested this is a misrecognition which arguably constitutes and legitimates symbolic violence.

My analysis of the framework as a leadership doxa, and its implications for leaders' practice and habitus dovetails with other research. There are for example studies of recruitment and selection (Blackmore et al., 2006; Gronn & Lacey, 2006; Grummell, Devine, & Lynch, 2009; MacBeath, Oduro, Jacka, & Hobby, 2006; Kwan & Walker, 2009) which point not only to the tendency to homophily – selecting people like me – but also that a narrow range of beliefs, knowledge and behaviour (doxa, capitals, practices and dispositions) are embedded in these processes. There are other studies of qualification frameworks and standards which come to similar conclusions (Anderson, 2001; English, 2000, 2006). My analysis of job advertisements (Thomson, 2009) suggested a prioritising by governing bodies of knowledge about and know-how of tests and inspections. Other empirical studies (Baker, 2005; Ball, 1999; Ball et al., 2012;

What do leaders need to know? 97

Gillbourn & Youdell, 2000; Maguire, Ball, & MacRae, 2001; Riddell, 2003) also show these conforming and performing practices and capitals in action.

Perhaps the most interesting aspect of my analysis of the NC qualification training framework lies in the shift away from aspects of core TLP beliefs – that around leadership. In the NC framework, leadership is a Trojan horse for a particular type of technical management. As I have argued, notions of vision, transformation and teachers' professional development are missing from the top level of the qualification documentation. There is an overwhelming emphasis on audit, measurement and monitoring improvement, all practices subject to central regulatory prescription and control. What are we to make of this? It is helpful to reconnect this shift away from what has been an orthodoxy of leadership practices with the overall changes occurring in the wider field of education.

The move from leader practices which might support more local determination of purposes and priorities occurred alongside the formation of the new Conservative government (2015), with its press to academise all schools. Reducing the capacity of individual schools and their leaders to deviate from the task of delivery of centrally mandated outcomes is central to this recent policy intervention. If schools buy into the NC leader qualifications, they will find that the capitals, dispositions and practices align neatly with current policy directions. The NC itself has also been marginalised in the field, and the qualification framework demonstrates the strategy that the National College has adopted in order to survive/train for what is now required. Offer no alternatives or critical perspectives.

And where to with this kind of Bourdieusian reading? While the analysis of the qualification framework is interesting, it is important not to assume a neat translation of capitals, practices and doxa into the actual practice of school leaders. That requires additional and separate empirical inquiry, and that is where we go in the next chapter.

6 New practices and old hierarchies

Academy conversion in a successful secondary school in England

Ruth McGinity and Helen M. Gunter

Introduction

We site our analysis in one secondary school in the north of England, and by drawing on in-depth interviews with the school leadership team, we bring analysis and perspective to professional practice at a time of rapid reform. The interviews were undertaken as part of a two-year ethnographic study. Using Bourdieu's (1989, 1990a, 1990b) conceptual tools we construct an understanding and explanations of the privatisation of public education through the expansion of the Academies Programme in England from 2010, and by doing so we examine how and why school leaders as individuals and as a team position themselves and the school within the field of educational policymaking. The findings suggest that there exists a complex interplay between external ideological demands and pragmatic internal opportunism enacted by the headteacher and deputies, where symbolic capital in the form of official recognition from the government is of utmost importance if the school is to present itself as a viable and legitimate player in the policy game. Our contribution is to engage with accounts of professional practice through a theory of power that enables powerfulness as an organisational narrative to be examined. This is significant because it not only demonstrates the role of research in uncovering the way the TLP operates, but also how field data requires social science thinking tools in order to ask important questions about ELMA.

Policy games

Kingswood High School (anonymised name) is an 11–18 school and is the only state funded secondary provision in the town located in the north of England. Our data set, produced from a year of intensive ethnographic study, provides an account of children and adults at work in a settled and locally endorsed good school. Nevertheless, the school is located in an intensive national and local performance regime based on published standards for pupils and teachers, targets, testing and data collection, and so there is a requirement to be extraordinary. Since the appointment of the current headteacher in 1997 the school has made year on year improvements as measured by the percentage of students attaining

New practices and old hierarchies 99

at least five A*–C grades at General Certificate of Secondary Education (GCSE) level. In 2011 the school inspectorate judged Kingswood as 'good with outstanding features'.

Our data show that there are historical narratives in play regarding how the headteacher and school leadership team have engaged with opportunities and major interruptions within national policy. Specifically, in 2004 the school received a grant from the now privatised Innovations Unit, in the then Department for Education and Skills (DfES). The grant was used to commission an evaluation study (Gunter & Thomson, 2004; Hollins, Gunter, & Thomson, 2006), where the school put emphasis on internal research as a method for renewing purposes and developing organisational processes (McGinity & Gunter, 2012). The stories surrounding this creative approach are linked to how the school has responded to two major policy changes. First is the Specialist Schools Programme (1993–2010), where the headteacher and school leadership team disagreed with the idea of a school adopting a specialism (e.g. Science or Languages) for all children. In 2002 Kingswood High School approached the DfES with the proposal of allowing individual students *within the school* to specialise, this was approved and the school became the first secondary school in England to offer individual student specialism rather than a whole school specialism. Second, the Academies Programme (2000 onwards) was expanded in 2010 to allow high-performing schools to convert, and in 2012 Kingswood High School became Kingswood Academy. Again the headteacher and school leadership team redesigned the policy, where the model proposed is based upon the school's earlier commitment to student personalisation of the curriculum. The academy model is known as the 'Professional School' and is based on agreements with local businesses and a national educational trust in order to offer pathways to students which link the curriculum and accreditation with employability.

These two examples illuminate some interesting issues about how educational professionals are positioned by radical reform proposals with regard to local policy development and how those professionals seek to position themselves through the reading and interpretation of such policies. Notably there are matters to do with the interplay between agency and structure, where there is a need to examine, in Ball et al's (2012) terms, "how schools do policy". Conceptualisations of such policy positioning and position taking within policy scholarship have generated an emerging view that educational professionals can and do engage with policy interrelated with their own values, experiences and context. Our project at Kingswood is sited within this tradition, where the daily practices that we have observed, read about in school documents and heard about in interviews are concerned with the core service of teaching and learning. So adults and children arrive in school, are timetabled into various rooms and engage in social relationships that are directly or indirectly about supporting pedagogic processes. In this sense the school is a field or arena of social practice where professionals, parents and pupils take up positions and are positioned in regard to exchanges over expertise, knowledge and accreditation of outcomes. Policies by successive governments over the past 30 years have sought to make interventions by

100   *New practices and old hierarchies*

engaging with the habitus revealed in daily practices as "structured structures", and seeking to impact on the "structuring structures" (Bourdieu, 1990b). So for example governments have sought to redesign professional structured structures through the structuring impact of marketisation. We have identified that while 'structuring' policy initiatives and projects have not been linear, have often failed and have generated incoherence for those required to implement them, there are trends that can be identified:

- An emphasis on modernisation with a lexicon of 'new' and 'improved' schools, with a clear intention to break with the past and do things differently.
- A cultural shift towards building 'can do' attitudes in ways that deem alternative narratives and agendas as unnecessary and indeed oppositional.
- Reworking professional knowledge, skills and values to make them suitable for radical change agendas, where those who take up roles in schools are not necessarily educationally qualified professionals.
- A model for school improvement and effectiveness is the 'independent' school autonomous from the local democratic accountability.
- An approach to teaching and learning based on neo-conservative belief systems about subject knowledge, teaching methods, behaviour and dress with neo-liberal demands for measurement data based on tests and value-added calculations.
- Preferred and imagined models of the good and effective teacher and leader are promoted and used within training and accreditation to control entry and career development.

Thomson (2005) has argued that the field of education has been breached, where a "synchrony of crises" in the fields of the economy, politics and media the "agents in the dominant field . . . breach(ed) the borders of dominated fields" (pp. 751–752). Consequently "agents in the superior field use administrative mechanisms, both policy and enacted policy via new regulations, jobs, procedures etc., to effect significant changes in the other fields . . ." (p. 752). Globalisation requires new markets in educational services with a flexible workforce, and so economic agents require political agents to remove barriers to markets and product development (particularly with regard to the terms and conditions of service of public sector workers). Importantly media agents need stories, whereby "agents of the state are increasingly in a synchronous relationship with agents in the field of the media, through which it/they seek to make visible and credible its/their activities" (p. 751). Hence, New Labour ministers (1997–2010) made bold statements about the relationship between investment in public services and accountability for outcomes, and Conservative ministers (in Coalition 2010–2015 and in majority government from 2015 onwards) are making claims about the relationship between system failure and the need to increase market penetration into service provision and delivery.

In Bourdieu's (1990a) terms, the game in play is the full-scale privatisation of educational services. This game is not new, and has gone through a range of

New practices and old hierarchies   101

reinventions, but has a number of features: first, the introduction of business models and practices to change workforce composition and professional practice from within, such as Local Management of Schools from 1988; second, the removal of local authority schools from local democratic control through the Grant Maintained Status 'opting out' process from 1988, and the Academies Programme from 2000; and, third, the setting up of educational provision outside of local authority democratic control through the City Technology Colleges from 1986, and Free Schools from 2010 (Courtney, 2016; Gunter, 2011). This game relies on the codification of "new practices and old hierarchies" (Thomson, 2005, p. 753), whereby elite adults in schools (and communities) are protected and strengthened through the adoption of entrepreneurial knowledge (e.g. strategic thinking), skills (e.g. language and negotiation deployment) and behaviours (e.g. charismatic commitment building). While research evidence has raised serious questions about the Academies Programme (Gunter, 2011; Gunter & McGinity, 2014) and the five-year study by PricewaterhouseCoopers (2008) found that there is no "academy effect" in regard to improvements, elite codification as a game strategy continues in a number of ways. Evidence is selected (e.g. DfE, 2010), enabling bold but clear claims to be made:

> [T]he Academies programme is not about ideology. It's an evidence-based, practical solution built on by successive governments – both Labour and Conservative . . . Research from the OECD and others has shown that more autonomy for individual schools helps raise standards . . . And from autonomous schools in Alberta, to Sweden's Free Schools, to the Charter Schools of New York and Chicago, freedom is proving an unstoppable driver of excellence.
>
> (Gove, 2012)

Headteachers have positioned themselves within the codification process by confirming claims about new freedoms generated through the reforms (e.g. Astle & Ryan, 2008; Daniels, 2011). This renders a school remaining under Local Authority control as failing to understand the game in play, and where Estelle Morris, a previous secretary of state for education, commented on the acceleration of the Academies Programme:

> The government seems to have stopped noticing successful schools unless they're academies. What a tragedy. Whatever else, one thing is certain: success and failure, innovation and creativity will be found in both academies and non-academies. There is not a school structure yet invented by a politician . . . that by itself can guarantee success.
>
> (Morris, 2011)

The school improvement model used by successive governments has been based on the identification of failure (in schools, teachers, children, parents and/or communities) with an integrated rescue narrative. The juxtaposing of the Gove

102 New practices and old hierarchies

and Morris accounts illuminates how the codification and strategising within the privatisation game has shifted from focusing on actual failure as measured by test data that underpinned the original Academies Programme, to a complex disposition that is partly located in a fear of failure through not converting combined with an expectation of rewards through converting.

While research has uncovered this privatisation game (Ball, 2007; Beckett, 2007; Gunter, 2011) it is not spoken about in those terms. The lexicon is one of 'choice', 'diversity', 'responsiveness' and 'personalisation', and it is played through various sub-games which are seductive for the profession and are common sense for parents (Gunter, 2012b). In this sense the sub-game is one of performance leadership which has been structured and shaped through waves of TLP, and which has spoken to notions of professional autonomy in ways that are consistent with demands for a restoration of autonomy. Professionals have a long history of organisational and educational leadership, and so the opportunities afforded by the Academies Programme can be read as a development of this, where they are "caught up in the game" with a leadership illusio "understood as a fundamental belief in the interest of the game and the value of the stakes which is inherent in that membership" (Bourdieu, 2000, p. 11). However, to paraphrase Thomson (2005), the doxa of performance leadership means that participants can "misrecognise" the game: professionals may not see how generic and transferrable knowledge, skills and behaviours is a form of deprofessionalisation, whereby they deliver outputs rather than lead on teaching and learning, and how accepted hierarchies are taking away the entitlement of all children in a community to an education.

These are matters that researchers have begun to examine in relation to the leadership field, whereby the claims made regarding the espoused agency of the leader, doing leading and exercising leadership have been subjected to critical analysis using Bourdieu's thinking tools (see Gunter & Forrester, 2010a). For example evidence from Australia by Addison (2009) examines what it means for the education field to be breached by the field of the economy and practice as a chief executive, and Eacott (2011b) considers what it means to be trained in the rules to play the game. What such studies are increasingly engaging with is the relationship between the logic of practice within the leadership sub-game and claims regarding autonomy. Studies from the early days of the privatisation game in England show how headteachers took up different positions with regard to claims about increased autonomy. Grace (1995) identified how freedom from the local authority was supported, but those who resisted the combined centralisation of the curriculum and decentralisation of the market from 1988 found themselves in an increasingly difficult situation, where "the policies to which they objected on philosophical and professional grounds were policies which, if adopted, could bring to their schools and their pupils considerable material and resource benefits" (p. 74). More recently, Thomson (2010b) has examined the logic within the claim for autonomy and how it is both created by and shapes the game in play (and can create rival games): "regardless of whether one is for or against policy, for or against the game, heads are key players and while they work to advantage their school and students, what they do – their agency – is

New practices and old hierarchies 103

always framed by a decision about whether they are prepared to play to their own positional detriment" (p. 17). This enables some serious questions to be asked about the academy conversion at Kingswood, not least how and why the headteacher and school leadership team worked for organisational autonomy rather than take a collaborative approach with other schools in the local authority or region regarding their collective interests in renewing the local authority or creating new democratic structures.

Capital exchanges

We intend in this section drawing on three in-depth interviews with the headteacher and three with the deputy headteacher, plus three one-off interviews with senior leaders (each with responsibilities for learning and achievement, and we have labelled them Leader 1, 2 and 3). The interviews took place between December 2011 and July 2012, the time when the decision to convert to an academy was most intense. We intend to read these data through Bourdieu's thinking tools so that we examine not only their interpretation of the policy but also how they position themselves and the school in relation to the policy trajectory of total academisation.

The feel for the game is embodied:

> [W]e're at the cutting edge of where schools are at nationally . . . It's an exciting time to be here. It feels like the beginning of something that could be growing arms and legs and could become a model for other schools around the country.
>
> (Interview School Leader 1: February 2012)

> It[']s quite exciting this place at the moment. It felt a bit down at heel when I got here and I'm not saying I turned that around, there's been an awful lot of things at this moment in time it feels like a really good place to be. Really exciting. Bit more money and a good idea.
>
> (Interview Deputy Head: July 2012)

Interestingly we have witnessed this enthusiasm in our examination of the internal policy process, and this illuminates localised strategising combined with a pragmatic opportunism to remodel and to innovate in response to perceived local needs within a centrally recognised and endorsed framework.

Our starting point is to give recognition to how the headteacher and the school leadership team had established Kingswood High School as an effective player within the leadership game, and specifically within the symbolic economy. The school had already accumulated symbolic capital:

> [T]hat Innovation Unit grant that we got was fantastic, it was an acknowledgement from central government that we were doing things really that most schools weren't in terms of personalization . . . the notion of kids specialising in a particular area . . . has proved really powerful. If you talk to kids

104 *New practices and old hierarchies*

they love the structure in year 9, staff do too. It's made year 9 much more positive because kids are doing, by and large what they are choosing to do. Last year's year 11, where as you know, we've had results way ahead of what we've achieved before, they were the first year that we did both the integrated curriculum and the [individual specialism]. And I think that's been one of the factors which has really been very positive in its impact.

(Interview with Headteacher: January 2011)

Through this process the headteacher at Kingswood High School accumulated significant symbolic capital through his experience of dealing with powerful policy actors and as such secured the school's position within the field, the process of which was to prove useful for the next stage of development.

The accumulation of this capital endows the agent with symbolic power which in turn contributes to the strength of the agent's position within the field. Bourdieu (1989) posited "objective relations of power tend to reproduce themselves in relations of symbolic power. In the symbolic struggle for the production of common sense, or more precisely, for the monopoly over legitimate naming, agents put into action the symbolic capital that they have acquired in previous struggles and which may be juridically guaranteed" (p. 21). The headteacher couched the decision to convert to academy status in terms which recognised the influence and impact of official legitimation:

We've had contact with the department. We ran a big project with the Innovation Unit . . . And we've had a lot of links with the Specialist Schools Trust and done a lot with and through them. But the Department as it currently is, following government policy obviously, is only interested in academies.

(Interview with Headteacher: January 2012)

In engaging with the Academies Programme the headteacher and school leadership team sought to deploy their accumulated capital through their interpretation of the policy and their construction of a 'Professional School':

You've got the whole thing around the Professional School, that it's something that I believe very strongly in. You cannot bring it about in a way that's valuable without support at the moment . . . and you won't get anything from the DfE or the Educational Trust if you're not an academy and I think that applies to other opportunities that might or might not come your way. As a school, currently the Department won't engage with schools that aren't academies . . . So the DfE wouldn't have dealt with us if weren't converting.

(Interview with Headteacher: January 2012)

Importantly, "support" was not articulated through devising and playing an alternative game. Indeed, the deputy head accepts top down dominance:

Largely because in my experience in teaching which [has] been largely the last administration and this one, whatever government decides, is what will

New practices and old hierarchies 105

happen. So we have pilots and we have consultations but generally the pilots go into being largely as they were . . . So our view, both [the head] and me, is that the academies programme is what will happen. A few years down the line we will all be academies so then the argument became, so, do you go now or do you wait until you're pushed.

(Interview with Deputy Headteacher: December 2011)

This is a very different narrative from schools that had been forced to convert as 'failures', where the predecessor school headteachers and leadership teams were positioned as capital poor and so were not recognised as legitimate players (Gunter, 2011). Kingswood as a successful school had been immune from this until the objective relations in the field changed with the shift in government from 2010, where in order to be recognised as a player successful schools had to convert. This was an opportunity to deploy and make gains in their symbolic capital, where the position taken was to convert on their terms rather than being left behind. It seems that a process of hysteresis (Bourdieu, 1986) is in play: Kingswood High School is trying to keep and maximise the value of its capital by making sure that revealed professional dispositions (unlike those professionals who they have seen be sacked or take early retirement or burn out) are not out of time and place. School leadership is a risky job (Thomson, 2009), but it requires risk in the form of reading how advantage and disadvantage operate in the field.

Such readings are located in the analysis of the logic of practice: for the head-teacher the experiences of working closely with national and business policy actors have generated a pragmatic and opportunistic disposition to succeed once again by proposing innovative approaches to the unfolding policy. For the deputy head this opportunity is located in a wider temporal process couched as inevitable. Bourdieu argues that these dispositions have developed out of doxic experience – that is taking for granted the social world based on experiences and previous knowledge – and thus, the headteacher's positioning within the field of educational policy is clarified within these terms:

In short, the art of estimating and seizing chances, the capacity to anticipate the future by a kind of practical induction or even to take a calculated gamble on the possible against the probable, are dispositions that can only be acquired in certain social conditions, that is, in certain social conditions.

(Bourdieu, 1990b, p. 64)

Thus, the headteacher has responded to the shift in academisation from 2010 by drawing on past experiences of interpreting reform in ways which have been deemed as innovative, and deploying this in the same way but with different players. The headteacher and senior leadership team had an agreed set of educational and school purposes through which all external reforms would be tested in regard to whether and how they were to be engaged with. In addition to this, strategy was seen to be a professional prerogative where the school could design and develop its own approach and use this to both read and potentially exceed what the department was directing. Dispositions identified within the

106 *New practices and old hierarchies*

data previously revealed enactments in which the head successfully accumulated symbolic and cultural capital to manoeuvre within the field and has capitalised on these dispositions to once again engage with the field by offering innovative strategic responses to policy. As such his engagement with the field is guided by his motivation in protecting his and the school's interests within the field. The headteacher's position with regards to this strategy, his 'calculated gamble' and thus his symbolic capital, in terms of his ability to secure meetings with policy actors within the field, was referred to in positive terms by one of the senior leaders interviewed:

> So everything that [the head] has done has been one step ahead of where everybody else seems to be. And given that he's had all these meetings with high-powered people clearly people see something in him. And I'm not aware and he's not aware of any other school thinking of doing things in this particular way.
>
> (Interview with School Leader 1: February 2012)

The deputy head also remarked upon the headteacher's sense of the sub-game of leadership, of surveying both the field of educational policy and the economic field of the country and making calculated estimations of how the challenges occurring within the youth employment market will continue to impact school provision:

> [W]hen you are in this job that's a very difficult question to be asking. What's the purpose of it at the end of the day? [The Head] thinks things are going to go around employers, big employers, taking people on at 18 and taking them through a training programme . . . What he's talking about there, will, I think, be exactly right if that's where we're going, we just don't really have a clue where we are going at the moment, at national level, it will drop out of what's going on, by necessity I think.
>
> (Interview with Deputy Headteacher: December, 2011)

While the deputy head acknowledges the lack of research evidence for the Academies Programme, and his own opposition to it, he handles this by conceding that the school could only make the significant structural changes necessary to develop the model of the 'Professional School' by taking a pragmatic stance and by acknowledging the advantage of the autonomy afforded to schools which convert to academy status and the legitimacy that goes hand in glove with it:

> So I'm actually ideologically opposed to it. But I'm also a pragmatist and that's where we're going . . . we couldn't have the same level of autonomy of what we're trying to do without becoming an academy. So my belief is for this school at this moment and for our staff at this moment, it's the right thing to do.
>
> (Interview with Deputy Headteacher: December 2011)

New practices and old hierarchies 107

Another member of the school leadership team commented on this position further, echoing the deputy head's stance that the decision to convert had been reconciled by a realistic necessity to bow to pragmatism and in so doing identifies a crucial relationship between adopting a pragmatic approach to decision making and the domination of neo-liberal ideology within the sociopolitical structures in which the school is operating:

> I think it's very driven by [the head]. I think he wanted it and if he didn't want it I don't think we would have become an academy . . . generally I think the SLT viewpoint was all schools will become academies eventually and you're better off being on board early on rather than later – I think it's a pragmatic approach. I think [the head] saw a possibility of *gaining a higher profile for the school* . . . it[']s very much his vision, he wanted to develop the concept of the professional school and there would be no way of developing that without being an academy. I think he was also a bit jaded with the relationship with the LA. *He wanted greater autonomy* for running the school. And in terms of marketing, the school has falling numbers and one way, was a fresh approach and being *particularly distinct from other schools*, and therefore encouraging more people to come to us.
>
> (Interview with School Leader 2: February 2012)

These excerpts crystallise the significance of Bourdieu's arguments that in order to understand practice (and practices as strategies), it is imperative to look to the relationship between the habitus revealed by an agent, the social field in which that agent is operating and the capital at stake within the field. The political field of education policy is internalised as being a space in which symbolic capital must be accrued, not only from the secretary of state and the Department for Education but also on a local level as a result of the privatisation agenda of establishing a framework of competition in which schools must attract students in order to survive in the marketplace. The head's interaction with the field in this sense, his internalisation of what is at stake means that he also successfully embodies the potential for exploiting opportunities to make pragmatic moves within the field, whilst reconciling this to his colleagues by framing its necessity as a means of survival. As Bourdieu (1990a) states, "in the game you can't do just anything and get away with it" (p. 64), and what we witnessed over the months in which decision-making took place is how pragmatism was used as an indicator of agency, but our analysis illuminates answers to Bourdieu's (1990a) question, "[H]ow can behaviour be regulated without being a product of obedience to rules?" (p. 65). It seems to us that the autonomy offered through the 2010 Academies Act is a powerful mechanism for encouraging schools to convert to academy status, and is part of a historical tradition within the field of education policy, as illustrated by the 1988 Education Reform Act and the introduction of Local Management of Schools (LMS) and Grant Maintained Schools (GMS), in citing autonomy as a means for advancing a school's position within the field (Thomson, 2010b). The logic of practice in Kingwood High School, and now in Kingwood Academy, is

108 *New practices and old hierarchies*

that as effective game players their capital can be deployed to deliver policy interventions on their terms. In protecting provision through securing academy status, the potential of Kingwood Academy being taken over and incorporated into one of the emerging academy chains as a means of branding autonomy or of a free school being set up in the future is not regarded as threats or a consequence of the dismantling of the local authority that academy conversion has contributed to.

As such this analysis must operationalise the significance of doxic experience along with a "constellation of dispositions" as embodiments of habitus which enable agents to act in ways which, in this case, enable them to not only secure but advance and therefore (re)produce their and the school's position within the field (Thomson, 2010b, p. 13). One of the school leaders described the interrelationship of professional dispositions displayed by the head and the deputy as essential constituents for the school's success in securing legitimation from other agents within the field:

> He's [the head] quite bold and innovative . . . (and) . . . that aspect of him, to be able to plough his own route and say this is what I think, and this is what I am going to do, is really good. I think what's also good is [the deputy] is a real asset to the team in the sense that he is very grounded in terms of his own practices in school and he is very school focussed, whereas [the head] is very wide focused and actually that gives a very powerful combination.
>
> (Interview with School Leader 3: January 2012)

The headteacher has led the school with a frank appraisal of the opportunities afforded by the codification of autonomy that is at the core of the 2010 Academies Act. A historically successfully innovative leader, the head receives support from members of his leadership team to take the risks articulated by his deputy because of his and their recognition of the weight of the symbolic economy within the field of educational policy. Where the deputy reconciles ideology against pragmatism and expresses concerns regarding the future impact of the academies policy trajectory, the headteacher articulates the potential the autonomy granted will have for redefining the school's culture, over and above any potential resourcing benefits:

> I think it[']s very indefinable but I think as an autonomous organisation you can develop a culture which is more dynamic, more responsive, I think that's at best and I think you've got to plan to exploit the potential of it to do that, but I think there are potentially over the medium term big advantages in terms of creating an organisation that's more fit for purpose, culturally and structurally because I think you shift the culture of the organisation partly by shifting its structures.
>
> (Interview with Headteacher: January 2012)

A school leader echoed this position:

> The professional school is coming about because we've been able to get the academy status so with that's got to come all the re-branding if you

New *practices and old hierarchies* 109

like, there's clearly the opportunities to say right we're starting with a new organisation, what's the ethos that we want, in particular with this professional thing.

(Interview with School Leader 1: February 2012)

We have argued that a privatisation game is in play that is being engaged with through a much more professionally acceptable game of leadership through which educational issues can be reorganised and re-cultured as business opportunities (see Courtney & Gunter, 2015). The Academies Programme is a neo-liberal privatisation project, and our data illustrate that the localised interpretation of the opportunities afforded by school reform in this example outweigh concerns regarding the potential damage that the atomisation of the school system may eventually create. In this sense there are shades of a 'survival of the fittest' discourse running throughout the decision and the subsequent proposal to develop the professional school model. Again, what the data suggest is that the symbolic economy in the field of education policy awards prizes of distinction to those schools who walk to the beat of the neo-liberal drum and that this discourse pervades and indeed is internalised by many of those with decision-making capacities at a local level:

And it's a good thing for the school in gross self interest marketing terms, because the school needs some sort of unique selling point, it's always had that because when most schools had very, very restricted choices for kids, we had a very sophisticated choice framework in the options because that, when the national curriculum sort of folded at key stage 4, everyone else went down that route so what was a big unique selling point for us disappeared, *this gives us that.*

(Interview with Head: June 2012)

In order to be able to structurally develop the school to be more 'responsive' to the economic field the headteacher and his senior leadership team perceived the way to achieve this was to convert to an academy, because the autonomy granted would gift them the freedom to act professionally with regard to localised policymaking. The school could not have made these changes without the legitimation of the policy actors in the field, without the "naming and framing" of the codification of the Academies Act as policy (Thomson, 2005, p. 745). The headteacher's role in the school's decision to convert must not be underestimated where the data reveal his disposition to play in the symbolic economy within the field of educational policy. The headteacher is a social agent, and through his professional role he is a policy enactor (Ball et al., 2012). The responses to changes within the field of educational policy at Kingswood High School, from the personalisation of the Specialist School Programme through to the development of the Professional School, have been driven by a leadership team, led by a deft and skilled headteacher, that understands the hierarchy of the field and has been able to accumulate and use symbolic capital to secure their position within the field.

110 *New practices and old hierarchies*

One of the successes is the way the school has responded to popular localised policies, such as students specialising in curriculum areas at an early stage, to form the basis for the next stage of school development. The current government scrapped the Specialist Schools Programme, but the school knew that their innovative and personalised response to the policy was popular with students and so endeavoured to incorporate into the new structures of the professional school:

> That was [the head's] fundamental belief – it should be the kid that specialises because they know what their strengths are. They know what they are interested in, and even if they're not you can still have the generalist route, which takes a little of everything so you're not doing anything that's detrimental to your choices later on. In a way I think him having this professional school dimension is another way of being able to afford students that chance to specialise again . . .
>
> (Interview with School Leader 1: February 2012)

This position illustrates a positive angle on the changes that are taking place at Kingswood School, in that this respondent identifies that the head and the leadership team are working within a field of power in which despite the pressure on the school to play the 'game' from the centre, still has spaces for these staff to reconcile their decisions by arguing that they are ultimately working with the best interests of the students. The deputy reminds us as well, that successful accumulation of symbolic capital within the field relies not just on agents and institutions playing the game but also actively anticipating and strategising ways which "to keep one step ahead of the game" (Interview with Deputy Head: July 2012). In this sense both the school as an institution and the students within it will maintain a position of privilege as a result of the recognition and accumulation of the right kind of capital within the field. Hence, the data also suggest that school leaders may make decisions that outwardly give distinction and acclaim to the importance of the formalised symbolic economy as they exchange their professional legitimation of the policy with the promised autonomy and status.

Summary

Our data show that located within seemingly rational strategising and decision-making about the legal and political location of a school in the post-1988 period in England are complex values judgements and assessments about political trends. Importantly, the case we outline is just one decision, albeit a significant one, amongst many that professionals in schools are working on at any one time, and therefore strategising is about how such competing options are prioritised as well as actioned. Our argument is that thinking with Bourdieu about these matters generates gains for researchers and professionals, not least that the codification of the TLP doxa is not an abstract deterministic suffocating process. By recognising a privatisation game in play, and the necessary sub-games that offer seductive opportunities for agency through being a leader, doing leading and exercising leadership, the entry into the game with positioning enables the power processes to be made transparent. The symbolic capital exchange between national policy 'makers' and local policy 'takers' is productive for both, whereby incoherent ideological tropes from ministers about autonomy and experiences of being at the receiving end of instructions to deliver by headteachers are reworked into treating professionals as professionals and professionals responding as creative policymakers.

Our data show that while professionals may not directly support the ideological position of the government of the time, they do not necessarily resist and oppose it through working for an alternative system to the privatised market that is emerging. Rather the accruing and investment of capital through the reading of events and opportunities over time enables the 'structured structures' within dispositions to be revealed and capital gains become 'structuring structures', where game playing is misrecognised as creative local policymaking. Thinking with Bourdieu enables scrutiny of the interplay of strategy to improve provision for local children with the pragmatism of the right thing to do in the circumstances. However, what is a limitation in this process is that the analysis could be characterised as pessimistic, not least because it enables description and explanation of leadership as a dominated social practice, but it does not of itself enable emancipation (see McGinity & Gunter 2012). Importantly, this makes doing research an activist project in two main ways: first, how we as researchers do important intellectual work, where in Apple's (2013) terms we "bear witness" to the politics of privatisation, and second, how our relationship with professionals needs to be subject to ongoing dialogues regarding the relationship among data, meaning and activity.

7 Thinking with and against Bourdieu

In this concluding chapter I return to the discussion of Bourdieu and the field of ELMA in general. I will consider some of the critiques that are made of Bourdieu and use these to focus on what a Bourdieusian approach may and may not do. After re-considering the issues related to the possible distinction accrued to critical ELMA scholars from engaging with Bourdieu, I then look at two aspects of ELMA practice which could benefit from the use of his thinking tools. I begin with some general comments about social theory.

The limits of social theory

This book, like others in this series, focuses on social theory. Social theory, such as Bourdieu's thinking tools, can be understood as a comprehensive framework for investigating and analysing society itself, changes in society, or a social problem, practice, puzzle, circumstance, experience or happening. We can think for example of Foucault and writings on discourse, discipline and governmentality (1972, 1977, 1988), Giddens and his work on reflexive modernisation (1990, 1991, 1994), Beck and risk society (1992, 1997, 1998), Castells and networked society (1996, 1997, 1998) and so on. These social theorists offer an empirically grounded lens through which to see the workings of the material and social world we live in. Raewyn Connell, in her book *Southern Theory* (2007), suggests that a general social theory is one which develops

> a broad vision of the social, and offers concepts that apply beyond a particular society, place or time. Such texts make propositions or hypotheses that are relevant everywhere, or propose methods of analysis that will work under all conditions.
>
> (p. 28)

A general social theory can be found in a text or set of texts in which a scholar has made a consistent and serious attempt to make sense of the world. A general social theory has ambition and sweep. It works to tidy up ideas, bring into line, codify and categorise them and establish causalities and connections. It generalises. It offers constructs for seeing a range of phenomena and for generating

Thinking with and against Bourdieu 113

sum and substance. It offers a logical and clear narrative thread which draws a rational border around that which is to be explained, eliminating mess and ill-fitting pieces (Thomas, 2007).

Connell suggests that general social theories make claims to apply everywhere, at all times and in all places – in other words, their makers construct a bid for universality. While this might appear to make sense if applied to, say, the laws of gravity, social life is less predictable. Different cultures make sense of things differently; the time in which things occur and are written about has an effect on how the world is understood and experienced; the place in which things are written also shapes what can be seen and said. Consider the ways in which a history of Alexander might be written differently from the Roman and Persian perspectives; one 'side' would see him as 'the great' and the other as an invader and a vandal. In contemporary social sciences we are accustomed to saying that knowledge is: partial, not universal; situated, that is coming from a given place and time; and, thus, particular, that is it carries with it specific limitations.

Problems arise for social scientists when they use general social theories assuming that they will automatically 'fit' all questions and all methods. In applying a general social theory as if it is a universal meaning-making tool, researchers may be tempted to leave out data which appear not to 'fit'. This is unfortunate, because phenomena which appear to be local, idiosyncratic and particular may alternatively be indicative of the limitations of the explanatory power of a particular social theory. It is always important to examine any social theory for its particularity and partiality and to understand that it has limited generalisability. This is particularly the case in transferring theories from one location to another. The vast majority of social theory used in contemporary social science has been produced in Europe, and it inevitably reads the world from that perspective. It sometimes relies on and assumes the applicability of its histories of intellectual thought to other contexts. The general social theories taught in English-speaking universities often ignore significant theoretical traditions from the misnamed 'periphery' of the European world.

But is the answer to these problems to abandon theory altogether? No. We still seek a way to have purchase on our research results beyond the singular, local and temporary. We still need social theory. But we need to handle social theories with caution, being careful about what we ask of and do with them, while we also expand our knowledge of other traditions of sense-making.

Connell provides reasons to continue to 'do theory' as a way of making sense of the world and the ways in which theory works variously in different places. She suggests that in current 'globalising' times (globalisation, of course, is another of those general theories to be held up to scrutiny), social science cannot afford to vacate the public space of meaning making and leave it open to politicians, market researchers, techno-rationalist economists and media. Rather, she suggests, there is a role for scholarship which:

1   generates compassion for those who are bearing the brunt of global social, economic, political and cultural changes;

114 *Thinking with and against Bourdieu*

2   interrogates the ideas and practices which perpetuate global and local injustices and
3   produces knowledge that are helpful to those who are attempting to change unjust practices and relations and which work to generate better, new, alternative and fairer ways to do things.

This might sound very utopian and potentially too activist for some. However, we all have to make up our own minds about where we stand in our research, and if we understand that knowledge is a social and cultural construction, we also understand that the very notion that social science research is neutral is a myth (Griffiths, 1998). Bourdieu certainly argued, at the end of his career, for an engaged social science that was highly rigorous and robust but clear about the interests it served. In his later life he also worked politically with anti-globalisation organisations (Bourdieu, 1998a, 2003), while producing work which showed the overall social suffering that globalised politics produced (Bourdieu et al., 1999). However, this did not mean abandoning the need for rigorous scholarship. As already noted earlier in the book, Bourdieu argued that effective political work relied on scholarly work that was not distorted by the fields of politics, government or media and was critical of its own self-interests and lacunae. Bourdieu's own anti-globalisation activism in the 1990s was, as Calhoun (2014) argues, not a retreat from his advocacy of institutional scholarly field autonomy but rather

> fully consistent with and understandable in terms of his scientific sociology, though they were not dictated by it. Bourdieu's challenge to the threatened collapse between scientific and economic (and for that matter, political and economic) fields in the 1990s and early 2000s is of a piece with his rejection of a collapse between academic and political fields in 1968 and both are informed by his theory of quasi-autonomous social fields and by his analysis of the disruption of traditional life and marginalization of former peasants in Algeria.

Concerns about the universalising tendencies of social theory do apply to Bourdieu, and it is thus important to consider in more detail how the specificity, particularity and partiality of his social theory might play out in ELMA research.

However, to start with it is important to note that a counter to universalisation also exists within Bourdieu's thinking toolkit. Bourdieu's thinking tools only become meaningful through their application to a specific project and the generation and analysis of particular data. What counts as capitals, field, habitus and so on shifts and changes depending on the problem addressed: they are developed through designed research and data generation. Using Bourdieu methodologically is not a tautologous exercise in which a researcher goes looking for, say, social capital and then triumphantly says at the end, 'It's social capital stupid'. Bourdieu's conceptual frame must be brought into conversation with particular data and used to make sense of a particular research question and to guide its empirical investigation. Bourdieu cannot be draped over data like a tablecloth.

The limitations of Bourdieu's toolkit

In this section I address some questions that might concern those in the field of ELMA. The first set of issues relates to the effects of Bourdieusian thinking tools and the second to the tool themselves.

Concerns about the effects of a Bourdieusian approach

The first issue is that of **context** – the particularities of time/space. The notions of field, habitus and capital, and their applications to various areas of social life, were developed in later 20th-century France. The French education system, both schooling and higher education, is organised differently than for example the system in England. The French school system is rooted in a political history in which there was a civil battle over principles of equality. The French school system has a more uniform curriculum and more didactic approaches to pedagogy than in many other locations and these have roots in historical commitments to a universal and common education. One must therefore be suspicious of transferring analytic details from Bourdieu's early work on schooling and higher education to other locations and different times. Nevertheless, researchers outside of France have found it very useful to ask questions prompted by Bourdieu; for example:

- In whose interests does this education system work?
- Are there 'inheritance' effects at work here?
- What is the logic of practice of this system?
- What capitals are at stake in this field?

Another frequently expressed concern is what is seen as **determinism** in the theory of production and reproduction of fields, capitals and habitus. Because of Bourdieu's focus, particularly in his early work, on the continuities of inequality in the school system and, in later studies, on the ways in which various social fields – science (Bourdieu, 2004), real estate (Bourdieu, 2005), journalism (Bourdieu, 1996) and so on – worked to produce and reproduce overall social inequalities, it seems from reading his work that he allows no way for radical social, economic and cultural change to occur. At best, it seems that there are minor shifts which may or may not change things for the better for those 'at the bottom' of society. It is as if, perhaps, we are mice trapped in a treadmill; we do not know how to stop.

Concerns about determinist reproduction in education are perhaps challenged by the evidence of some periods of social mobility via education. Halsey, Heath and Ridge (1980, in Goldthorpe, 2007) for instance traced the growth of secondary education in 20th-century Britain, and their work shows not only a massification – more people undertaking higher levels of schooling – but also overall intergenerational mobility via the acquisition of school credentials (symbolic capital). But there is debate about what these changes mean and Bourdieu

116 *Thinking with and against Bourdieu*

can help make sense of them. And even if overall hierarchies of social status are maintained during periods of educational expansion, more people getting higher levels of education and qualifications may change tastes and values. For instance it is suggested that working-class tastes and values (capitals and habitus) in England have changed to the point where many no longer see themselves as 'working class' (2007). Bourdieu helps us to make sense of this phenomenon.

And, of course, there are also many instances, often documented by EEIR scholars in ELMA, where change occurs within schools or clusters of schools. Again, how these are understood varies. Certainly the description offered in Chapter 6 of change in one school might be seen as producing better outcomes for some students, staff and the school. But a Bourdieusian lens suggests this may be a case of one site moving farther up the hierarchical ladder of distinction within the education field – not as an overall change in the field.

And Bourdieu *did* study change. He offered for example an analysis of the development of the art and literature markets and a new field position for critics, agents and brokers (Bourdieu, 1991, 1992, 1993a; Bourdieu et al., 1990). He showed the ways in which an avant-garde in art became a new elite position with 'avant-garde' cultural capital; this changed the rules of the art game, as well as who was advantaged and disadvantaged in it. Of course, this was not a change that led to greater social equity overall, but it was a change in the particular field which altered life chances for agents within it, according to the particular art field logics of contest over artistic capitals.

Bourdieu's task as a social scientist, as he saw it, was to explain why and how the social world worked and changed. He did not set out to produce a revolutionary manifesto. However, he did see political change as necessary. He saw change as having to occur in the field of politics, both through struggles over government and through wider social action, such as that taken by the anti-globalisation social movement (Wacquant, 2005).

Rather than seeing Bourdieu as exceptionally deterministic, it may be helpful to see his work as connected to other social scientists who seek to understand, explain, document and expose the ways in which society works. The social reality that Bourdieu addressed – and that as social scientists we must address too – was, and is, not one of increasing social and political justice. France did not become a more equal society during the period in which Bourdieu analysed it. The world in general has not become a more equal or indeed peaceful place in the last 50 or so years. The task of explaining how social and economic hierarchies have not only been maintained but actually increased – wealth is concentrated in fewer and fewer hands (Dorling, 2014; Piketty, 2014) – is that of social theorists in general, not just Bourdieu. And yes, it is depressing if we are interested in more, not less, justice.

It is important to consider whether the concerns about Bourdieu's apparent lack of a general theory of radical social change are an analytic category error – they are actually about the lack of change in society in relation to economic power and social relations, despite dramatic changes in technology, environment and culture. This is not the same as a social theory that seeks to empirically

Thinking with and against Bourdieu 117

research and document this reality. And it is important to note that Bourdieu strenuously rejected the notion that his work was deterministic: he argued that the habitus was a site for change within fields which were always engaged in ongoing contestation over power and ideas.

There has also been concern expressed about the ways in which Bourdieu dealt with **gender** (Adkins, 2003; Fowler, 1997; Lovell, 2000; Robinson & Garnier, 2000). Much of Bourdieu's work on education for example largely sidesteps the ways in which schools produce and reproduce particular masculinities, sexualities and femininities. Bourdieu did write one book about gender (Bourdieu, 2001) in which he suggested that the reproduction of masculine domination was a form of symbolic violence which operated via schools, the church, the family and the state. This particular text, *Masculine Domination* (Bourdieu, 2001), is generally seen by those who study gender as limited in its explanation of, inter alia, social divisions of labour, actual violence against women and gendered cultural practices (Fowler, 2003).

However, while Bourdieu's specific account of gendered relations is critiqued, his thinking tools have been helpful to many interested in questions of gender. Taking a lead from Moi (1991), who argues that feminists can and should 'appropriate' theoretical perspectives that are potentially generative, many feminist scholars have worked with Bourdieu's anti-essentialist thinking tools (Adkins & Skeggs, 2005). They have for example taken the notion of habitus and linked it to consciousness-raising (Chambers, 2005), working-class women's valuing of 'respectability' (Skeggs, 1997) and mothers' relationships with schooling (Reay, 1999). Lois McNay (2008) suggests that Bourdieu's approach to 'recognition' not only deals with power but also offers a way to understand the notion of structured agency, via 'habitus', which is far more adequate than other theorisations (e.g. Fraser & Honneth, 2003; Taylor, 1994). This feminist approach, thinking with Bourdieu, rather than taking Bourdieu's social theory as a blueprint to be laid across all contexts, is precisely what is advocated in this book in relation to ELMA.

Concerns about the thinking tools

As before, I consider issues pertinent to ELMA and some ways in which the concerns might be reframed.

1. Field

A common concern expressed about Bourdieu relates to the notion of **field**, one of the most generative, but also apparently the most frustrating of his thinking tools. Bourdieu suggests that fields not only are homologous to one another but also exist in relation to each other (see Chapter 1). They also interact. People occupy several fields and field positions at once. They move through various fields during their lifetimes. Bourdieu also uses the notion of 'field' to cover several different orders of social life – for example schools, universities, photography, art,

118 *Thinking with and against Bourdieu*

real estate and government. Some fields – schools and universities for example – can be seen as separate fields or as parts of one educational field; they are subfields with distinctiveness (relative autonomies) but also with strong field characteristics (homologies). And positions with fields, such as occupied by one school, can also be understood as a field in themselves – so each school is a field with its own idiosyncrasies and particularities but it also has commonalities with other schools and the broader schooling field. The notion of fields and subfields can create the impression of a dizzying set of receding mirrors, in which fields writ large and small are nested within one another.

To complicate matters further, the edges of fields are also indeterminate. Where does the education field begin and end? While schools and universities can be seen as having institutional borders, the presence of other educational spaces and places such as those opened up by Web 2.0, makes it almost impossible to establish clear outer edges of the education field. However, it is important to hold onto the Bourdieusian argument that field is a heuristic, not an absolute, not a law. It is the relations among agents, fields and capitals that are important, and it is the relations and practices that need to form the focus of empirical enquiry, not what constitutes a field per se.

This is not the only question related to fields. Amongst education scholars there is also a difference in view about whether education policy might constitute a field or whether policymaking is a practice of the political field views. Each option opens up different possibilities and creates its own set of problems. Thinking of policy as a field (see Lingard & Rawolle, 2004a, 2004b; and Thomson, 2005, for two different views) allows global players such as the OECD and World Bank to be brought together with national governments and schools so that the relationships between agents can be researched. The policy field approach renders highly accessible the knotty problems of how the political field influences the education field and the relations between the political field and national governments. On the other hand, focusing on a policy field smooths over important autonomies of the political and education fields, such as their separate doxa and the ways in which different players might work to different logics. Thinking of policy as a field in itself might then downplay the contestations across and within fields which might work to support and unsettle policy trajectories. However, scholars using Bourdieusian thinking tools are not confined to one policy project, there is not one best way of using the notion of field. It is possible to use the notion of field flexibly, as Bourdieu did himself, to attend to particular and different problems. The Bourdieusian toolkit is not a recipe, a blueprint, but a way of thinking and researching, as argued in Chapter 3.

The interaction among fields, as suggested earlier, can be troubling to those seeking to understand social life on a broader scale. The interaction between fields might concern ELMA scholars in particular as they seek to understand the ways in which for example:

- New Public Management (Hood, 1995a, 1995b, 1998), which originated in the public services, part of the field of politics – or government – came

Thinking with and against Bourdieu 119

to also frame the work of school, further education and university leaders (Gunter, Grimaldi, Hall, & Serpieri, 2016; Hall, 2012; Thomson, 1998).

- the ways in which the fields of business and education have become intertwined through processes of contracting out, sponsorship and philanthropy (see Ball, 2008b, 2012a; Gunter, Hall, & Apple, 2016).
- what the shift from government to governing (the fields of politics, business and education coming together) means for school administrators, local governing bodies and local authorities (see Ranson, 2006; Swyngedouw, 2005; Taylor, 2007).

Bourdieu himself often noted that many social fields – including education – were subordinate to the political field, and that all fields produced and reproduced the broader social field of power. However, because he did not specifically study education policy or ELMA we do not know how he would have tackled the questions above. He did, however, study the housing market and its logics (Bourdieu, 2005). He showed administrative regulations made in the political field framed the practices of real estate companies. We might similarly conclude that legislative, administrative rules and policy emanating from the political field intersect with a number of other fields including education and ELMA – perhaps even to the point of having some positions occupying intersectional spaces.

Similar concerns have been voiced over Bourdieu's apparent under-theorisation of interactions within fields; since these are productive of social relations as well as reproductive this is a critique which might be of interest to ELMA scholars. Bottero and Crossley (2011) for instance advocate bringing social network analysis to better understand the social connections between positions in a Bourdieusian field. But Bourdieu himself avoided these kinds of more abstract field interaction descriptions, opting instead for grounded elaborations of specific practice and relations in specific fields (see Gunter, 2012a). We might follow Bourdieu's lead instead of going down a rabbit hole seeking an ultimate definition of field operations.

One of Bourdieu's later research projects was directed to the field of power. It resulted in *The Weight of the World* (Bourdieu et al., 1999; see also Chapter 3). In this hefty volume we see different social groups of people who are similarly positioned in social space and in the overall field of power. We see how changes in the field of power – globalisation and deindustrialisation – play out in the everyday lives of French citizens and recent immigrants to France. In this text there is little discussion of fields, and much more of habitus and habitat as they appear in individual and collective lives, and much more about the relations in which agents are enmeshed. Through its focus on individual agents, the book counters criticism of Bourdieu as a covert structuralist, too concerned with broad social processes, ideologies and practices (Couldry, 2005). *The Weight of the World* refuses a simple binary between reproduction and freedom. The *Weight of the World* rejects an either/or position, showing instead that differently classed, raced and gendered lives are simultaneously and variously constrained and open. It is difficult to conclude from this book that Bourdieu is either a determinist and structuralist or a

120 *Thinking with and against Bourdieu*

radical showing how liberation might be achieved. This reading perhaps opens a way through the critiques of his work as ultimately pessimistic.

Bourdieu's emphasis on close studies of context is generative for many researchers. McLeod (2005) for instance argues that studying life trajectories as they live in and through social fields shows that gender norms can vary from field to field, producing gendered instability in the habitus. Skeggs's (1997) detailed study of working-class women and their life strategy of being 'respectable' counters populist deficit views by offering persuasive and detailed socially situated life/field analysis. These researchers do not claim that Bourdieu's thinking tools – including field – allow a completely comprehensive analysis but that there are benefits from engaging with it.

Rather than get bogged down in abstracted debates about Bourdieu's limitations, it is when the thinking tools are brought to actual empirical examples that researchers can assess conceptual difficulties – what the tools do not do – in the context of what they *do* make available. Bourdieu was clear that social science theories ought to be judged by how much insight they yielded, and for whose benefit, rather than on whether they are universal, perfect and unable to be critiqued (see Chapter 3). He specifically talked for instance about class as a metaphor, as a tool for understanding social life, rather than as a material social entity like trees and water. His thinking tools are aids to making meaning; they do not offer 'proofs', but instead 'truths'.

2. Capitals

Bourdieu's emphasis on the importance of cultural rather than economic capital must be placed in its historical context. At the time in France, most (but not all) of Bourdieu's contemporaries reduced discussions of social inequality to the economy. His emphasis on culture was therefore significant. The move to culture however has led to criticisms of the way in which Bourdieu conceived of economic capital. Critics suggest that he confuses value and use value, conflates capital with the creation of wealth through labour and ignores the power of labour (Rikowski, 2007). Bourdieu's thinking tools are regarded by some as not up to the task of explaining the continued expansion of capitalism and its various crises (Beasley-Murray, 2000; Calhoun, 1993).

There are also claims that Bourdieu deals in a reductionist and economistic manner with culture, seeing the distribution of cultural capitals in particular through their use value as determined through the habitus and fields (Sayer, 1999). There is also debate about how neatly the conception of cultural capitals fits in postcolonial societies, hybrid economies and in the increasingly connected spaces afforded by globalisation (see the collection edited by Hilgers & Mangez, 2015). But some scholars do now combine Bourdieu with other social theory in order to account for questions of race, gender and family; neo-liberal politics of austerity; and online cultures (e.g. Atkinson, 2016; Thatcher, Ingram, Burke, & Abrahams, 2016).

Like fields, the notion of capitals is also subject to extension into a wide variety of subcategories. Bourdieu discusses the importance of linguistic capital in

Thinking with and against Bourdieu 121

relation to schooling, political capital in relation to politics and scientific capital in relation to science. Bourdieu names specific cultural capitals in relation to the field in which they are valued and/or the practice with which they are concerned. Scholars working with Bourdieu have also used the notion of cultural capital in more specific ways – emotional capital (Reay, 2001b), subcultural capital (Thornton, 1996), spiritual capital (Verter, 2003), sexual capital (Martin & George, 2006), physical capital (Williams, 1995) and ethical capital (Williams, Woodby, & Drentea, 2010). And I have already referred to management knowledge as a capital (Chapter 3 and 6). There is clearly a danger of proliferating categories of capital, and ELMA scholars need to consider the relative benefits and problems with adding a subcategory to the overarching one of cultural capital for example. This, however, needs to be weighed against the necessity of naming what capitals are at stake in particular fields.

Another of the critiques of capital that might be of concern to students of ELMA is drawn from the familiar concerns about Bourdieu as a determinist and reductionist unable to conceptualise change. Giroux (1983) for example suggests that Bourdieu is largely unable to comprehend the kind of cultural capitals that make resistance possible. This is a contested view and one that I have already considered and return to later in this chapter.

3. Habitus

Habitus is one of the most frequently used of Bourdieu's concepts. It can be used to think about various positions in the field of education – headteachers, university lecturers, students and policymakers – and to show the ways in which the structures of the field are embodied and taken for granted. Economic, social and cultural capitals are variously accumulated, converted, exchanged, valued and devalued in each of these positional habituses as the agents occupying them play the game of the field.

The concept of habitus is not easy to define because it developed through Bourdieu's empirical analysis. He did not often explicitly address how an individual person's habitus is formed in a lifelong trajectory through various fields or how dispositions might mediate across the various fields in which they are embedded, at any one time. One place where he does do this is in relation to his own life story (Bourdieu, 2007). And Bourdieu did argue that the early years are very important and form a kind of 'primary' habitus which becomes the foundation for all other field-related dispositions (Bourdieu & Wacquant, 1992).

The concept of habitus has been widely used by researchers. Kenway and Macleod (2004) for example deliberately set out to pursue with the subjects of their study of gender formation across generations (mothers and daughters) what ambiguities and dissonances in the habitus they experienced within fields and across fields and what reflexive possibilities were available to them. And as noted earlier, researchers have shown that the clash between the primary habitus of academics with working class origins and the habitat of the university leads to visceral feelings of alienation, even if they are to all extents and purposes, very successful at the academic game (Plummer, 2000; Reay et al., 2005). Other

122 *Thinking with and against Bourdieu*

habitus studies include for example the institutional habitus in higher education (Thomas, 2002), vocational habitus (Colley, James, Dimend, & Tedder, 2007), organisational habitus (Diamond, Randolph, & Spillane, 2008), interpreting habitus (Inghilleri, 2005), resistance habitus (Crossley, 2010), circuit trainer's habitus (Crossley, 2004) and transnational habitus (Kelly & Lusis, 2006).

ELMA scholars who work with the notion of a 'leadership habitus' may have to exercise care to pay sufficient attention to the primary habitus and the life trajectory of different agents in leader positions. As Bourdieu (in Bourdieu & Chartier, 2010/2015, p. 52) notes that

> agents have a history and are the productive of an individual history and an education associated with a milieu, and . . . they are also the product of a collective history, and . . . their categories of thinking, categories of understanding, patterns of perception, systems of values. . . are the product of the incorporation of social structures.

The notion of a leadership habitus per se may be overgeneralising. While the idea of a leadership habitus may capture the common patternings between agents in leader positions, it also may miss important aspects of individual trajectories, as well as the ways in which specific horizontally distributed school positions, situated in particular hierarchised places in the educational field, produce and require specific dispositions. And habitus only exists when it is revealed; it does not exist outside of relational practice. Some of the work on habitus, including that of leadership habitus, arguably isolates and deals with the concept as if it is a 'thing'.

The apparent uncertainty about exactly how habitus is formed can lead to critiques of those who use it. Tooley with Darby (1998) for example in their highly contentious review of educational research, singled out Diane Reay's (e.g. Reay, 2001a; Reay & Lucey, 2000b; Reay & Wiliam, 1999) use of Bourdieu, arguing that it had nothing to offer practice, that her analysis of ethnographic data could stand by itself and that her work was a prime example of researchers idolising theory for its own sake. Nash's (1999) rebuttal of this critique specifically noted the difference between researchers seeking explanations (e.g. Reay) and those seeking predictable applications – that is what works. Nash argued that different researchers ask different kinds of questions; those concerned solely with effectiveness were not interested in the kinds of theoretical resources offered by Bourdieu and other social theorists. (This argument is made in Chapter 2.) Reay (2004) herself has been critical of the way that the notion of habitus has been used within educational research, suggesting that it is too often used as a kind of theory layer which is put over a set of analysed data rather than being a 'research method' which informs research topic selection and the questions which guide data generation and analysis.

The most consistent and most trenchant concern about habitus comes from considering whether habitus does indeed offer a resolution to understanding the ways in which structure and agency, objective social conditions and subjectivity, work together. Bourdieu argues that habitus is a structuring structure, acting

Thinking with and against Bourdieu 123

both inwards from the social to the individual and outwards from the individual to the social. However, many see in his own work a strong tendency to reduce human activity to predictable practices (Archer, 2007; Arnot, 2002; Butler, 1999). Calhoun (2003), noting that Bourdieu is often seen as a structuralist wolf in culturalist sheep's clothing (p. 303), suggests that

> [i]t is neither surprise nor indictment . . . that Bourdieu incorporated a great deal of structuralism; it is important to be precise in noting that he challenged the notion that semiotics (or cultural meanings) could adequately be understood autonomously from social forces and practices. Likewise, Bourdieu has labored against the notion that the meanings of behavior are transparent and manifested in purely objective interests or actors' own labels for their behavior. But this does not mean that he has ever sought to dispense with objective factors in social analysis.
>
> (p. 205)

Calhoun notes that Bourdieu's thinking was constantly evolving, and that it was incomplete. It was not, as already argued, a holistic, universal social theory. Rather, as Calhoun puts it, Bourdieu's social theory

> does have enduring motifs and recurrent analytic strategies as well as a largely stable but gradually growing conceptual framework. It does not have or ask for closure. Most basically, Bourdieu's theory asks for commitment to the creating knowledge – and thus to a field shaped by that interest.
>
> (p. 205)

Scholars in ELMA wishing to work with the notion of habitus as a central focus might note these concerns, particularly since it is all too easy to see the work of agents for example in leadership positions, dichotomously – as the working out of policy or as the result of a highly individual life trajectory. The concept of habitus, while imperfect, does direct attention to the ways in which the agent and social structures come together relationally to both produce and reproduce logics of practice.

4. Misrecognition and doxa

The concepts of misrecognition and doxa are important in Bourdieu's thinking toolkit. It is by 'seeing through' what is offered as reasons for particular practices that the game can be apprehended. Reflexivity, the habituated practice of asking critical questions in order to 'get at' the actual interests at stake in fields, is required. For some, this notion is discomforting as it is too reminiscent of the Marxist notion of 'false consciousness' (all the people of the working class need to do is realise their oppression and alienation and they will then become politicised). Bennett (2007) for instance suggests that in *Distinction*, and later work on aesthetic fields, Bourdieu's emphasis on the universality of class-fraction habitus

124 *Thinking with and against Bourdieu*

as 'taste' fails to account for the richness of working-class cultures and the ways in which practices of cultural consumption are mediated. Bennett suggests that the working class is ultimately seen by Bourdieu as culturally deprived, needing better educated intellectuals to include them in aesthetic debates and practices.

Jenkins (1992) is also concerned about the way in which the notion of misrecognition implicitly privileges the person/group/process uncovering the misrecognition. This is often a critical scholar who is there to enlighten the misguided. The critical scholar however faces a paradox – if those in the working class misrecognise their situation, then their words, on which an unveiling rests, are also inherently unreliable. There is also a moral question involved – on what basis does the critical theorist decide that they have the right to say what is 'good for you' (Gore, 1993). But there is a difference between false consciousness, which operates as a kind of ontological blindness, and misrecognition. Bourdieusian misrecognition draws attention to the practices which negatively name agents and their cultural capitals and strategies – street style, vernacular knowledge, tastes (McLaughlin, 1996) – and to how this naming justifies and accompanies strategies which actively penalise them.

But there are perhaps some warnings here about the ways in which ELMA scholarly analysis might misrecognise misrecognition itself, in order to produce moralising tracts – if only leaders would realise that what they are doing is, then a more equitable education system would result. This kind of scholarly analysis is unlikely to lead to the kinds of transformations that its ELMA makers hope. Reflexivity is the guard against this, as I conclude.

Implications for ELMA scholarship

There may seem to be a lot of concerns about Bourdieu and his social theory. This, however, is to be expected, in part because Bourdieu is one of the 20th century's most significant social scientists. But his work was, as suggested earlier, never intended to be a total theory, never intended to offer all of the answers to all problems. It is a set of interlocking theoretical tools – impressively consistent (Calhoun, 2014) – which are intended to guide empirical study. The toolkit is not to be dealt with in part, it is not a theory-lite in which a singular concept is applied to a pre-existing data set (James, 2015).

As we near a conclusion to the book, it is worth returning to two key concepts that Bourdieu has to offer ELMA scholars. They are (1) our own position in the field of knowledge production and the need for reflexivity and (2) a focus on practice.

1. Our own position in the field

Bourdieu was always conscious of himself as a higher education field member. He suggested that, as a researcher and a teacher, it was never possible to stand outside the field and comment on it. He saw himself invested in particular aspects of the field – he subscribed to the notion of the value and importance of education and the independence of scholarship for example. He suggested that it was

Thinking with and against Bourdieu 125

possible to offer a critique of the field from within, a critique concerned with the creation of elites and hierarchies on the basis of the knowledge (cultural capital) they produced and reproduced. It was equally possible to become part of an elite group within the field on the basis of producing that critical knowledge. It was important, he suggested, not to deny this but to use this understanding to always ask whether the academic work being undertaken was just self-serving, just about gaining distinction. The question was whether the scholarship had a wider social application and served equitable and more socially just interests by seeking to rigorously document the way that social life was organised.

Bourdieu advocated continual reflexivity. By this he did not mean the kind of self-conscious analysis of everyday modern life discussed by Beck and Giddens (Beck, 1992; Beck, Giddens, & Lash, 1994). Nor did he mean the kinds of reflexivity discussed in relation to research practice, where we routinely think about the ways in which we as researchers might be influencing the research process in order to produce the results that we want (Ellis & Bochner, 2000; Finlay, 2002; Guillemin & Gillam, 2004). Bourdieu *was* concerned about method but primarily about the ways in which researchers might privilege method over all else – what he often called looking for 'the things of logic, rather than the logic of things' (Bourdieu, 1990a, p. 61). Bourdieu saw social science as the quest to understand the ways in which the social world worked. Bourdieu urged researchers to always be aware of themselves as participating in a game in which the stakes were loaded against particular participants and in which research practice was always part of the field game. It was therefore critical, he suggested, to develop a scholarly practice in which the problems to be addressed were those which addressed important social phenomena (see Chapter 2) and which revealed how these were produced.

ELMA researchers interested in Bourdieu are thus directed to consider what it means to research the work that leaders do. Who benefits from ELMA scholarship which simply develops another adjective to describe leaders' work? Who benefits most from work which brings apparent examination successes from one country into another? Does critical ELMA scholarship constitute a horizontal avant-garde? How do ELMA scholarly activities address major social/educational problems?

2. A focus on practice

Bourdieu's emphasis on practice is a very helpful one for ELMA scholars. As Bourdieu explains it, a practice is an assemblage of organised, regular and repeated actions (thinking, doing, speaking, moving, feeling, relating) which occur in a given social, political and material context and which have a particular set of embedded meanings. This understanding of practice brings together

Theory and practice

Rather than seeing theory as something developed in advance of research, Bourdieu promoted understandings that all practice contains implied theory,

126 *Thinking with and against Bourdieu*

and theory, an implied practice; practical knowledge is not inferior to scholastic knowledge; practice is not the application of theory as rules but, rather, is more habituated, experiential and improvised. Practice as embodied theory has theory as concrete, not abstract. Calhoun (1993) notes that a focus on practice also means seeing through the lens of social actors and their strategic intentions and that Bourdieu's reconciliation of theory and practice equates to an action-centred sociology, not one focused on structures or things.

Following Bourdieu's take on practice not only means conducting empirical research but also research which moves beyond what people say. Research into practice in the field includes what agents do, where and with whom and to what effect. For ELMA scholars this means interrogating field specific abstract categories such as leadership, management, vision, mission and distribution. Bourdieusian ELMA scholars look for what actually is done/is said/is felt/occurs, using Bourdieu's thinking tools to focus the investigation and analysis.

Past, present and future

Working from practice means a different approach to time. Rather than seeing the past, present and future as three separate and distinct 'slots', the notion of practice always holds that what happens today is a result of what happened in the past; this history can be 'seen' and explained. All practice is historically produced and situated. Furthermore, practice today anticipates the future, the future is not out there in the distance, the present expects the future in the everyday. As Adkins (2003) observes, in thinking what Bourdieu might have to say to an analysis of recent global financial crises; time is not something that passes; practice actually makes time

> traded, contracted and mortgaged futures are made in the present, that is, that they are in fact made in and through the very practices of trading, contracting and mortgaging.
>
> (p. 355)

Understanding that the future is made and implied in the present suggests that ELMA researchers can make the future part of their empirical inquiry. Rather than simply looking at what leaders say that they want to do, researchers need to look to see what are the potential futures available from historically situated present practices in the field and its relational positions.

With reflexivity and time still in mind, I offer in conclusion some possibilities for a Bourdieusian ELMA agenda. This is not a conclusive list but some starting points for thinking.

A future ELMA agenda?

To conclude the chapter, and the book, I offer some beginning thoughts about a Bourdieusian-inspired ELMA agenda. This is not a definitive list but rather some places where it is obvious that more investigation would be fruitful.

Thinking with and against Bourdieu 127

There is further work to be done around the question of leadership per se. Leadership can be seen as a doxa in and of itself. What kind of game is 'leadership'? What are people in the position of a leader said to be, believe and do? Who says this, and why is it useful in the field at this time? What practices are seen to be 'leading', and what are not? Who benefits from 'leadership'? How has 'leadership' as doxa been produced? Who says what the game of leadership should be, how and why?

There is a great deal of work to be done simply to understand the diversity of practice involved in leading educational institutions – early childhood settings, schools, further education and higher education. A Bourdieusian research agenda would seek to build up a rich set of empirical studies of ELMA practices in a range of positions, plotting them vertically and horizontally. One focus for a detailed field study could be to assess the practices the differently positioned educational professionals need to 'play the game'. How did they get to be head-teachers (or further education directors or university vice chancellors)? What capitals and dispositions did they acquire in the long apprenticeship of becoming an educational professional in a leader post? How do they manage the various logics of practice across the various fields in which they are positioned, and how does this play out in the educational field? Is their practice reflexive, and if so how? How do the relations in the field affect what options and possibilities are available to agents?

There are also educators working in designated leadership positions in settings other than schools, colleges and universities – youth groups, galleries and museums, third-sector organisations – and in deinstitutionalised settings online. What does it mean to do educational leadership work in fields other than education? Are there practices that are common across positions? Common trajectories and capitals? What are the homologies between their positions and that of more orthodox educational leaders? What different strategies are available to them by virtue of being differently positioned relative to others in the field?

ELMA scholars might also expand research into the question of who becomes a designated educational leader, and whether there are homologies between their institutional position, their primary habitus and life trajectories. Are some people more disposed to be 'leaders' in inner urban schools or in elite universities for example? There is also the question of who does not get to be a designated leader and why. What does their refusal to play the game, or failure in the game, tell us about leadership practice and in whose interests it works? It would also be instructive to look across designated leadership roles in various professional, public policy and third-sector settings. Are there common leadership practices, trajectories, capitals and dispositions across fields; what effects does this have; and whose interests do they serve?

There is a great deal of work still to be done to trace how ELMA knowledge is generated, which knowledges is privileged, and how this becomes part of the capitals that count in the field. What practices of ELMA knowledge production and reproduction are privileged in higher education institutions and who benefits most from this? Which knowledge is sidelined and to what effects? How is ELMA knowledge actually connected with policymaking in the fields of politics

128   *Thinking with and against Bourdieu*

and media? How will the current shift in the hierarchy of ELMA knowledges between higher education and schools play out?

And there is an enormous amount of work to be done to understand how the game of leadership actually makes, or might make, a difference to the educational opportunities and benefits offered to children and young people whose families have typically been poorly served by educational institutions. How does practice in education connect with practices in other fields, welfare, housing and so on, in the same social space and place? How might counter–status quo practices be spread farther than single sites and clusters of sites? How might a greater focus on students' experiences of the educational game inform educational 'leadership' practices? How do designated 'leaders' work to reconcile the dilemmas of the imposition of classed/raced/gendered practices versus the importance of 'playing the game'?

It is this last question which goes to the heart of Bourdieu's major and lifelong concern about an education system which might do more than simply reproduce social inequalities and injustices. The contemporary school systems doxa is that the practices of making a difference in life chances for children and young people are equivalent to test result improvements and that 'leadership' which accomplishes equitable change is the same as making improvements in test results. But at the same time, higher education is becoming more and more expensive and out of reach, the youth labour market has collapsed and poverty is increasing. There is considerable urgency in generating other views of educational purposes, practices and possibilities. Taking up Bourdieu in ELMA scholarship to address these concerns could be a contribution to a more socially aware and responsive education field.

8 Finding out more about Bourdieu

This selected bibliography does not list all of the texts that Bourdieu wrote or those written about him. Bourdieu was a prolific author and wrote a great deal about a number of topics. This set of resources is intended to guide initial reading.

For the ELMA scholar new to Bourdieu it is probably best to begin with some books written about Bourdieu and then look at some of the ways in which his toolkit has been brought to educational questions. Once familiar with this, it is good to get immersed in his own writing, perhaps starting with his work on education before going onto his work on academic practice. Please note that the lists that follow largely refer to books and special issues of journals.

Introductions to Bourdieu

These books offer accessible explanations of Bourdieu's theoretical toolkit and major works.

Grenfell, Michael (2004) *Pierre Bourdieu: Agent provocateur.* London: Continuum
Grenfell, Michael Ed (2012) *Pierre Bourdieu: Key concepts* 2nd ed. London: Routledge
Grenfell, Michael (2014) *Pierre Bourdieu.* London: Bloomsbury
Harker, Richard, Mahar, Cheleen and Wilkes, Chris (1990) *An introduction to the work of Pierre Bourdieu: The practice of theory.* London: Palgrave Macmillan
Jenkins, Richard (1992) *Pierre Bourdieu.* London: Routledge
Lane, Jeremy (2000) *Pierre Bourdieu: A critical introduction.* London: Pluto Press
Webb, Jen, Schirato, Tony and Danaher, Geoff (2002) *Understanding Bourdieu.* London: Sage

Bourdieu on schooling

It is important to read primary source texts for yourself. It is generally good to read at least some of them before you read too many introductions or texts that use Bourdieu's work. Many of us read Bourdieu in translation, but if you can manage the originals in French, then do so.

Bourdieu, Pierre and Passeron, Jean Claude (1977) 1990 *Reproduction in society, education and culture.* (Trans R. Nice). London: Sage

130 *Finding out more about Bourdieu*

Bourdieu, Pierre and Passeron, Jean Claude (1979) *The inheritors: French students and their relation to culture.* (Trans R. Nice). Chicago: The University of Chicago Press

You may also like to read books which address the broader educational field and the ways in which schooling produces particular kinds of capitals and dispositions that are then important in further and higher education.

Bourdieu, Pierre, Passeron, Jean Claude and de Saint Martin, Monique (1965) *Academic discourse* (Trans R.Teese). Stanford, CA: Stanford University Press
Bourdieu, Pierre (1989/1996) *The state nobility* (Trans L. Clough). Stanford, CA: Stanford University Press
Bourdieu, Pierre (1998) *Homo academicus* (Trans P. Collier). Stanford, CA: Stanford University Press

Bourdieu and education

Costa, Cristina and Murphy, Mark (2015) *Bourdieu, habitus and social research: The art of application.* London: Palgrave Macmillan
English, Fenwick and Bolton, Cheryl (2016) *Bourdieu for educators: Policy and practice.* Thousand Oaks: Sage
Grenfell, Michael and James, David Eds (1998) *Bourdieu and education: Acts of practical theory.* London: RoutledgeFalmer
Murphy, Mark Ed (2013) *Social theory and education research: Understanding foucault, Habermas, Bourdieu and Derrida.* London: Routledge
Murphy, Mark and Costa, Cristina Eds (2016) *Theory as method in research: On Bourdieu, social theory and education.* London: Routledge

It is also helpful to look at educational books which use Bourdieu as method. The following are good places to start:

Ball, Stephen, Maguire, Meg and Macrae, Sheila (2000) *School choice, pathways and transitions: Post 16: New youth, new economies in the global city.* London: Routledge
Burnard, Pamela and Trulsson, Yiva (2015) *Bourdieu and the sociology of music education.* London: Routledge
Lareau, Annette (2011) *Unequal childhoods: Class, race and family life.* 2nd ed. Berkeley, CA: University of California Press
Reay, Diane, Crozier, Gill and James, David (2011) *White middle class identities and urban schooling.* London: Palgrave Macmillan
Reed Danahay, Deborah (1996) *Education and identity in rural France: The politics of schooling.* Cambridge, MA: Cambridge University Press

Bourdieu and language, literacy and education

The acquisition of linguistic capital was central to Bourdieu's concerns about the ways in which schooling reproduced class privilege. These books work from that premise and with the Bourdieusian toolkit.

Finding out more about Bourdieu   131

Albright, James and Luke, Allan (2008) *Pierre Bourdieu and literacy education*. London: Routledge
Grenfell, Michael (2011) *Language, ethnography and education*. London: Routledge
Grenfell, Michael (2012) *Bourdieu, language and linguistics*. London: Continuum
Grenfell, Michael, Bloome, David, Hardy, Cheryl, Pahl, Kate, Rowsell, Jennifer and Street, Brian (2011) *Language, ethnography and education: Bridging new literacy studies and Bourdieu*. London: Routledge

Bourdieu and ELMA

There is some work already in the ELMA field which mobilises Bourdieu. The following are some starting points.

The International Journal of Educational Leadership Volume 6, Issue 4, was a special issue devoted to Bourdieu, edited by Pat Thomson.

Eacott, Scott (2011). *School leadership and strategy in managerialist times*. Rotterdam, The Netherlands: Sense Publishers
Eacott, Scott (2015). *Educational leadership relationally: A theory and methodology for educational leadership*. Rotterdam, The Netherlands: Sense
Gunter, Helen (2001). *Leaders and leadership in education*. London: Paul Chapman
Gunter, Helen (2012). *Leadership and the reform of education*. Bristol: The Policy Press
Gunter, Helen (2016). *An intellectual history of school leadership practice and research*. London: Bloomsbury

Bourdieu on academic practice

Bourdieu wrote extensively about academic practice and social science. The following books elaborate his views on the conduct of independent, reflexive and rigorous scholarship.

Bourdieu, Pierre (1993) *Sociology in question* (Trans R Nice). London: Sage
Bourdieu, Pierre (1998) *Practical reason: On the theory of action*. Oxford: Blackwell
Bourdieu, Pierre (2000) *Pascalian meditations* (Trans R. Nice). Oxford: Polity Press
Bourdieu, Pierre, Chamberon, Jean Claude and Passeron, Jean Claude (1991) *The craft of sociology*. Berlin: de Gruyter
Bourdieu, Pierre and Wacquant, Loic (1992). *An invitation to reflexive sociology*. Chicago: University of Chicago Press

Extended reading about Bourdieu

If you wish to follow up writing about Bourdieu that offers examples of work with his toolkit across a wider range of disciplines, then you might check out:

Atkinson, Will (2016). *Beyond Bourdieu*. Bristol: Polity Press
Bennett, Tony, Emmison, Michael and Frow, John. (1999). *Accounting for tastes: Australian everyday cultures*. Cambridge: Cambridge University Press
Calhoun, Craig, LiPuma, Edward and Postone, Moishe Eds (1993). *Bourdieu: Critical perspectives*. Chicago: University of Chicago Press

132 *Finding out more about Bourdieu*

De Silva, Elizabeth and Warde, Alan (2010). *Cultural analysis and Bourdieu's legacy: Settling accounts and developing alternatives.* London: Routledge

Fowler, Bridget (1997). *Pierre Bourdieu and cultural theory: Critical investigations.* London: Sage

Gorski, Philip Ed (2013). *Bourdieu and historical analysis.* Durham: Duke University Press

Grenfell, Michael and Hardy, Cheryl (2007) *Art rules: Pierre Bourdieu and the visual arts.* Oxford: Berg

Hilgers, Mathieu, and Mangez, Eric Eds (2015) *Bourdieu's theory of social fields, Concepts and applications.* London: Routledge

Reed Danahay, Deborah (2005). *Locating Bourdieu.* Bloomington, IN: University of Indiana Press

Savage, Mike (2015). *Social class in the 21st century.* London: Penguin Books

Shusterman, Richard Ed (1999). *Bourdieu: A critical reader.* London: Blackwell Philosophy

Swartz, David (1997). *Culture and power: The sociology of Pierre Bourdieu.* Chicago: University of Chicago Press

Thatcher, Jenny, Ingram, Nicola, Burke, Ciaran, and Abrahams, Jessie Eds (2016) *Bourdieu: The next generation: The development of Bourdieu's intellectual heritage in contemporary times.* London: Routledge

References

Acker, S. (2010). Gendered games in academic leadership. *International Studies in Scoiology of Education, 20*(2), 129–152.

Addi-Raccah, A., & Ayalon, H. (2002). Gender inequality in leadership positions of teachers. *British Journal of Sociology of Education, 23*(2), 157–177.

Addison, B. (2009). A feel for the game – A Bourdieusian analysis of principal leadership: A study of Queensland. *Journal of Educational Administration and History, 41*(4), 327–341.

Adkins, L. (2003). Reflexivity: Freedom or habit of gender? *Theory, Culture & Society, 20*(6), 21–42.

Adkins, L., & Skeggs, B. (Eds.). (2005). *Feminism after Bourdieu*. Cambridge: Blackwell.

Adonis, A. (2012). *Education, education, education: Reforming England's schools*. London: Biteback Publishing.

Aguayo, R. (1990). *Dr Deming: The American who taught the Japanese about quality*. New York: Simon and Schuster.

Albright, J., & Luke, A. (Eds.). (2008). *Pierre Bourdieu and literacy education*. London: Routledge.

Althusser, L. (1971). *Lenin and philosophy and other essays* (B. Brewster, Trans.). London: New Left Books.

Amin, A. (1994). *Post Fordism: A reader*. Cambridge: Blackwell.

Anderson, G. (2001). Disciplining leaders: A critical discourse analysis of the ISLLC National Examination and Performance Standards in educational administration. *International Journal of Leadership in Education, 4*(3), 199–216.

Anderson, G. (2009). *Advocacy leadership: Towards a post reform agenda in education*. London: Routledge.

Anderson, G., & Herr, K. (2003). Violent youth or violent schools? A critical incident analysis of symbolic violence. *International Journal of Leadership in Education, 6*(4), 415–433.

Anderson, L., & Bennett, N. (2003). *Developing eductaional leadership: Using evidence for policy and practice*. Thousand Oaks: Sage.

Apple, M. (1979). *Ideology and curriculum*. London: Routledge & Kegan Paul.

Apple, M. (1982). *Cultural and economic reproduction in education*. London: Routledge & Kegan Paul.

Apple, M. (2013). *Education and power*. New York: Routledge.

Archer, L., & Francis, B. (2006). *Understanding minority ethnic achievement: Race, gender, class and 'success'*. London: Routledge.

134   *References*

Archer, L., Hutchings, M., & Ross, A. (2003). *Higher education and social class: Issues of exclusion and inclusion.* London: RoutledgeFalmer.

Archer, M. (2007). *Making our way through the world.* Cambridge: Cambridge University Press.

Arlestig, H., Day, C., & Johansson, O. (Eds.). (2016). *A decade of research on school principals: Cases from 24 countries.* Dordrecht, NL: Springer.

Arnot, M. (2002). *Reproducing gender? Essays on educational theory and feminist politics.* London: Routledge.

Arnot, M., & Mac An Ghaill, M. (Eds.). (2006). *The RoutledgeFalmer reader in gender and education.* London: Routledge.

Astle, J., & Ryan, C. (Eds.). (2008). *Academies and the future of state education.* London: CentreForum.

Atkinson, W. (1991). Cranford community school. In P. Mortimore & J. Mortimore (Eds.), *The secondary head: Roles, responsibilites and reflections* (pp. 143–160). London: Paul Chapman Publishing.

Atkinson, W. (2016). *Beyond Bourdieu.* London: Polity Press.

Avis, J. (2002). Imaginary friends: Managerialism, globalisation and post-compulsory education and training in England. *Discourse, 23*(1), 75–90.

Bacchi, C. (1999). *Women, policy and politics: The construction of policy problems.* London, Thousand Oaks, New Delhi: Sage.

Bacchi, C. (2009). *Analysing policy: What's the problem represented to be?* Frenchs Forest NSW: Pearson Australia.

Baker, B. (2005). *Transforming schools: Illusion or reality.* Stoke on Trent: Trentham.

Ball, S. (1999). School management myth: Good management makes good schools. In B. O'Hagan (Ed.), *Modern educational myths: The future of democratic comprehensive education* (pp. 88–106). London: Kogan Page.

Ball, S. (2006). *Education policy and social class: Selected works.* London: Routledge.

Ball, S. (2007). *Education plc: Understanding private sector participation in public sector education.* London: Routledge.

Ball, S. (2008a). *The education debate.* Bristol: The Policy Press.

Ball, S. (2008b). New philanthropy, new networks and new governance in education. *Political Studies, 56*(4), 747–765.

Ball, S. (2012a). *Global Education Inc: New policy networks and the neoliberal imaginary.* London: Routledge.

Ball, S. (2012b). *Networks, new governance and education.* Bristol: Policy Press.

Ball, S., Bowe, R., & Gewirtz, S. (1996). School choice, social class and distinction: The realisation of social advantage in education. *Journal of Education Policy, 11*(1), 89–112.

Ball, S., Macrae, S., & Maguire, M. (1999). Young lives, diverse choices and imagined futures in an education and training market. *International Journal of Inclusive Education, 3*(3), 195–224.

Ball, S., Maguire, M., & Braun, A. (2012). *How schools do policy: Policy enactments in secondary schools.* London: Routledge.

Ball, S., Maguire, M., & Macrae, S. (2000). *Choice, pathways and transitions post-16: New youth, new economies in the global city.* London: Falmer.

Barber, M., & Moffit, A. (2010). *Deliverology 101: A field guide for educational leaders.* Thousand Oaks: Corwin.

Barnett, C. (2010). Publics and markets: What's wrong with neoliberalism? In S. Smith, S. Marston, R. Pain, & J. P. Jones (Eds.), *The handbook of social geography* (pp. 269–296). London: Sage.

Barth, R. (1990). *Improving schools from within: Teachers, parents, and principals can make the difference.* San Francisco: Jossey Bass.

Bates, R. (1987). Corporate culture, schooling, and educational administration. *Educational Administration Quarterly, 23*(4), 79–115.

Bates, R. (1993). On knowing: Cultural and critical approaches to educational administration. *Educational Management and Administration, 21*(3), 171–176.

Bates, R., & Eacott, S. (2008). Teaching educational leadership and administration in Australia. *Journal of Educational Administration and History, 40*(2), 149–160.

Baum, F., Palmer, C., Modra, C., Murray, C., & Bush, R. (2000). Families, social capital and health. In I. Winter (Ed.), *Social capital and public policy in Australia* (pp. 250–275). Melbourne: Australian Institute of Family Studies.

Beare, H., & Slaughter, R. (1993). *Education for the twenty first century.* London: Routledge.

Beasley-Murray, J. (2000). Value and capital in Bourdieu and Marx. In N. Brown & I. Szeman (Eds.), *Pierre Bourdieu: Fieldwork in culture* (pp. 100–119). Lanham, MD: Rowman and Littlefield.

Beck, L. G. (1994). *Reclaiming educational administration as a caring profession.* New York: Teachers College Press.

Beck, U. (1992). *Risk society: Towards a new modernity.* London: Sage.

Beck, U. (1997). *The reinvention of politics: Rethinking modernity in the global social order* (M. Ritter, Trans.). Cambridge: Polity Press.

Beck, U. (1998). *Democracy without enemies* (M. Ritter, Trans.). Cambridge, Oxford: Polity Press.

Beck, U., Giddens, A., & Lash, S. (1994). *Reflexive modernisation: Politics, tradition and aesthetics in the modern social order.* Stanford, CA: Stanford University Press.

Beckett, F. (2007). *The great city academy fraud.* London: Continuum.

Bennett, T. (2007). Habitus clivé: Aesthetics and politics in the work of Pierre Bourdieu. *New Literary History, 38*(1), 201–228.

Bennis, W. (1993). *Beyond Bureaucracy.* San Francisco: Jossey Bass.

Berliner, D. (2009). *Poverty and potential: Out of school factors and school success.* Tempe, AR: Education Public Interest Centre, Arizona State University.

Berman, B. (1983). Business efficiency, American schooling and the public school superintendency: A reconsideration of the Callahan thesis. *History of Education Quarterly, 23*(3), 297–321.

Bernbaum, G. (1976). The role of the head. In R. S. Peters (Ed.), *The role of the head* (pp. 9–36). London: Routledge & Kegan Paul.

Bernstein, B. (2000). *Pedagogy, symbolic control and identity* (2nd ed.). London: Rowman & Littlefield.

Biesta, G. (2006). *Beyond learning: Democratic education for a human future.* Boulder, CO: Paradigm Publishers.

Blackmore, J. (1998). Self managing schools, the new educational accountability and the evaluative state. *South Australian Educational Leader, 9*(5).

Blackmore, J. (1999). *Troubling women: Feminism, leadership and educational change.* Buckingham: Open University Press.

Blackmore, J., & Sachs, J. (2007). *Performing and reforming leaders: Gender, educational restructuring and organisational change.* New York: State University of New York Press.

Blackmore, J., & Thomson, P. (2004). Just 'good and bad news'? Disciplinary imaginaries of head teachers in Australian and English print media. *Journal of Education Policy, 19*(3), 301–320.

136　*References*

Blackmore, J., Thomson, P., & Barty, K. (2006). Principal selection: Homo-sociability, the search for security and the production of normalised principals identities. *Educational Management, Administration and Leadership, 34*(3), 297–337.

Blatchford, R. (2015). *A practical guide, National standards of excellence for head-teachers.* Woodbridge: John Catt Publishing.

Bloom, C. M., & Erlandson, D. (2003). African American women principals in urban schools: Realities, (re)constructions, and resolutions. *Educational Administration Quarterly, 39*(3), 339–369.

Bobbitt, J. F. (1924). *How to make a curriculum.* Boston: Houghton Miflin.

Boden, R., Gummett, P., Coz, D., & Barker, K. (1998). Men in white coats . . . men in grey suits. New Public Management and the funding of science and technology services to the UK government. *Accounting, Auditing and Accountability Journal, 11*(3), 267–291.

Bolam, R. (1997). Management development for headteachers: Retrospect and pros-pect. *Educational Management and Administration, 25*(3), 265–283.

Bottero, W., & Crossley, N. (2011). Worlds, fields and networks: Becker, Bourdieu and the structures of social relations. *Cultural Sociology, 5*(1), 99–119.

Bourdieu, P. (1975). The specifity of the scientific field and the social conditions of the progress of reason. *Sociology of Science, 14*(6), 19–47.

Bourdieu, P. (1977). *Outline of a theory of practice* (R. Nice, Trans.). Cambridge: Cambridge University Press.

Bourdieu, P. (1984). *Distinction: A social critique of the judgment of taste* (R. Nice, Trans.). Boston: Harvard University Press.

Bourdieu, P. (1986). The forms of capital (R. Nice, Trans.). In J. Richardson (Ed.), *Handbook of theory and research for the sociology of education* (pp. 241–258). New York: Greenwood.

Bourdieu, P. (1988). *Homo academicus* (P. Collier, Trans.). Stanford, CA: Stanford University Press.

Bourdieu, P. (1989). Social space and symbolic power. *Sociological Theory, 7*(1), 14–25.

Bourdieu, P. (1990a). *In other words: Essays towards a reflexive sociology* (M. Adamson, Trans.). Stanford, CA: Stanford University Press.

Bourdieu, P. (1990b). *The logic of practice* (R. Nice, Trans.). Stanford, CA: Stanford University Press.

Bourdieu, P. (1991). *The love of art: European art museums and their public* (C. Beat-tie & N. Merriman, Trans.). Cambridge: Polity Press.

Bourdieu, P. (1992). *The rules of art: Genesis and structure of the literary field* (S. Ema-nuel, Trans.). Stanford, CA: Stanford University Press.

Bourdieu, P. (1993a). *The field of cultural production: Essays on art and literature.* Oxford: Polity.

Bourdieu, P. (1993b). *Sociology in question* (R. Nice, Trans.). London: Sage.

Bourdieu, P. (1996). *On television* (P. P. Ferguson, Trans.). New York: The New Press.

Bourdieu, P. (1998a). *Acts of resistance: Against the new myths of our time* (R. Nice, Trans.). Cambridge, Oxford: Polity Press.

Bourdieu, P. (1998b). *Practical reason: On the theory of action* (R. Johnson, Trans.). Oxford: Blackwell.

Bourdieu, P. (1998c). *The state nobility* (L. Clough, Trans.). Cambridge: Polity.

Bourdieu, P. (2000). *Pascalian meditations* (R. Nice, Trans.). Oxford: Polity Press.

Bourdieu, P. (2001). *Masculine domination* (R. Nice, Trans.). Stanford, CA: Stanford University Press.

Bourdieu, P. (2003). *Firing back: Against the tyranny of the market 2* (L. Wacquant, Trans.). New York: The New Press.

Bourdieu, P. (2004). *Science of science and reflexivity* (R. Nice, Trans.). Cambridge: Polity.

Bourdieu, P. (2005). *The social structures of the economy* (C. Turner, Trans.). Cambridge: Polity.

Bourdieu, P. (2007). *Sketch for a self-analysis* (R. Nice, Trans.). Cambridge: Polity.

Bourdieu, P., Boltanski, L., Castel, R., Chamboredon, J.-C., & Schnapper, D. (1990). *Photography: A middlebrow art* (S. Whitesicle, Trans.). London: Polity.

Bourdieu, P., Chamberon, J.-C., & Passeron, J. C. (1991). *The craft of sociology* (R. Nice, Trans.). Berlin: de Gruyter.

Bourdieu, P., & Chartier, R. (2010/2015). *The sociologist & the historian* (D. Fernbach, Trans.). London: Polity.

Bourdieu, P., et al. (1999). *The weight of the world: Social suffering in contemporary societies* (P. P. Ferguson, Trans.). Stanford, CA: Stanford University Press.

Bourdieu, P., & Passeron, J. C. (1977). *Reproduction in society, education and culture* (R. Nice, Trans.). London: Sage.

Bourdieu, P., & Passeron, J. C. (1979). *The inheritors, French students and their relation to culture* (R. Nice, Trans.). Chicago: The University of Chicago Press.

Bourdieu, P., Passeron, J.-C., & de Saint Martin, M. (1995). *Academic discourse* (R. Teese, Trans. 1965 ed.). Stanford, CA: Stanford University Press.

Bourdieu, P., & Wacquant, L. (1992). *An invitation to reflexive sociology*. Chicago and London: University of Chicago Press.

Bowles, S., & Gintis, H. (1976). *Schooling in capitalist America*. New York: Basic Books.

Briggs, A. R., Coleman, M., & Morrison, M. (2012). *Research methods in educational leadership and management* (3rd ed.). Thousand Oaks: Sage.

Brighouse, T., & Woods, D. (1999). *How to improve your school*. London: Routledge.

Bright, T., & Ware, N. (2003). *Were you prepared? Findings from a national survey of headteachers*. Nottingham: NCSL.

Brown, M. (1994). Competency based training: Skill formation for the workplace or classroom Taylorism? In J. Kenway (Ed.), *Economising education: The post-Fordist directions* (pp. 153–183). Geelong: Deakin University Press.

Brundrett, M., & Crawford, M. (Eds.). (2008). *Developing school leaders: An International perspective*. London: Routledge.

Brundrett, M., & Rhodes, C. (2014). *Reseaching eductaional leadership and management: Methods and approaches*. London: Sage.

Burch, P. (2009). *Hidden markets: The new education privatization*. New York: Routledge.

Bush, T. (1999). Crisis or crossroads? The discipline of educational management in the late 1990s. *Educational Management and Administration, 27*(3), 239–252.

Bush, T. (2000). The national professional qualification for headship: The key to effective leadership? *School Leadership & Management, 18*(3), 321–333.

Bush, T., Bell, L., Bolam, R., Glatter, R., & Ribbins, P. (1999). *Educational management: Redefining theory, policy and practice*. London: Paul Chapman Publishing.

Butler, J. (1999). Performativity's social magic. In R. Shusterman (Ed.), *Bourdieu: A critical reader* (113–128). Oxford: Blackwell.

Byrom, T., Thomson, P., & Gates, P. (2007). 'My school has been quite pushy about the Oxbridge thing': Voice and choice of higher education. *Improving Schools, 10*(1), 29–40.

138   *References*

Cahill, D., Edwards, L., & Stilwell, F. (Eds.). (2012). *Neoliberalism: Beyond the free market*. Cheltenham: Edward Elgar Publishing.

Caldwell, B. (1998, July 19). *Beyond the self managing school: Resourcing the New Agenda*. Paper presented at the Victorian Primary Principals Association, Mulwawa, Victoria.

Caldwell, B., & Hayward, D. (1997a). *The future of schools*. London: Falmer.

Caldwell, B., & Hayward, D. (1997b). *Previewing 'The Future of Schools'*. Paper presented at the ACEA Virtual Conference: The Shape of Future Schooling, http://www.acea.com.au/.

Caldwell, B., & Spinks, J. (1988). *The self managing school*. London: Falmer Press.

Caldwell, B., & Spinks, J. (1992). *Leading the self managing school*. London: Falmer Press.

Caldwell, B., & Spinks, J. (1998). *Beyond the self managing school: Student outcomes and the reform of education*. London: Falmer Press.

Calhoun, C. (1993). Habitus, field, and capital: The question of historical specificity. In C. Calhoun, E. LiPuma, & M. Postone (Eds.), *Bourdieu: Critical perspectives* (pp. 61–88). Chicago: University of Chicago Press.

Calhoun, C. (2003). Pierre Bourdieu. In G. Ritzer (Ed.), *The Blackwell companion to major contemporary social theorists* (pp. 274–309). Cambridge: Blackwell.

Calhoun, C. (2014). Pierre Bourdieu in context. http://www.nyu.edu/classes/bkg/objects/calhoun.doc: New York University. Accessed July 15, 2015.

Callahan, R. E. (1962). *Education and the cult of efficiency*. Chicago: University of Chicago Press.

Carrington, V., & Luke, A. (1997). Literacy and Bourdieu's sociological theory: A reframing. *Language and Education, 11*(2), 96–112.

Case, P., Case, S., & Catling, P. (2000). Please show you're working: A critical assessment of the impact of Ofsted inspection on primary teachers. *British Journal of Sociology of Education, 21*(4), 605–621.

Castagnoli, P., & Cook, N. (2004). *The impact of professional development on school improvement: Growing your own leaders*. Nottingham: NCSL.

Castells, M. (1996). *The information age: Economy, society and culture: The rise of the network society*. Oxford: Blackwell.

Castells, M. (1997). *The information age: Economy, society and culture: The power of identity*. Oxford: Blackwell.

Castells, M. (1998). *The information age: Economy, society and culture: End of the millenium*. Oxford: Blackwell.

Cerny, P. G. (2000). Restructuring the political arena: Globalisation and the pradoxes of the competititon state. In R. D. Germain (Ed.), *Globalisation and its critics: Perspectives from political economy* (pp. 117–138). Basingstoke: Palgrave Macmillan.

Chambers, C. (2005). Masculine domination, radical feminism and change. *Feminist Theory, 6*(3), 325–346.

Chapman, C., & Gunter, H. (Eds.). (2009). *Radical reforms: Public policy and a decade of educational reform*. Routledge: London.

Chevalier, A., & Conlon, G. (2003). Does it pay to attend a prestigious university? *IZA discussion Paper 848*. Retrieved from http://ftp.iza.org/dp848.pdf. Accessed June 6, 2015.

Chitty, C. (1997). Privatisation and marketisation. *Oxford Review of Education, 23*(1), 45–61.

Chouliaraki, L., & Fairclough, N. (1999). *Discourse in late modernity: Rethinking critical discourse analysis*. Edinburgh: Edinburgh University Press.

References 139

Coates, S. (2015). *Head strong: 11 lessons of school leadership.* Woodbridge: John Catts Publishing.

Codd, J. (1993). Managerialism, market liberalism and the move to self managing schools in New Zealand. In J. Smyth (Ed.), *A socially critical view of the self-managing school* (pp. 153–170). London: Falmer.

Cole, B. A., & Gunter, H. (2010). *Changing lives: Women, inclusion and the PhD.* Stoke on Trent: Trentham Books.

Coleman, A. (undated). *Collaborative leadership in extended schools: Leading in a multi-agency environment.* Nottingham: NCSL.

Coleman, J. S. (1966). *Equality of eductaional opportunity.* Washington, DC: United States Department of Health, Education and Welfare.

Coleman, M. (2005). *Gender and headship in the 21st century.* Nottingham: NCSL.

Colley, H., James, D., Dimend, K., & Tedder, M. (2007). Learning as becoming in vocational education and training: Class, gender and the role of vocational habitus. *Journal of Vocational Education and Training, 55*(4), 471–498.

Comber, B. (2012). Mandated literacy assessment and the reorganisation of teachers' work: Federal policy, local effects. *Critical Studies in Education, 53*(2), 119–136.

Comber, B., & Hill, S. (2000). Socioeconomic disadvantage, literacy and social justice: Learning from longitudinal case study research. *Australian Education Researcher, 27*(3), 151–166.

Common, R. (1998). Convergence and transfer: A review of the globalisation of new public management. *International Journal of Public Sector Management, 11*(6), 440–450.

Connell, R. W. (1993). *Schools and social justice.* Canada: Our Schools/ Ourselves Foundation. Australia: Pluto Press.

Connell, R. W. (2007). *Southern theory: The global dynamics of knowledge in social science.* Cambridge: Polity.

Connell, R. W., Ashenden, D., Kessler, S., & Dowsett, G. (1982). *Making the difference: Schools, families and social divisions.* Sydney: Allen & Unwin.

Considine, M., & Lewis, J. (1999). Governance at ground level: The frontline bureaucrat in the age of markets and networks. *Public Administration Review, 59*(6), 497–481.

Cook, A., & Mack, H. (1971). *The head teachers' role.* London: Macmillan.

Corrigan, P. (1977). *Schooling the smash street kids.* London: Paladin.

Couldry, N. (2005). The individual point of view: Learning from Bourdieu's 'The weight of the world'. *Cultural Studies Critical Methodologies, 5*(3), 354–372.

Court, M. (2003a). *Different approaches to sharing school leadership.* Nottingham: NCSL.

Court, M. (2003b). Towards democratic leadership: Co-principal initiatives. *International Journal of Leadership in Education, 6*(2), 161–183.

Court, M., & O'Neill, J. (2011). "Tomorrow's Schools" in New Zealand: From social democracy to market managerialism. *Journal of Educational Administration and History, 43*(2), 119–140.

Courtney, S. (2015). Corporatised leadership in English schools. *Journal of Educational Administration and History, 47*(3), 214–231.

Courtney, S. (2016). Mapping school types in England. *Oxford Review of Education, 41*(6), 799–818.

Courtney, S., & Gunter, H. (2015). Get off my bus! School leaders, vision work and the elimination of teachers. *International Journal of Leadership in Education, 18*(4), 395–417.

140 References

Crawford, M., & Earley, P. (2012). Personalised leadership development? Lessons from the pilot NPQH in England. *Educational Review, 63*(1), 105–118.

Crossley, M. (2010). Making sense of 'barebacking': Gay men's narratives, unsafe sex and the resistance habitus. *British Journal of Social Psychology, 43*(2), 225–244.

Crossley, N. (2004). The circuit trainer's habitus: Reflexive body techniques and the sociality of the workout. *Body and Society, 10*(1), 37–69.

Crow, G. (2001). *School leader preparation: A short review of the knowledge base.* London: National College for School Leadership.

Cullingford, C. (Ed.) (1999). *An inspector calls: Ofsted and its effect on school standards.* London: Kogan Page.

CUREE. (2003). *Leading the research engaged school: A literature review.* Nottingham: NCSL.

Cutler, T., & Waine, B. (1997). The politics of quasi-markets. *Critical Social Policy, 17*(2), 3–26.

Daniels, D. (2011). From reality to vision: The 'birth' of The Petchey Academy in Hackney. In H. Gunter (Ed.), *The state and education policy: The academies programme.* (pp. 92–104). London: Continuum.

Davies, B., & Ellison, L. (2003). *The new strategic direction and development of the school.* London: Routledge.

Day, C., Harris, A., Hadfield, M., Tolley, H., & Beresford, J. (2000). *Leading schools in times of change.* Buckingham: Open University Press.

Day, C., Sammons, P., Hopkins, D., Harris, A., Leithwood, K., Gu, Q., Penlington, C., Mehta, P., & Kington, A. (2007). *The impact of school leadership on pupil outcomes: Research Report DCSF-RR018.* London: DCSF.

Day, C., Sammons, P., Hopkins, D., Harris, A., Leithwood, K., Gu, Q., Brown, E., Ahtaridou, E., & Kington, A. (2009). *The impact of school leadership on pupil outcomes, DCSF Research Report -RR108.* London: Department for Children, Schools and Families.

Day, C., Sammons, P., Hopkins, D., Leithwood, K., & Kington, A. (2008). Research into the impact of school leadership on pupil outcomes, policy and research contexts. *School Leadership & Management, 28*(1), 5–25.

Day, C., Sammons, P., Leithwood, K., Hopkins, D., Gu, Q., Brown, E., & Ahtaridou, E. (2011). *Successful school leadership: Linking with learning and achievement.* Maidenhead: Open University Press.

Deal, T., & Peterson, K. (1999). *Shaping school culture: The heart of leadership.* San Francisco: Jossey Bass.

Dean, M. (1999). *Governmentality: Power and rule in modern society.* London: Sage.

Deem, R., & Morley, L. (2006). Diversity in the academy? staff peceptions of equality ppolicies in six contemporary higher education institutions. *Policy Future in Education, 4*(2), 185–202.

Deming, W. E. (1992). *The Deming management method.* Cambridge, MA: MIT Press.

Deming, W. E. (2000). *The new economics for industry, government and education.* Cambridge, MA: MIT Press.

DES. (1977). *A new partnership for our schools (the Taylor Report).* London: HMSO.

Devine, D. (2013). Practising leadership in a newly multi-ethic schools: Tensions in the field? *British Journal of Sociology of Education, 34*(3), 392–411.

DfE. (2010). *The case for school freedom: National and international evidence (Gove mythbuster 2).* http://www.education.gov.uk/news/news/freeschools: DfE. Accessed 2nd July 2010.

References 141

Diamond, J., Randolph, A., & Spillane, J. (2008). Teachers' expectations and sense of responsibility for students' learning: The importance of race, class and organisational habitus. *Anthropology and Education Quarterly, 35*(1), 75–98.

Dixon, J., Kouzmin, A., & Karac-Kakabadse, N. (1998). Managerialism – something old, something borrowed, little new: Economic prescription versus effective organisational change in public agencies. *International Journal of Public Sector Management, 11*(2/3), 164–187.

Donmoyer, R. (1999). The continuing quest for a knowledge base: 1976–1998. In J. Murphy & K. S. Louis (Eds.), *Handbook of research on educational administration: A Project of the American Educational Research Association* (pp. 25–44). San Francisco: Jossey Bass.

Dorling, D. (2014). *Inequality and the 1%*. London: Verso Books.

Dow, A., Jolliffe, D., Petherick, G., & O'Brien, G. (1996). Bureaucracy bad, devolution good? *Primary Focus, 10*(1), 6–10.

Du Gay, P. (2000). *In praise of bureaucracy: Weber, organisation, ethics*. Thousand Oaks: Sage.

Eacott, S. (2010a). Bourdieu's strategies and the challenge for educational leadership. *International Journal of Leadership in Education, 13*(3), 265–281.

Eacott, S. (2010b). Tenure, functional track and strategic leadership. *International Journal of Educational Management, 24*(5), 448–458.

Eacott, S. (2011a). Leadership strategies: Reconceptualising strategy for educational leadership. *School Leadership & Management, 31*(1), 35–46.

Eacott, S. (2011b). Preparing 'educational' leaders in managerialist times: An Australian story. *Journal of Educational Administration and History, 43*(1), 43–59.

Eacott, S. (2015). *Educational leadership relationally: A theory and methodology for educational leadership, management and administration*. Dordrecht, Netherlands: Springer.

Eagleton, T. (1991). *Ideology: An introduction*. London: Verso.

Earl, L., & Katz, S. (2006). *Leading schools in a data-rich world: Harnessing data for school improvement*. Thousand Oaks: Corwin Press.

Edmonds, E. L. (1968). *The first headship*. Oxford: Basil Blackwell.

Edward, P., & Green, A. (2003). Loosely coupled organizations, misrecognition, and social reproduction. *International Journal of Leadership in Education, 6*(4), 393–413.

Edwards, R. (2004). Present and absent in troubling ways: Families and social capital debates. *The Sociological Review, 52*(1) 1–21.

Eisenstein, H. (1984). *Contemporary feminist thought*. Sydney: Allen and Unwin.

Ellis, C., & Bochner, A. (2000). Autoethnography, personal narrative, reflexivity: Researcher as subject. In N. Denzin & Y. Lincoln (Eds.), *The Handbook of Qualitative Research* (pp. 733–768). Thousand Oaks: Sage.

Elmore, R. (2004). *School reform from the inside-out*. Cambridge, MA: Harvard University Press.

English, F. (2000). Psst! What does one call a set of non-empirical beliefs required to be accepted on faith and enforced by authority?(Answer: A religion: Aka the ISLLC standards). *International Journal of Leadership in Education, 3*(2), 159–167.

English, F. (2006). The unintended consequences of a standardized knowledge base in advancing educational leadership preparation. *Educational Administration Quarterly, 42*(3), 461–472.

English, F. (Ed.) (2011). *The SAGE handbook of educational leadership*. Thousand Oaks: Sage.

142   *References*

English, F. (2012). Bourdieu's misrecognition: Why educational leadership standards will not reform schools or leadership. *Journal of Educational Administration and History, 44*(2), 155–170.

Eraut, M. (1999). Head teachers' knowledge, practice and mode of cognition. In T. Bush, L. Bell, R. Bolam, R. Glatter, & P. Ribbins (Eds.), *Educational Management, Redefining Theory, Policy and Practice* (pp. 114–126). London: Paul Chapman Publishing.

Evans, R. (1999). *The pedagogic principal.* Edmonton, Alberta: Qual Institute Press.

Fairclough, N. (2002). Critical discourse analysis and the marketization of public discourse: The universities. In M. Toolan (Ed.), *Critical discourse analysis: Critical concepts in linguistics, Volume IV* (pp. 69–103). London: Routledge.

Fairclough, N. (2003). *Analysing discourse: Textual analysis for social research.* London: Routledge.

Fink, D. (1999). Deadwood didn't kill itself: A pathology of failing schools. *Educational Management and Administration, 27*(2), 131–141.

Finlay, L. (2002). Negotiating the swamp: The opportunity and challenge of reflexivity in research practice. *Qualitative Research, 2*(2), 209–230.

Fitzpatrick, K., & Santamaria, L. J. (2014). Disrupting racialisation: Considering critical leadership in the field of physical education. *Physical Education and Sport Pedagogy 40*(2), 532–546.

Forrester, G., & Gunter, H. (2009). School leaders: Meeting the challenge of change. In C. Chapman & H. Gunter (Eds.), *Radical reforms: Public policy and a decade of of educational reform* (pp. 69–79). London: Routledge.

Foster, W. (2004). The decline of the local: A challenge to educational leadership. *Educational Administration Quarterly, 40*(2), 176–191.

Foucault, M. (1972). *The archeology of knowledge* (A. Sheridan, Trans. 1995 ed.). Routledge: London.

Foucault, M. (1977). *Discipline and punish: The birth of the prison* (A. Sheridan, Trans. 1991 ed.). London: Penguin.

Foucault, M. (1988). *Technologies of the self: A seminar with Michel Foucault* (L. Martin, Trans.). London: Tavistock.

Fowler, B. (Ed.) (1997). *Pierre Bourdieu and cultural theory: Critical investigations.* London: Sage.

Fowler, B. (2003). Reading Pierre Bourdieu's Masculine Domination: Notes towards an intersectional analysis of gender, culture and class. *Cultural Studies, 17*(3–4), 468–494.

Francis, B., & Skelton, C. (Eds.). (2001). *Investigating gender: Contemporary perspectives in education.* Buckingham: Open University Press.

Fraser, N., & Honneth, A. (2003). *Redistribtion or recognition: A political-philosophical exchange.* London: Verso.

Frattura, E., & Capper, C. A. (2007). *Leading for social justice: Transforming schools for all learners.* Thousand Oaks: Corwin.

Freire, P. (1972). *Pedagogy of the oppressed.* Great Britain: Penguin.

Fullan, M. (2005). *Leadership and sustainabilty: System thinkers in action.* Thousand Oaks: Ontario Principals Council & Corwin Press.

Fullan, M. (2006). *Turnaround leadership.* San Francisco: Jossey Bass.

Fullan, M. (2011). *Change leader: Learning to do what matters most.* San Francisco: Jossey Bass.

Fuller, K. (2013). *Gender, identity and educational leadership.* London: Bloomsbury.

References 143

Gewirtz, S. (2002). *The managerial school: Post-welfarism and social justice in education*. London: Routledge.

Gewirtz, S., & Ball, S. (2000). From 'welfarism' to 'new managerialism': Shifting discourses of school headship in the education marketplace. *Discourse, 21*(3), 253–268.

Giddens, A. (1990). *The consequences of modernity*. Cambridge: Polity Press.

Giddens, A. (1991). *Modernity and self identity*. Stanford: Stanford University Press.

Giddens, A. (1994). *Beyond left and right: The future of radical politics*. California: Stanford University Press.

Gillborn, D., & Youdell, D. (2000). *Rationing education: Policy, practice, reform and equity*. Buckingham & Philadelphia: Open University Press.

Giroux, H. (1983). *Theory and resistance in education*. South Hadley, MA: Bergin & Garvey.

Glatter, R., & Kydd, L. (2003). 'Best practice' in educational leadership and management: Can we identify it and learn from it? *Educational Management and Administration, 31*(3), 231–243.

Gold, A., Earley, P., & Evans, P. (undated). *Leadership for transforming learning: NCSL's ten propositions and emergent leaders*.

Goldthorpe, J. (2007). "Cultural capital": Some critical observations. *Sociologica, 2,1–23*.

Gonzales, N., & Moll, L. (2002). Cruzanda el puente: Building bridges to funds of knowledge. *Educational Policy, 16*(4), 623–641.

Gonzales, N., Moll, L., & Amanti, C. (2005). *Funds of knowledge*. Mahwah, NJ: Lawrence Erlbaum.

Goodwin, F. J. (1968). *The art of the headmaster*. London: Ward Lock Educational.

Gorard, S., & Smith, E. (2004). An international comparison of equity in education systems. *Comparative Education, 40*(1), 15–28.

Gore, J. (1993). *The struggle for pedagogies: Critical and feminist discourses as regimes of truth*. New York: Routledge.

Gorely, T., Holroyd, R., & Kirk, D. (2003). Muscularity, the habitus and the social construction of gender: Towards a gender relevant physical education. *British Journal of Sociology of Education, 24*(2), 429–448.

Gove, M. (2012). Speech on academies [Press release]. http://www.education. gov.uk/inthenews/speeches/a00201425/michael-gove-speech-on-academies. January 4. Accessed June 12, 2015.

Grace, G. (1995). *School leadership: Beyond education management – An essay in policy scholarship*. London: Falmer Press.

Grant, C. (2011). Teacher leadership: Gendered responses and interpretations. *Agenda: Empowering Women for Gender Equity, 19*(65), 44–57.

Gray, J. (2004). School effectiveness and the other outcomes of secondary schooling: A reassessment of three decades of British research. *Improving Schools, 7*(2), 185–198.

Grek, S. (2009). Governing by numbers: The PISA 'effect' in Europe. *Journal of Education Policy, 24*(1), 23–38.

Grek, S., & Ozga, J. (2008). *Governing by numbers? Shaping education through data*. Edinburgh: Centre for Educational Sociology, The University of Edinburgh.

Grenfell, M. (1996). Bourdieu and initial teacher education – A poststructuralist approach. *British Educational Research Journal, 22*(3), 287–303.

Grenfell, M. (2007). *Pierre Bourdieu*. London: Bloomsbury.

144 *References*

Grenfell, M. (2008). Biography of Bourdieu. In M. Grenfell (Ed.), *Pierre Bourdieu: Key concepts* (pp. 11–25). Stocksfield, UK: Acumen.

Grenfell, M. (2010). Working with habitus and field: The logic of Bourdieu's practice. In E. Silva & A. Warde (Eds.), *Cultural analysis and Bourdieu's legacy: Setting accounts and developing alternatives* (pp. 14–27). London: Routledge.

Grenfell, M., Blackledge, A., Hardy, C., May, S., & Vann, R. (2011). *Bourdieu, language and linguistics*. London: Continuum.

Grenfell, M., Bloome, D., Hardy, C., Pahl, K., Rowsell, J., & Street, B. (2011). *Language, ethnography and education: Bridging new literacy studies and Bourdieu*. London: Routedge.

Grenfell, M., & Hardy, C. (2007). *Art rules: Pierre Bourdieu and the visual arts*. Oxford: Berg.

Grenfell, M., & James, D. (Eds.). (1998). *Acts of practical theory: Bourdieu and education*. London: Falmer Press.

Grenfell, M., & James, D. (2010). Change in the field – changing the field: Bourdieu and the methodological practice of educational research. *British Journal of Sociology of Education, 25*(4), 507–523.

Grenfell, M., & Lebaron, M. (Eds.). (2014). *Bourdieu and data analysis: Methodological principles and practice*. Oxford: Oxford University Press.

Griffiths, M. (1998). *Educational research for social justice: getting off the fence*. Buckingham: Open University Press.

Gronn, P. (2003). *The new work of educational leaders: Changing leadership practice in an era of school reform*. London: Paul Chapman Publishing.

Gronn, P., & Lacey, K. (2006). Cloning their own: Aspirant principals and the school-based selection game. *Australian Journal of Education, 50*(2), 102–121.

Gronn, P., & Ribbins, P. (1996). Leaders in context: Postpositivist approaches to understanding educational leadership. *Educational Administration Quarterly, 32*(3), 452–473.

Gruenewald, D. A., & Smith, G. A. (Eds.). (2008). *Place-based education in the global age: Local diversity*. New York: Lawrence Erlbaum.

Grummell, B., Devine, D., & Lynch, K. (2009). Appointing senior managers in education: Homosociability, local logics and authenticity in the selection process. *Educational Management, Administration and Leadership, 37*(3), 329–349.

Gu, Q., Rea, S., Smethem, L., Dunford, J., Varley, M., Sammons, P., Parish, N., Armstrong, P., & Powell, L. (2015). *Teaching schools evaluation. December 2015*. London, https://www.gov.uk/government/uploads/system/uploads/attachment_data/file/503333/Evaluation_of_Teaching_schools_FINAL_FOR_PUB_25_feb_final_.pdf: NCSL. Accessed February 2, 2016.

Guillemin, M., & Gillam, L. (2004). Ethics, reflexivity, and "ethically important moments" in research. *Qualitative Research, 10*(2), 261–280.

Gulson, K., & Symes, C. (Eds.). (2007). *Spatial theories of education: Policy and geography matters*. Abingdon, Oxon: Routledge.

Gunter, H. (1997). *Rethinking education: The consequences of Jurassic management*. London & Herndon: Cassell.

Gunter, H. (2000). Thinking theory: The field of education management in England and Wales. *British Journal of Sociology of Education, 21*(4), 623–635.

Gunter, H. (2001). *Leaders and leadership in education*. London: Paul Chapman Publishing.

Gunter, H. (2003). Intellectual histories in the field of education management in the UK. *International Journal of Leadership in Education, 6*(4), 335–349.

Gunter, H. (2004). Labels and labelling in the field of educational leadership. *Discourse, 25*(1), 21–41.

Gunter, H. (2005). *Leading teachers.* London: Continuum.

Gunter, H. (2010). Intellectual histories in the field of education manegement in the UK. *International Journal of Leadership in Education, 6*(4), 335–349.

Gunter, H. (2011). *The state and education policy: The academies programme.* London: Bloomsbury.

Gunter, H. (2012a). The field of educational administration in England. *British Journal of Educational Studies, 60*(4), 337–356.

Gunter, H. (2012b). *Leadership and the reform of education.* Bristol: Policy Press.

Gunter, H. (2015). Consultants, consultancy and consultocracy in education policymaking in England. *Journal of Education Policy, 30*(4), 518–539.

Gunter, H. (2016). *An intellectual history of school leadershi practce and research.* London: Bloomsbury.

Gunter, H., & Forrester, G. (2008). New Labour and school leadership 1997–2007. *British Journal of Educational Studies, 56*(2), 144–162.

Gunter, H., & Forrester, G. (2009). Institutional governance: The case of the National College for School Leadership. *The International Journal of Leadership in Public Services, 5*(3), 50–54.

Gunter, H., & Forrester, G. (2010a). New Labour and the logic of practice in educational reform. *Critical Studies in Education, 51*(1), 21–69.

Gunter, H., & Forrester, G. (2010b). School leadership and policymaking in England. *Policy Studies, 31*(1), 495–511.

Gunter, H., Grimaldi, E., Hall, D., & Serpieri, R. (Eds.). (2016). *New Public Management and the reform of education: European lessons for policy and practice.* London: Routledge.

Gunter, H., Hall, D., & Apple, M. (Eds.). (2016) *Corporate elites and the reform of public education.* Bristol: Policy Press.

Gunter, H., & McGinity, R. (2014). The politics of the Academies Programme: Natality and plurality in education policymaking *Research Papers in Education, 29*(3), 300–314.

Gunter, H., Rayner, S., Butt, G., Fielding, A., Lance, A., & Thomas, H. (2007). Transforming the school workforce: Perspectives on school reform in England. *Journal of Educational Change, 8*(1), 25–39.

Gunter, H., Rayner, S., Thomas, H., Fielding, A., Butt, G., & Lance, A. (2005). Teachers, time and work: Findings from the evaluation of the Transforming the School Workforce Pathfinder project. *School Leadership & Management, 25*(5), 441–454.

Gunter, H., & Thomson, P. (2004). *(Kingswood) High School Baseline Report 2004.* Report to Innovations Unit, DfES.

Hadfield, M. (2007). Co-leaders and middle leaders: The dynanic between leaders and followers in networks of schools. *School Leadership & Management, 27*(3), 259–283.

Hall, C., & Noyes, A. (2009). New regimes of truth: The impact of performative school self evaluation systems on teachers' professional identities. *Research Papers in Education, 24*(3), 311–334.

146   *References*

Hall, D. (2012). The strange case of the emergence of distributed leadership in schools in England. *Educational Review, 65*(4), 467–487. *ifirst*.

Hall, D. (2013). Drawing a veil over managerialism: Leadership and the discursive disguise of the New Public Management. *Journal of Educational Administration and History, 45*(3), 267–282.

Hall, D., Gunter, H., & Bragg, J. (2012). Leadership, New Public Management and the remodelling and regulation of teacher identities. *International Journal of Leadership in Education, 16*(2), 173–190.

Hall, V. (1999). Gender and education management: Duel or dialogue? In T. Bush, L. Bell, R. Bolam, R. Glatter, & P. Ribbins (Eds.), *Educational Management: Redefining theory, policy and practice* (pp. 155–165). London, Thousand Oaks & New Delhi: Paul Chapman Publishing.

Hallinger, P. (Ed.) (2003). *Reshaping the landscape of school leadershp development: A global perspective.* Lisse, NL: Swets and Zeitlinger.

Hallinger, P., & Bridges, E. M. (2007). *A problem based approach for management education: Preparing managers for action.* Dordrecht: Springer.

Halsey, A. H., Heath, A. F., & Ridge, J. M. (1980). *Origins and destinations.* Oxford: Clarendon Press.

Hampton, G., & Jones, J. (2000). *Transforming Northicote school: The reality of school improvement.* London: RoutledgeFalmer.

Harding, S. (1993). Rethinking standpoint epistemology: What is "strong objectivity"? In L. Alcoff & E. Potter (Eds.), *Feminist epistemologies* (pp. 49–82). New York: Routledge.

Hardy, I. (2010). Leading learning: Theorizing principal's support for teacher PD in Ontario. *International Journal of Leadership in Education, 13*(4), 421–436.

Hargreaves, A. (2003). *Teaching in the knowledge society: Education in the age of insecurity.* Buckingham: Open University Press.

Hargreaves, A. (2004). Distinction and disgust: The emotional politics of school failure. *International Journal of Leadership in Education, 7*(1), 27–41.

Hargreaves, A., & Fullan, M. (2012). *Professional capital: Transofrming teaching in every school.* London: Routledge.

Harris, A. (2008). *Distributed school leadership: Developing tomorrow's leaders.* London: Routledge.

Harris, A., & Chapman, C. (2002). *Effective leadership in schools facing challenging circumstances.* Nottingham: NCSL.

Harris, A., James, S., Gunraj, J., Clarke, P., & Harris, B. (2006). *Improving schools in exceptionally challenging circumstances: Tales from the frontline.* London: Continuum.

Harrison, T., & Kachur, J. (Eds.). (1999). *Contested classrooms: Education, globalisation and democracy in Alberta.* Edmonton: University of Alberta Press.

Hart, S., Dixon, A., Drummond, M. J., & McIntyre, D. (2004). *Learning without limits.* Buckingham: Open University Press.

Hart, S., Drummond, M. J., Swann, M., & Peacock, A. (2012). *Creating learning without limits.* London: Open University Press.

Hartley, D. (1997). The new managerialism in education: A mission impossible? *Cambridge Journal of Education, 27*(1), 47–57.

Hartley, F., & Thomas, K. (2005). *Growing tomorrow's school leaders: The challenge.* Nottingham: NCSL.

References 147

Harvey, D. (2005). *A brief history of neoliberalism*. Oxford: Oxford University Press.

Hatcher, R. (2005). The distribution of leadership and power in schools. *British Journal of Sociology of Education, 26*(2), 253–267.

Hatcher, R. (2014). Local authorities and the school system: The new authority-wide partnerships. *Educational Management, Administration and Leadership, 42*(3), 355–371.

Hattie, J. (2008). *Visible learning: A synthesis of over 800 meta-analyses relating to achievement*. London: Routledge.

Hattie, J. (2011). *Visible learning for teachers: Maximiising impact on leaders*. London: Routledge.

Hattie, J., & Rates, G. (2015). *Visible learning and the science of how we learn*. London: Routledge.

Hebert, E. (2006). *"The boss of the whole school." Effective leadership in action*. New York: Teachers College Press.

Henry, M., Lingard, B., Rizvi, F., & Taylor, S. (2001). *The OECD, globalisation, and education policy*. Oxford: Pergamon.

Higham, A. (1995). Banbury school, Oxfordshire. In D. Hustler, T. Brighouse, & J. Rudduck (Eds.), *Heeding heads: Secondary heads and educational commentators in dialogue* (pp. 56–64). London: David Fulton Publishers.

Higham, R. (2013). Free schools in the Big Society: The motivations, aims and demography of the free school proposers. *Journal of Education Policy, 29*(1), 122–139.

Hilgers, M., & Mangez, E. (Eds.). (2015). *Bourdieu's theory of social fields, Concepts and applications*. London: Routledge.

Hill, S., Comber, B., Louden, B., Reid, J., & Rivalland, J. (1998). *100 Children go to school: Connections and disconnections in the literacy experience prior to school and in the first year of school. Vols 1–3*. Canberra: Department of Education, Employment, Training and Youth Affairs.

Hirsch, D. (2007). *Experiences of poverty and educational disadvantage*. New York: Joseph Rowntree foundation.

Hollins, K., Gunter, H., & Thomson, P. (2006). Living improvement: A case study of a school in England. *Improving Schools, 9*(2), 141–152.

Holt, J. (1964). *How children fail* (1972 ed.). London: Penguin.

Hood, C. (1995a). Emerging issues in public administration. *Public Administration, 73*(Spring), 165–183.

Hood, C. (1995b). The "New Public Management" in the 1980s: Variations on a theme. *Accounting, Organisations and Society, 20*(2/3), 93–109.

Hood, C. (1998). *The art of the state: Culture, rhetoric and public management*. Oxford: Clarendon Press.

Hopkins, D. (2001). *School improvement for real*. London: RoutledgeFalmer.

Hopkins, D., Ainscow, M., & West, M. (1994). *School improvement in an era of change*. London: Cassell.

Hsieh, H.-F., & Shannon, S. A. (2005). Three approaches to qualitative content analysis. *Qualitative Health Research, 15*(9), 1277–1288.

Huber, S., & Hiltmann, M. (2010). The recruitment and selection of school leaders – first findings of an international comparison. In S. Huber (Ed.), *School leadership – internaitonal perspectives. Vol 10* (pp. 303–330). Dordrecht: Springer.

Imai, M. (1997). *Gemba Kaizen: A commonsense, low-cost approach to management*. New York: Mc Graw Hill.

148   *References*

Inghilleri, M. (2005). Mediating zones of uncertainty: Interpreter agency, the interpreting habitus and political asylum adjudication. *The Translator, 11*(1), 69–85.

Ingram, N., & Abrahams, J. (2016). Stepping outside oneself: How a cleft habitus can lead to greater reflexivity through occupying "third space". In J. Thatcher, N. Ingram, C. Burke, & J. Abrahams (Eds.), *Bourdieu: The next generation: The development of Bourdieu's intellectual heritage in contemporary UK sociology* (pp. 140–156). London: Routledge.

Ingvarson, L., Anderson, M., Gronn, P., & Jackson, A. (2006). *Standards for school leadership: A critical review of the literature.* Melbourne: ACER.

Jackson, B. (1960). *Life in classrooms.* New York: Holt, Rhinehart &Winston.

Jackson, B., & Marsden, D. (1966). *Education and the working class.* London: Penguin.

James, D. (2015). How Bourdieu bites back: Recognising misrecognition in the education and educational research. *Cambridge Journal of Education, 45*(1), 97–112.

Janks, H. (2009). *Literacy and power.* New York: Routledge.

Jenkins, R. (1992). *Pierre Bourdieu.* London: Routledge.

Jones, A. (1978). *The influence of the freedom and authority memorandum on education policy in South Australia.* Armidale: University of New England.

Jones, A. (1980). *Decentralisation in the central state: Some aspects of the policy -making profcess in South Australia.* Parkville, ACT: Centre of the Study of Higher Education, University of Melbourne.

Jones, K., & Thomson, P. (2008). Policy rhetoric and the renovation of English schooling: The case of creative partnerships. *Journal of Education Policy, 23*(6), 715–728.

Jones, N. (1999). The changing role of the primary school head: Reflections from the front line. *Educational Management and Administration, 27*(4), 441–451.

Kachur, J. (1999). Privatising public choice: The rise of charter schooling in Alberta. In T. Harrison & J. Kachur (Eds.), *Contested Classrooms* (pp. 107–122). Edmonton: University of Alberta Press.

Kaminsky, J. (1981). The "Freedom and Authority Memorandum": A philosophical addendum in educational administration. *Journal of Educational Administration, 19*(3), 187–200.

Karabel, J., & Halsey, A. (1977). *Power and ideology in education.* Oxford: Oxford University Press.

Kelly, P., & Lusis, T. (2006). Migration and transnational habitus: Evidence from Canada and the Phlippines. *Environment and Planning A, 38*(5), 831–847.

Kelsey, J. (1999). *Reclaiming the future: New Zealand and the global economy.* Wellington: Bridget Williams Books.

Kemp, L. (undated). Technical high schools were now in the forefront of educational change. 1964–1972. In E. Jolley (Ed.), *A broader vision:* Adelaide: Lythrvm Press. http://www.lythrvmpress.com.au/vision/255.html. Accessed 5th May 2009.

Kenway, J. (1990). Education and the Right's discursive politics: Private versus state schooling. In S. Ball (Ed.), *Foucault and education: Disciplines and knowledge* (pp. 167–206). London: Routledge.

Kenway, J., & McLeod, J. (2004). Bourdieu's reflexive sociology and 'spaces of points of view': Whose reflexivity, which perspective? *British Journal of Sociology of Education, 25*(4), 525–544.

Kilvert, P. (2001). Partnerships 21. *International Education Journal, 2*(1), http://iej.cjb.net/. Accessed 30 April, 2009.

References 149

Knight, J., & Lingard, B. (1996). Ministerialisation and politicisation: Changing practices of educational policy production. In B. Lingard & P. Porter (Eds.), *A national approach to schooling in Australia? Essays on the development of national policies in schools education*. Canberra, Australia: Australian College of Education.

Koh, A., & Kenway, J. (2012). Cultivating national leaders in an elite school: Deploying the transational in the national interest. *International Studies in Sociology of Education, 22*(4), 333–351.

Kooiman, J. (2003). *Governing as governance*. London: Sage.

Kozol, J. (1968). *Death at an early age*. London: Penguin.

Kwan, P., & Walker, A. (2009). Are we looking through the same lens? Principal recruitment and selection. *International Journal of Educational Research, 48*(1), 51–61.

Ladwig, J. (1996). *Academic distinctions: Theory and methodology in the sociology of school knowledge*. New York: Routledge.

Lareau, A. (2000). *Home advantage: Social class and parental intervention in elementary education* (2nd ed.). London, Boulder, New York & Oxford: Rowman & Littlefield.

Lareau, A. (2003). *Unequal childhoods: Class, race and family life*. Berkeley: University of California Press.

Lather, P. (2007). *Getting lost: Feminist efforts toward a double(d) science*. New York: State University of New York Press.

Leadbetter, C. (2004). *Personalisation through participation: A new script for public services*. London: Demos.

Lebaron, F. (2009). How Bourdieu quantified: The geometric modelling of data. In Robson, K., & Sanders, C. (Eds.), *Quantifying theory: Pierre Bourdieu* (pp. 11–30). Dordrecht: Springer.

Leithwood, K., Day, C., Sammons, P., Harris, A., & Hopkins, D. (2006). *Seven strong claims about successful school leadership*. Nottingham: NCSL.

Leithwood, K., & Jantzi, D. (2005). A review of transformational school leadership research 1996–2005. *Leadership and Policy in Schools, 4*, 177–199.

Leithwood, K., & Reihl, C. (2003). *What we know about successful school leadership*. Nottingham: National College for School Leadership.

Levin, H. (1970). *A new model of school effectiveness*. Stanford, CA: Stanford University.

Liker, J. (2004). *The Toyota way: 14 management principles from the world's greatest manaufacturer*. New York: McGraw Hill.

Lingard, B., & Christie, P. (2003). Leading theory: Bourdieu and the field of educational leadership: An introduction and overview to this special issue. *International Journal of Leadership in Education, 6*(4), 317–333.

Lingard, B., Christie, P., Hayes, D., & Mills, M. (2003). *Leading learning: Making hope practical in schools*. Buckingham: Open University Press.

Lingard, B., & Rawolle, S. (2004b). Mediatising education policy: The journalistic field, science policy and cross-field effects. *Journal of Education Policy, 19*(6), 353–372.

Lingard, B., & Rawolle, S. (2013). *Bourdieu and the field of education policy: Understanding globalisation, mediatisation, implementation*. London: Routledge.

Lingard, B., Rawolle, S., & Taylor, S. (2005). Globalising policy sociology in education: Working with Bourdieu. *Journal of Education Policy, 20*(6), 759–777.

150 *References*

Lingard, B., Sellar, S., & Baroutsis, A. (2015). Researching the habitus of global policy actors in education. *Cambridge Journal of Education, 45*(1), 25–42.

Lingard, B., Thompson, G., & Sellar, S. (Eds.). (2015). *National testing in schools: An Australian perspective*. London: Routledge.

Loader, D. (1997). *The inner principal*. London: Falmer.

Lovell, T. (2000). Thinking feminism with and against Bourdieu. *Feminist Theory, 1*(1), 11–32.

Lubienski, C., & Weitzel, P. (Eds.). (2010). *The charter school experiment: Expectations, evidence and implications*. Boston: (Vol. Harvard Education Press).

Luke, A. (1992). The body literate: Discourse and inscription in early literacy training. *Linguistics and Education, 4*(1), 107–129.

Lumby, J., Crow, G., & Pashiardis, P. (2008). *International handbook on the preparation and development of school leaders*. London: Routledge.

Lumby, J., & English, F. (2010). *Leadership as lunacy and other metaphors for educational leadership*. Thousand Oaks: Corwin.

Lupton, R. (2003). *Poverty street: The dynamics of neighbourhood decline and renewal*. Bristol, UK: The Policy Press.

Lupton, R. (2004). *Schools in disadvantaged areas: Recognising context and raising performance. CASE paper 76*. London: Centre for Analysis of Social Exclusion, London School of Economics.

Lyman, L., Strachan, J., & Lazaridou, A. (Eds.). (2012). *Shaping social justice leadership. Insights of women educators worldwide*. Lanham, CO: Rowman & Littlefield.

Macbeath, J. (2006). *School inspection and self-evaluation: Working with the new relationship*. London: Routledge.

Macbeath, J., & Mortimore, P. (Eds.). (2001). *Improving school effectiveness*. London: RoutledgeFalmer.

MacBeath, J., Oduro, G., Jacka, J., & Hobby, R. (2006). *Leading appointments: The selection and appointment of headteachers and senior leaders: A review of the literature*. Nottingham: NCSL.

Maguire, M., Ball, S., & MacRae, S. (2001). 'In all our interests': Internal marketing at Northwark Park School. *British Journal of Sociology of Education, 22*(1), 35–50.

Maguire, S., & Robinson, J. (2006). Two years on: The destinations of young people not in education, employment or training at 16. *Journal of Youth Studies, 8*(2), 187–201.

Mahony, P., & Zmroczek, C. (1997). *Class matters: "Working class" women's perspectives on social class*. London: Taylor and Francis.

Manning, P. K., & Cullum-Swan, B. (1998). Narrative, content, and semiotic analysis. In N. K. Denzin & Y. S. Lincoln (Eds.), *Collecting and interpreting qualitative materials* (pp. 246–274). London, New York and New Delhi: Sage.

Marginson, S. (1997). *Markets in education*. Sydney: Allen and Unwin.

Marginson, S. (2008). Global field and global imagining: Bourdieu and worldwide higher education. *British Journal of Sociology of Education, 29*(3), 303–315.

Martin, J. L., & George, M. (2006). Theories of sexual stratification: Towards an analytics of the sexual field and a theory of sexual capital. *Sociological Theory, 24*(2), 107–132.

Maton, K. (2005). A question of autonomy: Bourdieu's field approach and higher eduction policy. *Journal of Education Policy, 20*(6), 687–704.

Maton, K. (2014). *Knowledge and knowers: Towards a realist sociology of education*. London: Routledge.

References 151

McDowell, L. (2000). Learning to serve? Employment aspirations and attitudes of young working class men in an era of labour market restructuring. *Gender, Place and Culture, 7*(4), 389–416.

McGinity, R., & Gunter, H. (2012). Living improvement 2: A case study of a secondary school in England. *Improving Schools, 15*(3), 228–244.

McInerney, P. (2005). *Making hope practical: School reform for social justice.* Brisbane: Postpressed.

McKenley, J., & Gordon, G. (2002). *Challenge plus: The experience of black and minority ethnic school leaders.* Nottingham: NCSL.

McKenzie, L. (2014). *Getting by: Estates, class and culture in austerity Britain.* Bristol: Policy Press.

McLaughlin, T. (1996). *Street smarts and critical theory: Listening to the vernacular.* Madison, Wisconsin: University of Wisconsin Press.

Mclean, M., & Abbas, A. (2011). The 'biographical turn' in university sociology teaching: A Bersteinian analysis. *Teaching in Higher Education, 14*(5), 529–539.

McLeod, J. (2005). Feminists re-reading Bourdieu: Old debates and new questions about gender habitus and gender change. *Theory and Research in Education, 3*(1), 11–30.

McNay, L. (2008). *Against recognition.* Cambridge: Polity Press.

Meier, D. (1995). *The power of their ideas: Lessons for America from a small school in Harlem.* Boston: Beacon Press.

Meier, D. (2002). *In schools we trust: Creating acts of learning in an era of testing and standardisation.* Boston: Beacon Press.

Meier, D., Sizer, T., & Sizer, N. (2004). *Keeping school: Letters to families from principals of two small schools.* Boston: Beacon Press.

Melville, W., Hardy, I., Weinburgh, M., & Bartley, A. (2014). A logic of "linking learning": Leadership practices across schools, subjects departments and classrooms. *Cogent Education, 1*(1), 1–18.

Mitchell, C., & Sackney, L. (Eds.). (2000). *Profound improvement: Building capacity for a learning community.* The Netherlands: Swets & Zeitlinger.

Moi, T. (1991). Appropriating Bourdieu: Feminist theory and Pierre Bourdieu's sociology of culture. *New Literary History, 22*(4), 1017–1049.

Monroe, L. (1997). *Nothing's impossible: Leadership lessons from inside and outside the classroom.* New York: Public Affairs.

Moos, L., & Macbeath, J. (2004). *Democratic learning: The challenge to school effectiveness.* London: RoutledgeFalmer.

Morgan, C., Hall, V., & Mackay, H. (1983). *The selection of secondary school headteachers.* Milton Keynes: Open University Press.

Morgan, R. (2003). *A country report: Australia's experience in self-managing schools: A case study based on experience in a self-governing school for nearly fifty years.* Paper presented at the World Reform Conference, Bangkok, Thailand. http://www.worldreform.com/intercon3/third/f-rexmorgan.pdf. Accessed 12 April, 2009.

Morris, E. (2011, 25 October). Stephen Twigg will not rush to judge on Education Policy. *Education Guardian.* Available at http://www.guardian.co.uk/education/2011/oct/24/stephen-twigg-free-schools-education-policy. Accessed 1st March 2012.

Morrison, M. (2009). *Leadership and learning: Matters of social justice.* Charlotte, NC: Information Age Publishing.

152 *References*

Mouzelis, N. (2010). Habitus and reflexivity: Restructuring Bourdieu's theory of practice. *Sociological Research Online, 12*(6), http://www.socresonline.org.uk/12/16/19.html. Accessed August 26, 2012.

Murphy, J. (2002). Reculturing the profession of educational leadership: New blueprints. In J. Murphy (Ed.), *Yearbook of the National Society for the Study of Education* (pp. 65–82). New York: National Society for the Study of Education.

Murphy, J. (2005). Unpacking the foundations of ISLLC Standards and addressing concerns in the academic community. *Educational Administration Quarterly, 41*(1), 154–191.

Murphy, J., & Louis, K. S. (Eds.). (1999). *Handbook of research on educational administration. Second Edition: A project of the American Educational Research Association.* San Francisco: Jossey Bass.

Murphy, M. (Ed.) (2013). *Socal theory and educational research: Understanding Foucault, Habermas, Bourdieu and Derrida.* London: Routledge.

Murphy, M., & Costa, C. (Eds.). (2015). *Bourdieu, habitus and social resarch: The art of application.* London: Palgrave Macmillan.

Murphy, M., & Costa, C. (Eds.). (2016). *Theory as method in research: Bourdieu, social theory and education.* London: Routledge.

Naidoo, R. (2004). Fields and institutional strategy: Bourdieu on the relationship between higher education, inequality and society. *British Journal of Sociology of Education, 25*(4), 457–471.

Nash, R. (1999). Bourdieu, habitus and educational research: Is it all worth a candle? *British Journal of Sociology of Education, 20*(2), 175–187.

National College for School Leadership. (2002). *Making the difference: Successful leadership in challenging contexts.* Nottingham: NCSL.

National College for School Leadership. (2005). *Executive headship: A study of heads who are leading two or more secondary or special schools.* Nottingham: NCSL.

Newman, J. (2001). *Modernising governance: New Labour, policy and society.* London: Sage.

Niesche, R. (2011). *Foucault and educational leadership: Disciplining the principal.* London: Routledge.

Niesche, R., & Thomson, P. (in press). Freedom to what ends – school autonomy in neoliberal times. In F. English & D. Waite (Eds.), *The International handbook of school leadership.* New York: Wiley Blackwell.

Normore, A. H. (Ed.) (2008). *Leadership for social justice: Promoting equity and excellence through inquiry and reflective practice.* Charlotte, North Carolina: Information Age Publishing.

Offe, C. (1996). *Modernity and the State: East, West.* Cambridge: Polity.

Osborne, D., & Gaebler, T. (1993). *Reinventing government: How the entrepreneurial spirit is transforming the public sector.* New York: Plume, Penguin.

Ozga, J. (2009). Governing education through data in England: From regulation to self evaluation. *Journal of Education Policy, 24*(2), 149–162.

Penn, H. (2002). "Maintains a good pace to lessons": Inconsistencies and contextual factors affecting Ofsted inspections of nursery schools. *British Educational Research Journal, 28*(6), 879–888.

Perry, L.-A. (2006). *The impact of risk management on the changing nature of principal's work. Ed D dissertation.* Queensland University of Technology, Brisbane.

Perry, L.-A., & McWilliam, E. (2007). Accountability, responsibility and school leadership. *Journal of Educational Enquiry, 7*(1), 32–43.

Perryman, J. (2005). School leadership and management after Special Measures: discipline without the gaze? *School Leadership & Management, 25*(3), 281–297.

Peters, R. S. (Ed.) (1976a). Introduction: the contemporary problem. In *The role of the head* (pp. 1–8). London: Routledge & Kegan Paul.

Peters, R. S. (Ed.) (1976b). *The role of the head.* London: Routledge & Kegan Paul.

Pierre, J. (1999). Models of urban governance: The institutional dimensions of urban politics. *Urban Affairs Review, 34*(3), 372–396.

Pierre, J., & Peters, B. G. (2000). *Governance, politics and the state.* New York: St Martins Press.

Piketty, T. (2014). *Capital in the twenty first century.* Boston, MA: Harvard University Press.

Piven, F. F. (1992). Reforming the welfare state. *Socialist Review, 22*(1), 69–82.

Plummer, G. (2000). *Failing working class girls.* Stoke on Trent: Trentham Books.

Pollitt, C. (2011). *Public management reform: A comparative analysis: New public management, governance and the neo-Weberian state* (3rd ed.). Oxford: Oxford University Press.

Popkewitz, T. (1996). Rethinking decentralisation and the state/civil society distinctions: The state as a problematic of governing. *Journal of Education Policy, 11*(1), 27–51.

Portelli, J., & Foreman, D. (Eds.). (2015). *Key questions for educational leaders.* Burlington, ON: Edphil Books.

Portes, A. (1998). Social capital: Its origins and applications in modern sociology. *Annual Review of Sociology, 24,* 1–24.

Poster, C. (1976). *School decision making: Educational management in secondary schools.* London: Heinemann Educational.

PricewaterhouseCoopers. (2008). *Academies evaluation: Fifth annual report.* DCSF: London.

Pusey, M. (1991). *Economic rationalism in Canberra: A nation building state changes its mind.* Cambridge: Cambridge University Press.

Putnam, R. (1993). *Making democracy work: Civic traditions in modern Italy.* Princeton: Princeton University Press.

Putnam, R. (2000). *Bowling alone: The collapse and revival of American community.* New York: Simon & Schuster.

Raco, M. (2002). The social relations of organisational activity and new local governance in the UK. *Urban Studies, 39*(3), 437–456.

Rae, J. (2009). *The old boys network: A headmaster's diaries 1970–1986.* London: Short Books.

Raffo, C., Dyson, A., Gunter, H., Hall, D., Jones, L., & Kalambouka, A. (2008). *Education and poverty: A critical review of theory, policy and practice.* New York: Joseph Rowntree Foundation.

Ranson, S. (2006). *Governance, good practice and service structures: State of knowledge. Paper 8 on governance and engagement.* Birmingham: University of Birmingham.

Ranson, S. (2012). The state and education policy: The academies programme. *Journal of Education Policy, 27*(5), 694–696.

Ravitch, D. (2011). *The death and life o the great American school system: How testing and choice are undermining education.* New York: Basic Books.

154 *References*

Rawolle, S., & Lingard, B. (2013). Bourdieu and educaional research: Thinking tools, relational thinking, beyond epistemological innocence. In M. Murphy (Ed.), *Social theory and education research: Understanding Foucault, Habermas, Bourdieu and Derrida* (pp. 117–137). London: Routledge.

Rawolle, S., Rowlands, J., & Blackmore, J. (2015). The implications of contractualism for the responsibilisation of higher education. *Discourse*, DOI:10.1080/0159 6306.2015.1104856.

Reay, D. (1998a). 'Always knowing' and 'never being sure': Familial and institutional habituses and higher education choice. *Journal of Education Policy, 13*(4), 519–529.

Reay, D. (1998b). *Class work: Mother's involvement in their children's schooling*. London: University College Press.

Reay, D. (1998c). Engendering social reproduction: Mothers in the educational marketplace 11. *British Journal of Sociology of Education, 19*(2), 195–209.

Reay, D. (1998d). Surviving in dangerous places: Working class women, women's studies and higher education. *Women's Studies International Forum, 2*(1), 11–19.

Reay, D. (1999). Linguistic capital and home-school relationships: Mother's interactions with their children's primary school teachers. *Acta Sociologica, 42*(2), 159–168.

Reay, D. (2001a). Finding or losing yourself? Working class relationships to education. *Journal of Education Policy, 16*(4), 333–346.

Reay, D. (2001b). A useful extension of Bourdieu's conceptual framework? Emotional capital as a way of understanding mother's involvement in their children's education? *The Sociological Review, 48*(4), 568–585.

Reay, D. (2004). 'It's all becoming a habitus': Beyond the habitual use of habitus in educational research. *British Journal of Sociology of Education, 25*(4), 431–444.

Reay, D., & Ball, S. (2000). Essentials of female management: Women's ways of working in the education market place? *Educational Management and Administration, 28*(2), 145–159.

Reay, D., Crozier, G., & Clayton, J. (2009). 'Strangers in paradise'? Working class students in elite universities. *Sociology, 43*(6), 1103–1121.

Reay, D., David, M., & Ball, S. (2005). *Degrees of choice: Class, race, gender and higher education*. Stoke on Trent: Trentham.

Reay, D., & Lucey, H. (2000a). Children, school choice and social differences. *Educational Studies, 26*(1), 83–100.

Reay, D., & Lucey, H. (2000b). "I don't really like it here but I don't want to be anywhere else": Children and inner city housing estates. *Antipode, 32*(4), 410–428.

Reay, D., & Wiliam, D. (1999). "I'll be a nothing': Structure, agency and the construction of identity through assessment. *British Educational Research Journal, 25*(3), 343–354.

Reed-Danahay, D. (2005). *Locating Bourdieu*. Bloomington, ID: Indiana University Press.

Rhodes, R. A. W. (1994). The hollowing out of the state: The changing nature of the public service in Britain. *The Political Quarterly, 65*(2), 138–151.

Ribbins, P. (1999). Producing portraits of leaders in education: Cultural relativism and methodological absolutism? *Leading and Managing, 5*(2), 78–99.

Ribbins, P., & Gunter, H. (2002). Mapping leadership studies in education towards a typology of knowledge domains. *Educational Management & Administration, 30*(4), 359–385.

References   155

Riddell, R. (2003). *Schools for our cities: Urban learning in the 21st century*. Stoke on Trent: Trentham.

Rikowski, G. (2007). Bourdieu on capital. http://www.flowideas.co.uk/print.php?page=314 Accessed December 1, 2012

Riley, K. (1998). Creating the leadership climate. *International Journal of Leadership in Education, 1*(2), 137–153.

Rizvi, F., & Lingard, B. (2009). *Globalising education policy*. London: Routledge.

Robertson, J. (1999). Principals working with principals: Keeping education at the centre of practice. *SET, One*(9), 1–4.

Robinson, R., & Garnier, M. (2000). Class reproduction among men and women in France: Reproduction theory on its home ground. In D. Robbins (Ed.), *Pierre Bourdieu* (pp. 144–153). London: Sage.

Robinson, V. (2007). *School leadership and student outcomes: Identifying what works and why*. Melbourne: Australian Council for Educational Leaders.

Robinson, V., & Hargreaves, A. (2011). *Student centered leadership*. San Francisco, CA: Jossey-Bass.

Rose, N. (1991). Governing by numbers: Figuring out democracy. *Accounting, Organisations and Society, 16*(7), 673–692.

Rose, N. (1993). Government, authority and expertise in advanced liberalism. *Economy and Society, 22*(3), 288–299.

Rutter, M., Mortimore, P., & Maugham, B. (1979). *Fifteen thousand hours: Secondary schools and their effects*. Boston: Harvard University Press.

Ryan, J. (2005). *Inclusive leadership*. San Francisco, CA: Jossey Bass.

Sahlberg, P. (2006). Raising the bar: How Finland responds to the twin challenges of secondary education. *Profesorado: Revista de curiculum y formacion del profesorado, 10*(1), 1–26.

Sahlberg, P. (2012). *Finnish lessons: What can the world learn from educational change in Finland?* London: Routledge.

Samier, E., & Bates, R. (Eds.). (2006). *Aesthetic dimensions of educational administration and leadership*. London: Routledge.

Sandlin, J., Schultz, B., & Burdick, J. (Eds.). (2010). *Handbook of public pedagogy*. New York: Routledge.

Savage, G. C. (2012). *Imagination, governance, community: Making education, making difference*. Melbourne, VA: University of Melbourne.

Sayer, A. (1999). Bourdieu, Smith and disinterested judgment. *The Scoiological Review, 47*(3), 403–431.

Seddon, J. (2003). *Freedom from command and control: A better way to make the work work*. New York: Vanguard Publishing.

Seddon, T. (1997). Markets and the English: Rethinking educational restructuring as institutional design. *British Journal of Sociology of Education, 18*(2), 165–185.

Sergiovanni, T. (1992). *Moral leadership: Getting to the heart of school improvement*. San Fransisco: Jossey Bass.

Sharp, R., & Green, A. (1975). *Education and social class*. London: Routledge & Kegan Paul.

Sheffield, J. (2007). *Teacher, teacher! The alternative school log book 1977–1978*. London: Corgi.

Sheffield, J. (2008). *Mister teacher: The alternative school log book 1978–1979*. London: Corgi.

156   *References*

Shields, C., & Edwards, M. (2005). *Dialogue is not just talk: A new ground for educational leadership*. New York: Peter Lang.

Simmons, R., & Thompson, R. (2011). *NEET young people and training for work: Learning on the margins*. Stoke on Trent: Trentham Books.

Sirianni, C., & Friedland, L. (1995). Social capital and civic innovation: Learning and capacity building from the 1960s to the 1990s. http://epn,org/cpn/sections/new_citizenship/theory/socialcapital_civicinnov.html. Accessed 3 May 1996.

Skeggs, B. (1997). *Formations of class and gender: Becoming respectable*. London: Sage Publications.

Skinner, B. F. (1968). *The technology of teaching*. Englewood Cliffs, NJ: Prentice Hall.

Skorobohacz, C., Billiot, J., Murray, S., & Khong, L. (2016). Metaphors as expressions of followers' experiences with academic leadership. *Higher Education Research & Development, 35*(5), 1053–1067.

Skrla, L., & Scheurich, J. J. (Eds.). (2003). *Educational equity and accountability: Policies, paradigms and politics*. New York: RoutledgeFalmer.

Slee, R. (1995). *Changing theories and practices of discipline*. London: Falmer.

Slee, R., Weiner, G., & Tomlinson, S. (Eds.). (1998). *School effectiveness for whom? Challenges to the school effectiveness and school improvement movements*. London: Falmer.

Smithson, A. (1983). Kaminsky's addendum to the "freedom and authority" memorandum: A philosophical investigation in a contextual vacuum. *Journal of Educational Administration, 21*(1), 79–92.

Smulyan, L. (2000). *Balancing acts: Women principals at work*. New York: State University of New York Press.

Smyth, J. (Ed.) (1993). *A socially critical view of the self managing school*. London: Falmer Press.

Smyth, J., & Hattam, R. (2004). *Dropping out, drifting off, being excluded: Becoming somebody without school*. New York: Peter Lang.

Sorens, J. (2000). The failure to converge: Why globalisation doesn't cause deregulation. *Critical Review: A Journal of Politics and Society, 14*(1), 19–33.

Southworth, G. (1995). *Looking into primary headship: A research based interpretation*. London: The Falmer Press.

Southworth, G. (1998). Change and continuity in the work of primary headteachers in England. *International Journal of Educational Research, 29*, 311–321.

Southworth, G. (1999). Continuities and changes in primary headship. In T. Bush, L. Bell, R. Bolam, R. Glatter, & P. Ribbins (Eds.), *Educational Management. Redefining Theory, Policy and Practice* (pp. 29–42). London: Paul Chapman Publishers.

Spillane, J. (2006). *Distributed leadership*. San Francisco, CA: Jossey Bass.

Spillane, J., & Diamond, J. B. (Eds.). (2007). *Distributed leadership in practice*. New York: Teachers College Press.

Stahl, G. (2013). Habitus disjunctures, reflexivity and white working class boys' conceptions of status in learner and status identities. *Sociological Research Online, 18*(3), http://www.socresonline.org.uk/18/13/12.html. Accessed August 18, 2014.

Stahl, G. (2015). *Identity, neoliberalism and aspiration: Educating white working class boys*. London: Routledge.

Starr, K. (2001). *The roar behind the silence: Women principals and their work*. Unpublished doctoral thesis. Adelaide: University of South Australia.

Starratt, R. (2003). *Centering educational administration: Cultivating meaning, community, responsibility*. Mahwah, NJ: Lawrence Erlbaum.

References 157

Stenson, K., & Watt, P. (1999). Governmentality and the "the death of the social"? A discourse analysis of local government texts in South-east England. *Urban Studies, 36*(1), 189–201.

Stoker, G. (1998). Governance as theory: Five propositions. *International Social Science Journal, 50*(1), 17–28.

Stoll, L., & Fink, D. (1996). *Changing our schools: Linking school effectiveness and school improvement.* Buckingham: Open University Press.

Stoll, L., & Myers, K. (Eds.). (1998). *No quick fixes: Perspectives on schools in difficulty.* London: Falmer.

Strachan, J. (1993). Including the personal and the professional: Researching women in educational leadership. *Gender and Education, 5*(1), 71–80.

Strachan, J. (1999). Feminist educational leadership in a New Zealand neo-liberal context. *Journal of Educational Administration, 37*(2), 121–138.

Stubbs, M. (2003). *Ahead of the class: How an inspiring headmistress gave children back their future.* London: John Murray.

Swartz, D. (2010). Pierre Bourdieu's political sociology and public sociology. In E. Silva & A. Warde (Eds.), *Cultural analysis and Bourdieu's legacy: Settling accounts and developing alternatives* (pp. 45–59). London: Routledge.

Swyngedouw, E. (2005). Governance innovaton and the citizen: The Janus face of governance-beyond-the-state. *Urban Studies, 42*(11), 1192–2006.

Syal, R. (2012, January 20). Cameron's 'bonfire of the quangoes' to cost double original estimate. *The Guardian*, pp. http://www.guardian.co.uk/politics/2012/jan/2020/cameron-bonfire-quangos-double-estimate. Accessed June 6, 2012.

Symes, C. (1998). Education for sale: A semiotic analysis of school prospectuses and other forms of educational marketing. *Australian Journal of Education, 42*(2), 133–152.

Taylor, C. (1994). *Multiculturalism and "the politics of recognition".* Princeton: Princeton University Press.

Taylor, C. (2000, September 7–10). *Hierarchies and 'local' markets: The geography of the 'lived' market place in secondary education provision.* Paper presented at the British Education Research Association, Cardiff.

Taylor, F. W. (1911/1947). *Scientific management.* New York: Harper & Brothers.

Taylor, M. (2007). Community participation in the real world? Opportunities and pitfalls in new governance spaces. *Urban Studies, 44*(2), 297–317.

Teddlie, C., & Reynolds, D. (Eds.). (2000). *The international handbook of school effectiveness.* London: Falmer.

Teese, R. (2000). *Academic success and social power.* Melbourne: Melbourne University Press.

Teese, R., Davies, M., Charlton, M., & Polesel, J. (1995). *Who wins at school? Boys and girls in Australian secondary education.* Melbourne: Melbourne University Press.

Teese, R., & Polesal, J. (Eds.). (2003). *Undemocratic schooling: Equity and quality in mass secondary education in Australia.* Sydney: Allen & Unwin.

Thatcher, J., Ingram, N., Burke, C., & Abrahams, J. (Eds.). (2016). *Bourdieu: The next generation: The development of Bourdieu's intellectual heritage in contemporary times.* London: Routledge.

Thomas, G. (2007). *Education and theory: Strangers in paradigms.* Maidenhead: Open University Press.

Thomas, L. (2002). Student retention in higher education: The role of institutional habitus. *Journal of Education Policy, 17*(4), 423–442.

158 *References*

Thompson, G., & Cook, I. (2014). Manipulating the data: Teaching and NAPLAN in the control society. *Discourse, 35*(1), 129–142.

Thomson, P. (1994). *Local decision making and management.* South Australian Secondary Principals Association: Adelaide, South Australia.:

Thomson, P. (1998). Thoroughly modern management and a cruel accounting: The effect of public sector reform on public education. In A. Reid (Ed.), *Going Public: Education policy and public education in Australia* (pp. 37–46). Canberra: Australian Curriculum Studies Association.

Thomson, P. (2000). Like schools, educational disadvantage and 'thisness'. *Australian Educational Researcher, 27*(3), 151–166.

Thomson, P. (2002). *Schooling the rustbelt kids: Making the difference in changing times.* Sydney: Allen & Unwin (Trentham Books UK).

Thomson, P. (2005). Bringing Bourdieu to policy sociology: Codification, misrecognition and exchange value in the UK context. *Journal of Education Policy, 20*(6), 741–758.

Thomson, P. (2008a). Answering back to policy? Headteachers' stress and the logic of the sympathetic interview. *Journal of Education Policy, 23*(6), 649–668.

Thomson, P. (2008b). Leading schools in high poverty neighbourhoods: The National College for School Leadership and beyond. In W. Pink & W. Noblit (Eds.), *The international handbook of urban education* (pp. 1049–1078). Dordrecht: Springer.

Thomson, P. (2009). *School leadership – heads on the block?* London: Routledge.

Thomson, P. (2010a). Bringing Bourdieu to 'widening prticipation policies in higher education: A UK case analysis. In M. Apple, S. Ball, & L. A. Gandin (Eds.), *The Routledge handbook of the sociology of education* (pp. 318–328). London: Routledge.

Thomson, P. (2010b). Headteacher autonomy: A sketch of Bourdieuian field analysis of position and practice. *Critical Studies in Education, 51*(1), 1–16.

Thomson, P. (2011a). Creative leadership: A new category or more of the same? *Journal of Educational Administration and History, 43*(4), 249–272.

Thomson, P. (2011b). 'The local' and its authority: The coalition, governance and democracy. In R. Hatcher & K. Jones (Eds.), *No country for the young: Education from new labour to the Coalition* (pp. 85–99). London: Tuffnell Press.

Thomson, P. (2011c). *Whole school change: A reading of the literatures* (2nd ed.). London: Creative Partnerships, Arts Council England.

Thomson, P. (2014). 'Scaling up' educational change: Some musings on misrecognition and doxic challenges. *Critical Studies in Education, 55*(2), 87–103.

Thomson, P., Blackmore, J., Sachs, J., & Tregenza, K. (2003). High stakes principalship: Sleepless nights, heart attacks and sudden death accountabilities: Reading media representations of the US principal shortage. *Australian Journal of Education, 47*(2), 118–132.

Thomson, P., & Hall, C. (2008). Opportunities missed and/or thwarted? 'Funds of knowledge' meets the English national curriculum. *Curriculum Journal. 19*(2), 87–103.

Thomson, P., Hall, C., & Jones, K. (2010). Maggie's day: A small scale analysis of English education policy. *Journal of Education Policy, 25*(5), 639–656.

Thomson, P., & Holdsworth, R. (2003). Theorising change in the educational 'field': Re-readings of 'student participation' projects. *International Journal of Leadership in Education, 6*(4), 371–391.

Thomson, P., Jones, K., & Hall, C. (2009). *Creative whole school change: Final report.* London: Creativity, Culture and Education Arts Council England.

References 159

Thomson, P., & Russell, L. (2009). Data data everywhere: But not the ones that count? Mapping the provision of alternatives to exclusion. *International Journal of Inclusive Education, 13*(4), 423–438.

Thornton, S. (1996). *Club cultures: Music, media and subcultural capital.* Middletown, CT: Wesleyan University Press.

Thrupp, M. (1998). Exploring the politics of blame: School inspection and its contestation in New Zealand and England. *Comparative Education, 34*(2), 195–208.

Thrupp, M. (1999). *Schools making a difference: Lets be realistic! School mix, school effectiveness and the social limits of reform.* Buckingham: Open University Press.

Thrupp, M. (2005a). The National College for School Leadership: A critique. *Management Education, 19*(2), 13–19.

Thrupp, M. (2005b). *School improvement: An unofficial approach.* London: Continuum.

Thrupp, M., & Wilmott, R. (2003). *Educational management in managerialist times: Beyond the textual apologists.* Buckingham: Open University Press.

Tillman, L., & Scheurich, J. J. (Eds.). (2013). *Handbok of research on educational leadership for equity and diversity.* New York: Routledge.

Tomlinson, H. (2004). *Educational leadership: Personal growth for professional development.* London: Sage.

Tomlinson, S. (2001). *Education in post-welfare society.* Buckingham: Open University Press.

Tompkins, J. (1998). *Teaching in a cold and windy place: Change in an Inuit school.* Toronto: University of Toronto Press.

Tooley, J., & Darby, D. (1998). *Educational research: A critique.* London: Ofsted.

Tranter, S. (undated). *Talent spotting: Recognising and developing leadership potential.* Nottingham: NCSL.

Triventi, M. (2013). Stratification in higher education and its relationship with social inequality: A comparative study of 11 European countries. *European Sociological Review, 29*(3), 489–502.

Venugopal, R. (2015). Neoliberalism as a concept. *Economy and Society, 44*(2), 165–187.

Verter, B. (2003). Spiritual capital: Theorising religion with Bourdieu against Bourdieu. *Sociological Theory, 21*(2), 150–174.

Vickers, M., & Kouzmin, A. (2001). New managerialism and Australian police organisations. *The International Journal of Public Sector Management, 14*(1), 7–26.

Wacquant, L. (1989). Towards a reflexive sociology: A workshop with Pierre Bourdieu. *Sociological Theory, 7*(1), 26–63.

Wacquant, L. (2004). *Body and soul: Notebooks of an apprentice boxer.* New York: Oxford University Press.

Wacquant, L. (Ed.) (2005). *Pierre Bourdieu and democratic politics.* Cambridge: Polity.

Wacquant, L. (2016). A concise geneology and anatomy of habitus. *The Sociological Review, 64*, 64–72.

Walker, A., Stott, K., & Cheng, Y. C. (2003). Principal supply and quality demands: A tale of two Asia-pacific states. *Australian Journal of Education, 47*(2), 197–208.

Walkerdine, V., Lucey, H., & Melody, J. (2001). *Growing up girl: Psychosocial explorations of gender and class.* London: Palgrave.

Wang, Y., & Bowers, A. (2016). Mapping the field of educational administration research: A journal citation network analysis. *Journal of Educational Administration, 54*(3), 242–269.

160 *References*

Waters, D. (1979). *Management and headship in the primary school*. London: Ward Lock Educational.

Watts, J. (1976). Sharing it out: The role of the head in participatory government. In R. S. Peters (Ed.), *The role of the head* (pp. 127–136). London: Routledge & Kegan Paul.

Weindling, D. (2004). *Funding for research on school leadership*. Nottingham: National College for School Leadership.

Welch, A. R. (1998). The cult of efficiency in education: Comparative reflections on the reality and rhetoric. *Comparative Education, 34*(2), 157–175.

West, M., Ainscow, M., & Stanford, J. (2006). Achieving sustainable improvements in urban schools. In M. Ainscow & M. West (Eds.), *Improving urban schools: Leadership and collaboration* (pp. 46–57). Buckingham: Open University Press.

West-Burnham, J. (2005). Leadership for personalisation. In J. West-Burnham & C. Max (Eds.), *Personalised learning: Transforming education for every child* (pp. 98–114). Stafford: Network Educational Press.

Whitaker, K. S. (2003). Principal role changes and influence on principal recruitment and selection: An international perspective. *Journal of Educational Administration, 41*(1), 37–54.

Whitaker, P. (1983). *The primary head*. London: Heinemann Educational Books.

Whitehead, S. (1998). Disrupted selves: Resistance and identity work in the managerial area. *Gender and Education, 10*(2), 199–216.

Whitty, G. (2002). *Making sense of education policy*. London: Paul Chapman Publishing.

Whitty, G., Anders, J., Hayton, A., Tang, S., & Wisby, E. (2016). *Research and policy in education*. London: UCL IOE Press.

Whitty, G., Power, S., & Halpin, D. (1998). *Devolution and choice in education: The school, the state and the market*. Buckingham: Open University Press.

Wilkins, A. (2011). School choice and the commodification of education: A visual approach to school brochures and wesbites. *Critical Social Policy, 32*(1), 69–86.

Williams, B., Woodby, L., & Drentea, P. (2010). Ethical capital: "What's a poor man got to leave?' *Sociology of Health and Illness, 32*(6), 880–897.

Williams, S. J. (1995). Theorising class, health and lifestyle: Can Bourdieu help us? *Sociology of Health and Illness, 17*(5), 577–604.

Winkley, D. (2002). *Handsworth revolution: The odyssey of a school*. London: Giles De La Mare.

Wolcott, H. (1973). *The man in the principal's office: An ethnography*. Prospect Heights, ILL: Waveland Press.

Woodrow, C., & Brennan, M. (1999). Marketised positioning of early childhood: New contexts for curriculum and professional development in Queensland, Australia. *Contemporary Issues in Early Childhood, 1*(1), 78–94.

Woods, P. (2005). *Democratic leadership in education*. London: Paul Chapman.

Woods, P., Woods, G., & Gunter, H. (2007). Academy schools and entrepreneurialism in education. *Journal of Education Policy, 22*(2), 237–259.

World Bank Social Capital Initiative. (1999). Working paper five: Social capital: Conceptual frameworks and empirical evidence. *An annotated bibliography*. http://www.worldbank.org/poverty/scapital/wkrppr/index.htm. Accessed June 16, 2012.

Wrigley, T. (2004). 'School effectiveness': The problem of reductionism. *British Educational Research Journal, 30*(2), 227–244.

Wrigley, T. (2006). Schools and poverty: Questioning the effectiveness and improvement paradigms. *Improving Schools, 9*(3), 273–290.

Wylie, C. (1999). *Ten years on: How schools view educational reform*. Wellington: New Zealand Council for Educational Research.

Yeatman, A. (1990). *Bureaucrats, technocrats, femocrats: Essays on the contemporary Australian state*. Sydney: Allen and Unwin.

Yeatman, A. (1993). Corporate managerialism and the shift from the welfare to the competition state. *Discourse, 13*(2), 3–10.

York-Barr, J., & Duke, K. (2004). What do we know about teacher leadership? Findings from two decades of scholarship. *Review of Educational Research, 74*(3), 255–316.

Young, M. (Ed.) (1971). *Knowledge and control*. London: Collier-MacMillan.

Zipin, L., & Brennan, M. (2003). The suppression of ethical disposiions through mangerial governmentality: A habitus crisis in Australian higher education. *International Journal of Leadership in Education, 6*(4), 351–370.

Index

Abbas, A. 10
Abrahams, J. 16, 120
academies: shift to 25, 27, 69, 77, 96, 99,100–102, 104, 106
Acker, S. 55
Addi-Raccah A. 36
Addison, B. 102
Adkins, L. 117, 126
Adonis, A. 77
Aguayo, R. 93
Ainscow, M. 41–2
Albright, J. 51
Althusser, L. 14
Amanti, C. 95
Amin, A. 91
Anders, J. 57
Anderson, G. 43, 53, 96
Anderson, L. 76
Anderson, M. 35
Apple, M. 5, 119
Archer, L. 51, 95, 123
Archer, M. 38
Arnot, M. 95, 123
Ashenden, D. 94
Astle, J. 101
Atkinson, W. 66, 120
Avis, J. 25
Ayalon, H. 36

Bacchi, C. 19
Baker, B. 96
Ball, S. 18, 24, 26, 28, 51, 54, 64, 77, 96, 97, 99, 102, 109, 119
Barber, M. 80
Barker, K. 73
Barnett, C. 24
Barth, R. 37
Bartley, A. 55
Barty, K. 36
Bates, R. 31, 36, 37, 40

Baum, F. 13
Beare, H. 64
Beasley-Murray, J. 120
Beck, L. 35
Beck, U. 112, 125
Beckett, F. 25, 102
Bell, L. 31
Bennett, N. 76
Bennett, T. 16, 123
Bennis, W. 31
Beresford, J. 40
Berliner, D. 5
Berman, B. 90
Bernbaum, G. 63
Bernstein, B. 87
Biesta, G. 57
Billiot, J. 39
Blackledge, A. 52
Blackmore, J. 10, 25, 35, 36, 43, 57, 65, 96
Blatchford, R. 33
Bloom, C. 35
Bloome, D. 51
Bobbit, J. 90
Bochner, A. 125
Boden, R. 73
Bolam, R. 31, 78
Bottero, W. 119
Bourdieu: approach to inequality 5; concern with democracy 3; early life 1–2; epistemological relativism 46; key texts on education 4; as methodology 48–50; research choices 3
Bourdieusian approach: commitment to rigour 46–47; context concerns 117–120; capitals, concerns with 120–121; concerns with 105–124; field, concerns with 117–120; and gender 117; habitus, concerns with

164 *Index*

121–123; a hypothetical study 55–59; misrecognition, concerns with 123–124; misuse of 44–45; ontological orientation 45–46; reflexivity 47–48; tensions for researchers 58–59; use in educational research 50–52; use in ELMA research 52–55
Bowe, R. 51
Bowles, S. 5
Bragg, J. 26
Braun, A. 28
Brennan, M. 26, 53
Bridges, E. 35
Briggs, A. 37, 39
Brighouse, T. 31
Bright, T. 79
Brown, M. 91
Brundrett, M. 37, 76
Burch, P. 25
Burdick, J, 51
Burke, C. 120
Bush, R. 13, 31, 32, 78
Butler, J. 123
Byrom, T. 10

Cahill, D. 24
Caldwell, B. 34, 64
Calhoun, C. 114, 120, 123, 124,126
Callahan, R. 90, 91
capitals 11–13; concerns about 120–121; cultural 11–12; economic 11; exchange of 103–110; exchange use and value 12, 13; management 88–89; symbolic 11–12
Capper, C. 36
Carrington, V. 51
Case, P. 27
Case, S. 27
Castagnoli, P. 79
Castells, M. 112
Catling, P. 27
Cerny, P. 24
Chambers, C. 117
change 17, 21–22, 116
Chapman, C, 36, 39
Charlton, M. 51
Cheng, Y, 36
Chevalier, A. 10
Chitty, C. 65
Chouliaraki, L. 76
Christie, P. 40, 43, 53
Clarke, P. 41
Clayton, J. 16
Coates, S. 34

Codd, J. 27
Cole, B. 16
Coleman, A. 39
Coleman, M. 36, 37, 39
Colley, H. 52, 122
Comber, B. 18, 68
Common, R. 73
Conlon, G. 10
Connell, R. 94, 95, 111, 112, 113
Considine, M. 73
content analysis of training framework 81–88
Cook, A. 63
Cook, I. 68
Cook, N. 79
Corrigan, P. 5
Costa, C. 52
Couldry, N. 119
Court, M. 35, 57
Courtney, S. 29, 77, 101, 109
Coz, D. 73
Crawford, M. 76, 96
Crossley, M. 122
Crossley, N. 119, 122
Crow, G. 36, 76
Crozier, G. 16
Cullingford, C. 28
Cullum-Swan, B. 81
CUREE 39
Cutler, T. 26

Daniels, D. 101
Darby, D. 122
David, M. 18
Davies, B 34
Davies, M. 51
Day, C. 33, 40, 42
Deal, T. 39
Dean, M. 24
Deem, R. 10
Deming, J.E. 92
DES 64
determinism 116–117
Devine, D. 96
DfE 101
Diamond, J. 122
Dimend, K. 122
Diment, K. 52
disciplines in ELMA 30–40
Dixon, A. 19
Dixon, J. 26
Donmoyer, R. 32
Dorling, D. 116
Dow, A. 66
Dowsett, G. 94

doxa 18
Drentea, P. 121
Drummond, M.J. 19
Du Gay, P. 29
Duke, K, 38

Eacott, S. 36, 54, 102
Earl, L. 34
Earley, P. 39, 96
Educational Effectiveness and Improvement Research (EEIR) 41–42
educational research: Bourdieusian studies 50–52
Edward, P. 53
Edwards, L. 24
Edwards, M. 36, 43
Edwards, R. 13
Eisenstein, H. 19
ELAM scholarship: and methodologies 37–42
Ellis, C. 125
Ellison, L. 34
ELMA field 31–32
ELMA research: Bourdieusian studies 52–55
ELMA scholarship 32–42; disciplinary bases 39–40; effectiveness 41–42; focus on practice 125–126; focus on time 126; a future agenda 126–128; and governing 32; improvement 41–42; positioning as scholar 124–125; questions and concerns 32–37
Elmore, R. 34
English, F. 37, 43, 54, 96
Eraut, M. 35
Erlandson, D. 35
Evans, A, 39
Evans, R. 35

Fairclough, N. 76
feel for the game 103
field 8–11; as game 11; concerns about 117; education, changes in 29–30; ELMA, characteristics of 31–32; homology 9; positions in 9; positions as sub-field 10; relative autonomy 9; of schooling 60–70, 72; three steps for analysis 49; vertical and horizontal hierarchies in 9–10, 11
Fink, D. 32, 41
Finlay, L. 125
Fitzpatrick, K. 55
Foreman, D. 37

Forrester, G. 54,102
Foster, W. 33
Foucault, M. 14, 112
Fowler, B. 117
Francis, B. 95
Fraser, N. 117
Frattura, E. 36
Freire, P. 5
French school system 3–4
Friedland, L. 13
Fullan, M. 34, 56, 88
Fuller, K. 36

Gaebler, T. 24
Garnier, M. 117
Gates, P. 10
George, M. 121
Gerwirtz, S. 26, 51, 65, 95
Giddens, A. 112, 125
Gillam, L. 125
Gillborn, D. 28, 96
Gintis, H. 5
Giroux, H. 121
Glatter, R. 31, 79
Gold, A. 39, 79
Goldthorpe, J. 115, 116
Gonzales, M. 95
Goodwin, F. 63
Gorard, S. 5
Gordon, G. 79
Gore, J. 124
Gorely, T. 52
Gove, M. 101
governance 24–25; and educational leadership 26–27; English context 77–78, 99–102; key interventions 27–28; tools of 25–26; use of EEIR 42–43; use of leadership studies 42–43
Grace, G. 65, 91,102
Grant, C. 54
Gray, J. 42
Green, A. 5, 53
Grek, S. 23, 26
Grenfell, M. 3, 45, 49, 51, 52, 73
Griffiths, M. 114
Grimaldi, E. 119
Gronn, P. 35, 37, 43, 96
Gruenewald, D. 95
Grummell, B. 96
Gu, Q. 56
Guillemin, M. 125
Gulson, K. 94
Gummett, P. 73
Gunraj, J. 41

166 *Index*

Gunter, H. 16, 25, 26, 27, 29, 32, 36, 40, 43, 53, 54, 57, 68, 77, 78, 79, 99, 101, 102, 105, 109, 111, 119

habitus 13–17; as spring 17, 72; cleft 16; concerns about 121–123; definition 14; dispositions 14,16; primary 16
Hadfield, M. 39, 40
Hall, C. 28, 57, 95
Hall, D. 26,119
Hall, V. 36, 66
Hallinger, P. 35
Halpin, D. 25
Halsey, A. 5, 115
Hampton, G. 34, 68
Harding, S. 38
Hardy, C. 49, 52, 72
Hardy, I. 54, 55
Hargreaves, A. 32, 34, 56, 57
Harris, A. 31, 33, 38, 39, 40, 41, 94
Harris, B. 41
Harrison, T. 77
Hart, S. 19
Hartley, D. 31
Hartley, F. 79
Harvey, D. 24
Hatcher, R. 54, 69
Hattam, R. 94
Hattie, J. 57
Hayes, D. 40, 43
Hayton, A. 57
Hayward, D. 34, 64
head teacher: autonomy, as phenomenon 60–69, 107; dispositions 108; field positions 89–90; freedom, 62–63; logic of practice 70; position in field 70
Heath, A. 115
Hebert, E. 33
Henry, M. 23
Herr, K. 53
Higham, A. 65
Higham, R. 69
Hilgers, M. 120
Hill, S. 18
Hiltmann, M. 76
Hirsch, E. 5
Hobby, R. 96
Holdsworth, R. 53
Hollins, K. 99
Holroyd, R. 52
Holt, J. 5
Honnetth, A. 117
Hood, C. 26, 118

Hopkins, D. 33, 41
Hsieh, H-F. 81
Huber, S. 76
Hutchings, M. 51

illusio 20
Imai, M. 92
Inghilleri, M. 122
Ingram, N. 16, 120
Ingvarson, L. 35

Jacka, J. 96
Jackson, A. 35
Jackson, B. 5
James, D. 49, 52, 58, 59, 122, 124
James, S. 41
Janks, H. 95
Jenkins, R. 124
Jolliffe, D. 66
Jones, A. 61
Jones, J. 34, 68
Jones, K. 28, 57

Kachur, J. 25, 77
Kaminsky, J. 61
Karabel, J. 5
Karac-Kakabadse, N. 26
Katz, S. 34
Kelly, P. 122
Kelsey, J. 25
Kemp, L 62
Kenway, J. 55, 96, 121
Kessler, S. 94
Khong, L. 39
Kilvert, P. 64
Kington, A. 33
Kirk, D. 52
Knight, J. 29
Koh, A. 55
Kooiman, J. 24
Kouzmin, A. 26, 73
Kozol, J. 5
Kwan, P. 96
Kydd, L. 79

Lacey, K. 96
Ladwig, J. 51
Lareau, A. 18, 51
Lash, S. 125
Lather, P. 38
Lazaridou, A. 41
Leadbetter, C. 80
leaders: titles, changes in 27
leadership as doxa: 90–94, 96; shift to management 97

Index 167

leadership studies 38–41
Lebaron, M. 49, 50
Leithwood, K. 33, 39
Levin, H. 5
Lewis, J. 73
Liker, J. 92
Lingard, B. 23, 29, 40, 43, 52, 53, 54, 68, 118
Loader, D. 33, 35, 68
logics of autonomy 72–75
Louden, B. 18
Louis, K.S. 32
Lovell, T. 117
Lubienski, C. 25
Lucey, H. 41, 51, 122
Luke, A. 51
Lumby, J. 43, 76
Lupton, R. 42, 94
Lusis, T. 122
Lyman, L. 41
Lynch, K. 96

Mac An Ghaill, M. 95
Macbeath, J. 27, 42, 66, 96
McDowell, L. 21
McGinity, R. 99, 101, 111
McInerney, P. 95
McIntyre, D. 19
Mack, H. 63
Mackay, H. 66
McKenley, J. 79
McKenzie, L. 12
McLaughlin, T. 124
Mclean, M. 10
McLeod, J. 120, 121
McNay, L. 117
Macrae, S. 51, 97
McWilliam, E. 67
Maguire, M. 28, 51, 97
Maguire, S. 10
Mahony, P. 16
Mangez, E. 120
Manning, P. 81
Marginson, S. 26, 51
Marsden, D. 5
Martin, J. 121
Maton, K. 46, 52
Maugham, B. 5
May, S. 52
Meier, D. 34
Melody, J. 41
Melville, W. 55
mental/manual binary 19
meritocracy 18–19
methodologies, ELMA 37–42

methodology, Bourdieu as 48–50
Mills, M. 40, 43
misrecognition 21, 94–96; concerns about 123–124
Mitchell, C. 42
Modra, C. 13
Moffit, A. 80
Moi, T. 117
Moll, L. 95
Monroe, L. 34
Moos, L. 42, 66
Morgan, C. 66
Morgan, R. 68
Morley, L. 10
Morris, E. 101
Morrison, M. 36, 37, 39, 40, 43
Mortimore, P. 5, 42
Mouzelis, N. 17
multiple correspondence analysis 49–50
Murphy, J. 32, 35, 43
Murphy, M. 14, 52
Murray, C. 13
Murray, S. 39
Myers, K. 34

Naidoo, R. 51
Nash, R. 122
National College for School Leadership, 39, 76; and ELMA research 78–80; history 78–80
Newman, J. 24
Niesche, R. 36, 43, 68, 69
Normore, A. 36
Noyes, A. 28

O'Brien, G. 66
Oduro, G. 96
Offe, C. 24
O'Neill, J. 57
ontology 45–46
Osborne, D. 24
Ozga, J. 26

Palmer, C. 13
Pashiardis, P. 76
Peacock, A. 19
Penn, H. 28
Perry, L-A. 67
Perryman, J. 28
Peters, B. 24
Peters, R.S. 62, 63
Peterson, K. 39
Petherick, G. 66
Pierre, J. 24
Piketty, T. 116

168 *Index*

Piven, F. 24
playing the game 14
Plummer, G. 16, 121
Polesal, J. 51
Pollitt, C. 26
Popkewitz, T. 27
Portelli, J. 37
Portes, A. 13
position 9
Poster, C. 63
Power, S. 25
practice, logic of 17–21
PricewaterhouseCoopers 84, 101
privatization, game of 102, 109
Pusey, M. 24
Putnam, R. 13

Raco, M. 25
Rae, J. 33, 68
Raffo, C. 5
Randolph, A. 122
Ranson, S. 68, 119
Rates, G. 57
Ravitch, D. 26
Rawolle, S. 25, 52, 118
Reay, D. 16, 18, 44, 51, 54, 117,
    121, 122
Reed-Danahay, D. 2
reflexivity 22, 47–48
Reid, J. 18
Reihl, C. 39
reproduction 2, 18, 21–22, 34, 73,
    115, 119
research questions, ELMA 32–37
research, rigour in 46–47
Reynolds, D. 41
Rhodes, C. 37
Rhodes, R. 24
Ribbins, P. 31, 33, 36, 37
Riddell, S. 97
Ridge, J. 115
Rikowski, G. 120
Riley, K. 78
Rivalland, J. 18
Rizvi, F. 23
Robertson, J. 76
Robinson, J. 10
Robinson, R. 117
Robinson, V. 34, 57
Rose, N. 24, 26
Ross, A. 51
Rowlands, J. 25
Runnymede Trust 10
Russell, L. 26
Rutter, M. 5, 41

Ryan, C. 101
Ryan, J. 36, 43

Sachs, J, 10, 36, 57
Sackney, L. 42
Sahlberg, P. 56, 88
Samier, E. 37
Sammons, P. 33
Sandlin, J. 51
Santamaria, L. 54
Savage, G. 28
Sayer, A. 120
Scheurich, J. 36, 37
school based management 64–69
school effectiveness 5
School Effectiveness and School
    Improvement (SESI) 41–42
schooling field, changes in 72–74
schools doing policy 98–103
Schultz, B. 51
Seddon, J. 92
Seddon, T. 27
self-managing school 25, 27, 64–69
Sellar, S. 68
Sergiovanni, T. 37
Serpieri, R. 119
Shannon, S. 81
Sharp, R. 5
Sheffield, J. 62
Shields, C. 36, 43
Simmons, R. 10
Sirianni, C. 13
Sizer, N. 34
Sizer, T. 34
Skeggs, B. 117, 120
Skelton, C. 95
Skinner, B.F. 91
Skorobohacz, C. 39
Skrla, L. 36
Slaughter, R. 64
Slee, R. 42, 43, 95
Smith, E. 5
Smith, G. 95
Smithson, A. 61
Smulyan, L. 35
Smyth, J. 27, 65, 95
social mobility 18
social theory: definition 112; uses of
    112–114
Sorens, J. 24
Southworth, G. 33, 66, 78, 40
Spillane, J. 31, 38, 122
Spinks, J. 34, 64
Stahl, G. 21
Stanford, J. 42

Index 169

Starr, K. 33
Starratt, R. 37
Stenson, K. 24, 25
Stilwell, F. 24
Stoker, G. 24
Stoll, L. 34, 41
Stott, K. 36
Strachan, J. 41
structure-agency 14
Stubbs, M. 34, 68
Swann, M. 19
Swartz D. 47
Swyngedouw, E. 119
Syal, R. 80
symbolic violence 21
Symes, C. 28, 94

Tang, A. 57
Taylor, Charles 117
Taylor, Chris 26
Taylor, F. W 90, 91
Taylor, M. 119
Taylor, S. 23, 52
Taylorism 90–91
teaching schools 55–58
Tedder, M. 52, 122
Teddlie, C 41
Teese, R. 51
Thanh and Vicky 6–7, 12, 15, 18
Thatcher, J. 120
thinking tools, 8, 48–50, 52, 53, 60, 98, 102
Thomas, G. 113
Thomas, K. 79
Thomas, L. 51, 121
Thompson, G. 68
Thompson, R. 10
Thomson, P. 6, 10, 25, 26, 28, 29, 35, 36, 42, 48, 53, 54, 57, 66, 68, 69, 73, 77, 79, 80, 94, 95, 96, 99, 100, 101,102, 105,107, 108, 109, 118
Thornton, S. 121
Thrupp, M. 27, 42, 47, 64, 79
Tillman, L. 36, 37
Tolley, H. 40
Tomlinson, H. 76
Tomlinson, S. 42, 65
Tompkins, J. 34
Tooley, J. 122
TQM 92–93
Tranter, S. 79
Tregenza, K. 36
Triventi, M. 10

university entrance 19
uses/misuses of Bourdieu 44–45

Vann, S. 52
Venugopal, R. 24
Verter, B. 121
Vickers, M. 73
virtual school bag 6–7

Wacquant, L. 12, 15, 16, 46, 58, 116
Waine, B. 26
Walker, A. 36, 96
Walkerdine, V. 41
Ware, N. 79
Waters, D. 66
Watt, P. 24, 25
Watts, J. 63, 66
Weinburgh, M. 55
Weindling, D. 42
Weiner, G. 42
Weitzel, P. 25
Welch, A. 91
West, M. 41, 42
West-Burnham, J. 34, 80
Whitaker, K. 35
Whitaker, P. 63
Whitehead, S. 35
Whitty, G. 25, 27, 57, 65
Wiliam, D. 51, 122
Wilkins, A. 28
Williams, B. 121
Williams, S. 121
Wilmott, R. 47
Winkley, D. 33, 67
Wisby, E. 57
Wolcott, H. 33, 40
Woodby, L. 121
Woodrow, C. 27
Woods, D. 31
Woods, G, 25
Woods, P. 25, 66
World Bank Social Capital Initiative. 13
Wrigley, T. 42, 43
Wylie, C. 64

Yeatman, A. 19, 25
York-Barr, J. 38
Youdell, D. 28, 96
Young, M. 5

Zipin, L. 53
Zmroczek, C. 16